A DANGEROUS LEGACY

A DANGEROUS LEGACY
Judaism and the Psychoanalytic Movement

Hans Reijzer

Translated by Jeannette K. Ringold

KARNAC

First published in Dutch as HET GEVAAR VAN DE JOODSE ERFENIS by
Prometheus Bv Uitgeverij Bert Bakker
Uitgeverij
Nederlands

This translated English edition, published in 2011 by
Karnac Books Ltd
118 Finchley Road
London NW3 5HT

HET GEVAAR VAN DE JOODSE ERFENIS
Copyright © Hans Reijzer, 2008

Translation copyright © 2011 Jeannette K. Ringold

Publication of *A Dangerous Legacy: Judaism and the Psychoanalytic Movement* was made possible with the financial support from the Dutch Foundation for Literature

The right of Hans Reijzer to be identified as the author of this work has been asserted in accordance with §§ 77 and 78 of the Copyright Design and Patents Act 1988.

All rights reserved. No part of this publication may be reproduced, stored in a retrieval system, or transmitted, in any form or by any means, electronic, mechanical, photocopying, recording, or otherwise, without the prior written permission of the publisher.

British Library Cataloguing in Publication Data

A C.I.P. for this book is available from the British Library

ISBN-13: 978-1-85575-858-2

Typeset by Vikatan Publishing Solutions (P) Ltd., Chennai, India

Printed in Great Britain

www.karnacbooks.com

CONTENTS

ACKNOWLEDGEMENTS	vii
ABOUT THE AUTHOR	xi
EPIGRAPH	xiii
PRELUDE	1
CHAPTER ONE Introduction	9
CHAPTER TWO Freud: a Jew in Europe	29
CHAPTER THREE Pfister and Freud, a friendship	51
CHAPTER FOUR Freud and the man Moses, the man Moses and Freud	67

CHAPTER FIVE
Jerusalem and Hamburg: two congresses   83

CHAPTER SIX
Two incidents in the Netherlands   107

CHAPTER SEVEN
International   129

CHAPTER EIGHT
The battle of Durban   165

CHAPTER NINE
Conclusion   185

REFERENCES   197

INDEX   213

ACKNOWLEDGEMENTS

Many people helped me while I was writing this book, and I owe thanks to all of them. The first ones to whom I showed the manuscript were Jaap Sajet and Solange Leibovici. Jaap had only one question: In what way do psychoanalysts differ from all other professionals? That question has hovered in front of me during the whole time that I worked on this book. Now I know: They are different because of where they come from. Solange's advice was firm: Throw out all that personal rubbish. I have done that, or not really.

My four readers have made a labour-intensive contribution. The fact that I asked them to do this was evidence of the trust I had in the quality of our relationship and in their expertise. That trust has grown. The first two readers were Marian Beijk-Docter and Wouter Gomperts, both psychoanalysts and both members of the "group of five" that will be encountered in chapter 6. They tried to look at the text in an even-handed way. I believe that they have succeeded. The other two readers were Henk Hillenaar and Bas van Gent. Henk Hillenaar is a scholar of Romance languages and literatures and an authority on psychoanalytic literature whom I met as editor of the *Tijdschrift voor Psychoanalyse* (Journal for Psychoanalysis). He was often considerably more charitable than I was about the text. That helped me to overcome many difficulties. I have known Bas for a long time as a very bright colleague, a social psychologist who became a professor in adult educational theory. He was endlessly amused and amazed at what members of the strange psychoanalyst species were up to with one another and their surroundings.

My PhD thesis supervisor Abram de Swaan read the manuscript in a later stage and added meaningful comments and fortunately appreciation. I gave parts of one of the last versions to the *Schaamteclub* (Shame Discussion Group), for many years under the leadership of Louis Tas, and received oral and written comments from the participants. Iki Halberstadt-Freud was as sharp and widely read as ever. In his opinion of this book Harry Stroeken was intimate and detached and above all precise and professional. Heleen Terwijn managed to summarize my subject matter in one sentence: The psychoanalysts, by distancing themselves from the Jewish roots of psychoanalysis, made them more blatantly visible. Randolph Wörner helped me to find my way in the quagmire of the behaviour of German psychoanalysts during the Second World War. Wim Kortenoeven (CIDI) was my guide in searching for difficult-to-find literature, and I asked Paul Gabriner, a literary scholar, his opinion about the passages about Edward Said. He said that they were sound. There were people who supported me occasionally. Walter Schönau helped me out several times when I did not understand a text. Michael Chayes helped me in thinking about some excerpts.

I cherish grateful memories of my visit to Janine Chasseguet-Smirgel who received me for an interview in Paris six months before her death. Mr W. van Manen looked at the text to check for possible legal problems. Nina Kaplan and Jan van der Linden ensured that Jan's house in Aix-en-Provence would be vacant so that I was able to work there without interruption for the entire month of December 2003. Petra Kaas unerringly managed to find the good Dutch translation of all the Freud texts I quoted.

Special thanks go to Evelien Gans and Ronny Naftaniel (CIDI). At two very different moments, the transformation of manuscript to book was close to failure. They came to my aid very effectively at the beginning and at the end of this long haul.

I thank Earl Hopper for his ideas and constant advice and for drawing attention to the psychological and sociological background of the dealings of the principal characters and myself. All this has now become part of our long friendship.

What a pleasure to be able to thank all these people for their efforts.

* * *

Finally, as I come from a decimated family, it has not been simple to maintain the Jewish tradition. The fact that this has been possible for me is thanks to Lottie, who has been my wife for more than 40 years. It is obvious that she has been my most important consultant as this book came into being.

I dedicate this book to her and to the gang that she, as matriarch, watches over: José Reijzer, David Keyson, Ezra Reijzer, Rivka Eljon, Jonathan Keyson, Nadav Keyson, Moran Reijzer, Yaniv Reijzer, Gideon Keyson, Tsiporah Reijzer, and Naftali Benjamin Keyson.

ABOUT THE AUTHOR

Hans Reijzer is a psychoanalyst in Amsterdam. From 1995 to 2003, he was general editor of the *Tijdschrift voor Psychoanalyse*, established by seven Dutch and Flemish psychoanalytic organizations. From 2003 to 2008, he was chairman of the joint Scientific Committee of three Dutch psychoanalytic organizations.

EPIGRAPH

The discussion about the impact the extermination of European Jewry had on the "Jewish psychology", psychoanalysis (and psychoanalysts), and what to do with it clinically is almost certainly not over. I would argue it has barely begun. It appears at times as if the profession wished—and here I am generalizing, of course—Freud's last name had indeed been Oberhuber (Maurice Preter).[1]

---

[1] This is the contribution to an internet discussion about Perel Wilgowics (1999). This reaction of Maurice Preter cannot be found in the report of the internet discussion by Paul Williams, the general editor (1999).

PRELUDE

For 25 years the French photographer Frédéric Brenner roamed the world in search of Jews to photograph. That yielded a beautiful coffee table book (2003a) with an accompanying book of texts with free associations that sometimes contain an explanation (2003b). The whole is held together in a sturdy slipcase. The guiding principle of the book is that the destiny of those who were photographed was to a large extent determined by the fact that they were Jews or were seen as Jews. It is also an attempt to be ahead of the archaeologists. All sorts of clubs and individuals are depicted, and you can practically see the photographer think: record this before it is too late.

On page 212 we see a puzzling group. It looks like a religious gathering. All eyes look straight into the lens and look attentive, serious. The leader is obviously sitting in the front at the right. He has a beard, and you might think that he was leading a prayer service. Jews require ten adult men for this, and that exact number was reached. Except, this photo is not correct for a synagogue service because there are four women among these men. That is impossible during an Orthodox service, and these men are too solemn in an old-fashioned way to be members of a Reform synagogue. A chaise longue dominates the photo. The room is overcrowded with photos, busts, and filing cabinets. Shelves filled with books and journals leave little room for the people.

What the viewer sees here is a number of members of the New York Psychoanalytic Society. I assume that they are senior training analysts or even the executive committee, because they could not have looked much more distinguished and self-possessed in 1994—hands in their laps, serious-looking eyes that promise a smile, cheerful strictness mixed with compassion. It is not a Jewish institute, not even an institute for Jews—what is Brenner doing there? He is taking photos there! Because it is very Jewish.

For those who are not convinced by the photo, the commentators place it exactly in the centre of the subject matter of the photo book. Sartre's former secretary, Benny Lévy, writes: "They are Jews because psychoanalysis is Jewish, and psychoanalysis is Jewish because its inventor was Jewish. That's it". Brenner, the photographer, details what he saw: "The New York Psychoanalytic Society; the holy of holies of Freudians: busts of Freud decorate the bookshelves around the room; Vienna in New York; a memory of Europe in the heart of America". And Tsvi Blanchard adds: "Nervous, I ask myself, 'What is the answer?' and then, like Gertrude Stein, I ask again, 'What was the question?'" (Brenner, 2003a, pp. 212–213; 2003b, pp. 96–97).[1]

My topic and my thesis are hidden in that book, in that photo, in those questions, and in those playful commentaries. The subject is the triangle consisting of Freud, psychoanalysis, and its Jewish legacy. The thesis is that this linking has led to complications within the psychoanalytical world and in the relation of psychoanalysis to its surroundings. The Jewish legacy can be seen as a danger. Analysts have always felt the threat that a transference would land on them and their work, as if their profession were Jewish. With this I mean that there are elements in this relationship that are also present in the way that people think and feel about Jews and how they are treated.

In the same vein psychoanalysis is seen as extremely interesting, with connections to esoteric insights that non-analysts will never attain. In addition, it continues to be characterized as strange, almost ordinary but in fact quite extraordinary. Psychoanalysis, analogous to the position of Jews, is experienced as threatening, creepy, and suspect. Psychoanalysis is reproached for being engaged in matters that are none of its business and that it knows nothing about; after all, psychoanalysis is outside normal life. Another reproach is the obsession with money. In a negative review of the book *Ein Jahrhundert*

Psychoanalytische Bewegung in Deutschland: die Psychotherapie unter dem Einfluß Freuds by Annemarie Dührssen, Yigal Blumenberg, a psychoanalyst from Berlin, notes how Dührssen uses centuries-old anti-Jewish stereotypes to discount psychoanalysis. She characterizes it as fundamentalist, fanatical, undemocratic, totalitarian, contemptuous of people, and violent (Blumenberg, 1995). Freud always feared this kind of approach. Hence his statement (quoted in Dezoncle, 2006) to his American follower Smiley Blanton: "As a science, psychoanalysis is neither Jewish, nor Catholic, nor pagan".

By analysing a number of incidents, this book shows how the Jewish connection is treated in psychoanalysis. The fact that there is awareness of this connection has had consequences for the position of psychoanalysis and for the dynamics inside the psychoanalytic movement. I will try to show a number of the large and small consequences. I will follow the actions of psychoanalysts and of people who have connections to psychoanalysis and their manoeuvres in the borderline area where psychoanalysis, Judaism, Jewish origin, Jewish identity, and the idea that psychoanalysis might be Jewish are in danger of touching.

At the origin of the indicated transference is the fact that the founders of psychoanalysis were Jews and that much of the inner logic of psychoanalysis has its roots in a Jewish way of thinking. This Jewish-analytic entanglement has had far-reaching consequences for the reception of psychoanalysis and for the internal organizations of psychoanalysts. Let us first look at what was really happening in the New York Psychoanalytic Society portrayed by Brenner. There is quite a bit of literature about it that is in a concealed way about the above-mentioned triangle. To examine this I used, in addition to Brenner's book of photos, solid research by Janet Malcolm (1982) and a scholarly study by Kirsner (2000).

When Janet Malcolm wanted to write an extensive article for *The New Yorker* about psychoanalysis and its practitioners, she created a figure that she used for her story. The imaginary character she describes is called Aaron Green, a composite of a number of New York psychoanalysts. He is a 46-year-old psychiatrist. She adds, quite unnecessarily, that he looks Jewish. Green was trained at the New York Psychoanalytic Institute, is now a member of the New York Psychoanalytic Society, and is conscious of his dignity. He looks down unabashedly on the training at other institutes, especially if they train psychologists. Malcolm lets Green tell about being accepted into training:

> When I received my letter of acceptance from the New York Psychoanalytic Institute, it was as if I had been given an injection of adrenaline, amphetamine, and heroin. I have seldom in my life felt so triumphant. I knew that my life was going to be the way I wanted (1982, p. 47).

During his tour of the leading psychoanalytic institutes in the United States, Kirsner calls the New York Psychoanalytic Institute *The Anointed* (2000, p. 13). Whoever is an instructor there belongs to the psychoanalytic elite of the United States and the world. It is the oldest and has for years been the most important psychoanalytic institute in the United States. From this description one may assume that it is an autocratic and authoritarian establishment that pretends to have direct access to Truth, the special knowledge that is attributed to psychoanalysts and that they sometimes possess. It was the institute to which Jewish analysts—invariably described in the literature as *European* analysts—fled in the Thirties and Forties of the 20th century. Yet they were not entirely welcome, not even there. In this connection Kirsner cites the analyst and well-known author Margaret Mahler who recounts that many experienced analysts felt less than well disposed towards the large number of famous analysts who eyed New York as a place to establish themselves. Although they nominally sympathized with the refugees and were helpful with their move, the leaders of the group made it clear that they would be happier if their European colleagues would establish themselves outside New York City (Kirsner, 2000, p. 17).

On the next page, Kirsner quotes from earlier research (Langer & Gifford, 1978) and adds his own scathing comment:

> When the president of the NY Society was asked for affidavits to sponsor Viennese analysts to migrate to the US after the *Anschluss*, he refused, with the reply: "What in the world would we do with all these additional analysts?" Fortunately, affidavits for the Viennese analysts could be collected outside psychoanalytic circles.

The story of the New York Psychoanalytic Institute in the Fifties and Sixties of the 20th century runs parallel to the life of Otto Isakower (1899–1972). He was one of the newcomers from Vienna. In 1943 he became a member of the institute and rapidly became a central figure within it. He determined in general who became a training analyst, which training candidate went into analysis with which training analyst, who gave which course. He was an instructor and an institute leader who published little. His most important theoretical contribution was in the area of supervision. Within that he concentrated on the preconscious reaction of the analyst to the patient. He called it the analysing instrument. Anyone who did not possess this difficult-to-describe skill was not a real analyst. The way the myth worked was that you were admitted to the training if Isakower and his friends determined that you had this instrument available to you. The degree of having that quality determined how high you could rise in the organization.

According to Kirsner, it was in reality how faithful you were to an inner circle, which determined whether you were regarded as an established insider or as an outsider. Association with the analysing instrument meant association with group loyalty. This last decided who belonged to the Anointed and who did not. Partly out of dissatisfaction with the arbitrariness of the authorities in their evaluation of their fellow analysts, the atmosphere in the institute was wretched during the third quarter of the 20th century. Kirsner places much of the blame for this at the feet of *the Europeans*. According to him, they felt that as Freud's spiritual heirs they were the only ones who knew what psychoanalysis was about and what it meant in all respects. They looked down on the Americans, as Freud himself had done.

What united all of them was worry about the institute. It required constant upkeep of the building and continual acquisitions for the library. Bankruptcy was always lurking, and to avoid that it was necessary to have slightly too many patients per analyst. Working at the institute meant living for, through, and in the institute. Fellow workers were asked for financial contributions in the form of donations and gifts. There is an interesting aside to all that disinterested love. When Isakower died, he left behind a considerable sum of money. He had not only earned well as an analyst, but he had also invested shrewdly. The result of all these efforts, the fruit of his investor's instinct, was not for his faithful companions at the institute but for his distant beloved Jerusalem. Hebrew University was named as his beneficiary. His close colleague Lillian Malcove made a similar gesture; she left her valuable collection of Russian icons to the Museum of Toronto. One can only guess about their motives. Kirsner maintains that they wanted to leave nothing to their American colleagues. For Isakower one may assume that in his last will and testament he wanted to assert his first love, but it was also a gesture against what the institute had become. Kirsner, who in his book comes across as a cool observer of all sorts of fights inside psychoanalytic societies, suddenly becomes vehement in his aversion to *the Europeans* when he talks about the totally poisoned atmosphere of the New York Institute:

> Given the trauma and terror suffered by the Europeans during the 1930s together with common background, it was understandable why they grouped together socially in the US. But this carried over to professional matters, leading to a climate of paranoia in the Institute which affected all its members (2000, p. 36).

Let us return to Janet Malcolm, her creation Aaron Green, and his career. At the age of 46 he is a young man on this way to the top, but Janet Malcolm does not tell us whether he will ever get there and become a training analyst or, even more desirable, a member of the training committee. You would think that he would. He knows theory, is ambitious, thinks carefully about his profession, and is didactically very clear when talking to Malcolm, his interviewer. Anyone who projects that Green will get a position as training analyst assumes that there are normal criteria for acceptance: knowledge, experience, trustworthiness, and didactic skills. But all the other factors that deal with group loyalty and affection, views about psychoanalysis and origins, make the outcome very uncertain.

And there is something else: in describing social and psychological phenomena it is useful to pay attention to what is not said. In the three sources that I consulted (Brenner, 2003b; Malcolm, 1982; and Kirsner, 2000), being Jewish is normal. Take for example the researcher who is presented by Malcolm. He figures in the book under his own name, Hartvig Dahl. He is the concession made by the institute to "pure research" (1982, p. 84). He calls himself the "Shabbes goy" (Yerushalmi, 1991, p. 53) for the orthodox members. Malcolm adds as a matter of course:

The once nastily anti-Semitic characterization of psychoanalysis as "the Jewish science" is today good-humoredly accepted by analysts as an accurate comment on the great predominance of Jews in the profession, and on the parallel between Talmudic and analytic hermeneutics.

She acts as if the expression "the Jewish science" is a perfectly ordinary one, but it is not—and not only because it dates from the Nazi era. Also pay attention to her use of the word "orthodox" in Dahl's description of himself: it is an adjective that can refer to certain analysts as well as to certain Jews. She removes the tension between non-Jewish and Jewish. She attributes no symbolic value to the destination of Isakower's estate. She does not recognize the tension, described several times by Ostow, between "proper" Jews, Western Jews accepted by non-Jews, and "Ostjuden", East European Jews who did not go through the acculturation and assimilation process in the West (as described among others in Ostow, 1982 and 1997). The first group sees the second one as an obstacle to their own acceptance. In the end Malcolm leaves out the fact that for some non-Jews there is no such thing as an acceptable Jew. These people, who are called anti-Semites, also exist among psychoanalysts, and we will encounter them in this book. An identical assumption is the basis for the joke with which Frosh (2005) opens his book *Hate and the Jewish Science*: "It has sometimes been suggested that books on psychoanalysis, rather than being shelved in psychology sections in bookshops and libraries should instead be listed under 'Jewish Studies'".

That would not be logical and would be contrary to the facts. But this thought has determined much of the history of psychoanalysis, internally as well as externally.

Note

1. As an aside: Psychoanalysts do not call themselves Freudians, and according to the membership handbook and the roster of the International Psychoanalytical Association (IPA), the organization on the photo is called the New York Psychoanalytic Society and Institute. None of the busts on the shelves is of Freud. The only depiction of Freud in that room is an etching.

CHAPTER ONE

Introduction

> Although modern psychoanalysis is, of course, independent today of its founder, and as a science stands apart from any religious creed (not to speak of racist *Weltanschauungen*), nevertheless an analyst is necessarily born into a Jewish genealogy and acquires his professional identity through identification with Freud's work (Eickhoff, 1989, p. 324).

The above sentence, written by the German psychoanalyst Eickhoff, contains one of the main points from the introduction to a clinical consideration of the second-generation problem of descendants of Nazis. The article was originally written in English and contains one German word. At first I read it with approval because I thought I encountered in Eickhoff's ideas an aspect of the theme of this book: its Jewish origin has left many traces in psychoanalysis as a whole. And not only in psychoanalysis itself, but also in the world around it. That includes its methods and body of thought, but also the way it was received.

However, when I read the quote more carefully, I encountered a problem. The writer sets down "racist *Weltanschauungen*" (world views) as an intensification of religious convictions and of

Judaism in particular. Religion can now be seen as obscuring the view of reality, an obstacle to reaching the truth. The same is true for racism. But those are two very different impediments to the extension of knowledge. Human mortality, the helpless beginning as baby and child, and the need to find meaning play an essential role in religion—in racism it is fear and hate of the unfamiliar.

I have corresponded about this with the author. Eickhoff let me know that on further consideration he shared my objection and on second thought he felt that his use of the expression showed *a certain naïveté*. He wrote me that he, in turn, had taken the text from the handbook by Thomä and Kächele (1986). He had used the English edition. To clarify he mentioned that Thomä is a "passionate scholar, but also someone who discounts the specifically Jewish genealogy of psychoanalysis in his considerations". This too is a contrast that is not self-evident. Being a passionate scholar is not inconsistent with paying attention to the Jewish origin of psychoanalysis. In this way a quote that I initially saw as a clarification of my formulation of the problem became an example of the lack of clarity that appears when the so-called Jewish identity is linked to psychoanalysis. The whole thing surprised me all the more because I had come to know Eickhoff as a sensible man. During a psychoanalytic conference in Hamburg (for more about this see chapter five) he presented a case of a young woman who grew up under the shadow of a father who was an active Nazi (1986). His contribution was planned as the echo of two other lectures. Those (Klein, 1986; and Kogan, 1986) presented a treatment and some theoretical concepts about people who as victims or as children of victims during the Second World War had been treated by a psychoanalyst. Eickhoff's presentation was sensible and sympathetic, without extreme outrage about or hidden identification with Nazi ideology.

* * *

The Jewish origin of psychoanalysis is a problem that still causes confusion. Of course a form of science or psychological treatment is not Jewish or non-Jewish, but the history of psychoanalysis with its Jewish founders and reputation invites treating psychoanalysis and Jews at the same time; symbiotically bound together in love and hate, linked by perceptions of analysts and non-analysts, and involved in a fight to disentangle one from the other. Thomä and Kächele are neither the first nor the last to wonder whether the

Jewish origin of psychoanalysis has consequences in the present. Frosh cites Lowenstein's comment (1952, p. 38): "At some point in the course of analysis almost all non-Jewish patients will manifest varying degrees of anti-Semitism". Frosh himself adds:

> Almost always, the Jew is regarded as a figure of fear and hate, and in the transference these feelings become directed towards the analyst, especially (though not only) if she or he is Jewish. Presumably, the ethnicity of the analyst is not a crucial factor here because psychoanalysis itself is so strongly perceived as "Jewish"; that is, *all* analysts are Jewish in the minds of their necessarily anti-Semitic patients (2005, p. 154).

This kind of observation and other facts that will still be discussed lead to the basic point of this book:

> *A web of transferences rests on psychoanalysis as well as on the individual analyst, the analytic association, and the analytic institute. The thought that psychoanalysis might be Jewish colours the character of this transference, determines it, and extends it. Such a strong transference should include countertransference, equally irrational and fed by the wish not to be stereotyped but to be judged on one's own acts.*

* * *

It is undesirable for psychoanalysis to be seen as Jewish in transference or countertransference. As a consequence it is necessary for *The Movement* to distance itself from any appearance of being Jewish, or more precisely, to keep as great a distance from it as possible in real world actions. Psychoanalysis should not be a *Jewish science*. That is what the Nazis called it, and then they burned Freud's books. From the beginning of psychoanalysis, psychoanalysts have strived to create a universal area of knowledge—even though everything that Freud and the circle around him discovered was the result of what Jewish patients told Jewish psychoanalysts during their treatment.

* * *

The historian Dennis Klein has written about the beginning of the psychoanalytic movement (1985, pp. IXff.). He, too, has researched the influence of the Jewish founders on the reception and the practice of psychoanalysis. He has determined that earlier researchers dealt in two ways with the context in which psychoanalysis was created. On the one hand there is a tendency to describe it as universal and human, but there is also the tendency to see it as Jewish. Those who emphasize its universal character make the Jewish part as small as possible. When the Jewish part is emphasized, it is often to show that obscurantism and provincialism are hidden inside psychoanalysis.

The Berlin psychoanalyst Yigal Blumenberg, who earlier put forward the idea of Jewish transference on psychoanalysis, indicates what it is about.[1] According to him affluence, power, knowledge of "the secret", and humanity are attributed to psychoanalysis. On the other hand it is seen as dirty and narrow. It is held responsible for disrupting the social order.

Psychoanalysis can be seen as a part of the struggle for emancipation in anti-Semitic Vienna. Jews strove to be accepted by society, and they took economic as well as ideological routes to accomplish this. As their unique contribution, psychoanalysts offered to free humanity from *neurosis*. Their self-image was that of an elite with a mission. They translated the prison of their real lack of freedom as Jews into the equally real lack of freedom of every human being with his or her unfulfilled desires. The historian Zaretsky expresses this as follows:

> The founding idea of psychoanalysis, the idea of a dynamic or *personal unconscious* reflected this new experience of personal life. [...] Thus, there was no direct or necessary connection between one's social condition and one's subjectivity (2004, p. 5).

Psychoanalysis was not alone in its struggle with its Jewish background. In a study devoted to this subject, the French psychoanalyst and psychologist Chemouni (1987, 1988) examines what Jewish organizations Freud belonged to. He mentions that other new disciplines or scientific knowledge were also set aside as Jewish knowledge. In this connection he recounts a web of fantasies about sociology but also about the theory of relativity. He quotes from Philippe Frank's book (1968), *Einstein, sa vie, son temps*. Frank had found reviews in which the theories of Einstein were rejected as a product of the Jewish mind. Well before the Nazi era a smear campaign was carried out against him and his theory. This is very clear from Einstein's correspondence with his colleague Marcel Grossman. Worried and alarmed, he writes from Zurich: "At present every coachman and every waiter argues about whether or not the relativity theory is correct. A person's conviction on this point depends on the political party he belongs to" (Isaacson, 2007, p. 267). Chemouni also recounts how Philippe Ariès remembers that in his youth he rejected sociology because its most important founders were Jews. We should remember that Ariès came from an extremely reactionary family.

The idea that if something is Jewish it cannot be good has had some tragic consequences. In the middle of the 19th century, doctors interested in science, proud of their work ethos, would go straight from an autopsy to the delivery room to assist with a delivery. The consequences were terrible: women in labour were infected with bacteria from the dead bodies and died a few days later from the feared childbed fever. In 1847 Ignace Semmelweis discovered that these painful and tragic deaths could be avoided if the doctors would wash their hands thoroughly before examining women in labour. Although Semmelweis worked in academic hospitals, he never managed to get this measure adopted during his lifetime. Even his book *Die Aetiologie, der Begriff und die Prophylaxis des Kindfiebers*, published in 1861, did not have the desired effect. It was not until 1890 that Lester, a Quaker who was more socially skilled, managed to obtain general acceptance for making hands sterile around childbirth. By then Semmelweis had died, and Lester did not hear until later about his life and his death. According to the medical historian Nuland (2003), the Jewish-sounding name Semmelweis had been one of the reasons why that strange Hungarian did not get his simple, practical measure introduced in the relevant medical circles.

This book is about Jews, non-Jews, and psychoanalysis in a non-Jewish environment. It is not a chronological history but an examination of the interaction of those four elements from Freud's time until the present. A small incident from my own life can serve as a demonstration of the constrained relationship between Jews and psychoanalysis.

In 2003 I became involved in a small controversy because of an attack on circumcision by two psychoanalysts, De Klerk and Schalkwijk.[2] This attack had little substance or foundation: all kinds of circumcision, in various stages of development of the circumcised, Jewish and not Jewish, baby and adolescent were mixed up in order to show how traumatic it is. Even Freud's addiction to his cigar was connected to it. I felt that the Journal for Psychoanalysis (*Tijdschrift voor Psychoanalyse*) should never have published an article of that level. I presented the draft of my reaction to psychoanalyst X who made some quite appropriate remarks, and thanks to his help I improved my text. I wanted to thank him for his suggestions in a footnote, but I first asked him if I should do this. He refused without any hesitation. The reason was clear and commendable: in the future X would need space to manoeuvre for quite different psychoanalytical projects, and a too close connection to a Jewish article would make him more eccentric than was desirable.

* * *

When I state that a Jewish transference has landed on psychoanalysis and that a strong countertransference is part of it, I am introducing terms that seem clear but still need an explanation. I have to give transference, countertransference, and Jewish the meaning that makes them relevant in the scope of this book. I will do this briefly because they are the instrument of my study and not its subject. Psychoanalysis itself seems an obvious notion, although that is not so in the least. I will consider three concepts: a profession with its own practices and institutions; a group of colleagues; and a theory about human functioning. My emphasis is on the first two aspects that concern the profession. The entire development of the profession, the improvement of treatment, and the formation of a theory—Freud called those *die Sache*. Brinkgreve (1984) sees first of all an establishment struggle, and the struggle for professionalization is a part of it. Inside the profession the struggle to develop usable theories takes place so that the right intervention can be used for the patient at the right moment.

* * *

Transference is a central concept in the formation of psychoanalytic theory and the practice of psychoanalysis and psychoanalytic psychotherapy.[3] In the course of the years its meaning has shifted.[4] It is a term created by Freud for a phenomenon that occurs in the treatment situation. When Freud began to develop his course of treatment, it consisted primarily of an explanation of the cause of the complaint. In the early years of psychoanalytic thinking, Freud assumed that when the analyst told the patient how his problem had started, the *insight* obtained through this would lead to recovery. However, the *psychic reality* of the patient prevented the latter from understanding what the analyst actually said.

Reality as perceived by the patient is distorted by a mix of passions, fantasies, and conflicts that is the sum total of the processing of earlier experiences. According to theory, these conflicts were primarily created by the experience of contact with mother, father, or other primary caregivers, brothers and sisters, or you could say the rest of one's social milieu. The patient looks at the here and now through coloured glasses. This bias is between hearing and understanding what the psychoanalyst says in the treatment situation, and it works like a screen of incomprehension between analyst and patient. Freud called this transference. Transference can be intense, positively or negatively biased, or both at the same time. Lacan's fine definition, pulled from Stroeken's psychoanalytic dictionary (2000, p. 15), is as follows: "Transference is the unconscious in action".

In later developments transference was no longer considered as a hindrance but instead became an important tool in treatment. In 1923 Freud writes:

> This *transference* alike in its positive and in its negative form is used as a weapon by the resistance; but in the hands of the physician it becomes the most powerful therapeutic instrument and it plays a part scarcely to be over-estimated in the dynamics of the process of cure (p. 247).

What takes place in the here and now of treatment and the discussion of it became from then on one of the most important instruments of psychoanalysis. Transference is not limited to treatment. It even plays an important role in social intercourse. In it a different significance is attached to the other that he does not have as a person but that is ascribed to him or her by the imagination.

* * *

Countertransference is also a concept that has come a long way. Freud mentions patients who fall in love with one psychoanalyst after the other, and he then warns about the countertransference lying in wait for the analyst—that he is as capable and attractive as his patients think. He stated that infatuation of patients for the analyst cannot always be avoided and that the analyst should therefore not be afraid of it. However, the analyst should not think that this love has anything to do with him and his outstanding qualities, but should be prepared for the fact that the analytical situation stimulates it (Freud, 1914a).

The definition of *countertransference* is analogous to that of transference. Except that it is about the web of passions, fantasies, and conflicts that make it difficult but also possible for the analyst to understand the patient. When Freud introduced the concept of countertransference in *Observations on Transference Love*[5] in 1915, it quickly became a negatively charged concept. This was because in the beginning countertransference in fact meant love and/or hate for the patient by the analyst. If the analyst suffered too often or too intensely from it, then he was supposed to continue and to deepen his self-analysis. If that was insufficiently successful, then he had to go back into psychoanalysis, *re-analysis*, in order to make his irrational feelings for the patient manageable again. In this way *technical neutrality* could again be reached.

Later, the definition of the concept of countertransference was broadened to *all of the analyst's reactions to the patient*. In addition, countertransference has experienced a reversal of reputation. It is no longer seen as an obstacle in treatment but has become an important source of information about patient and analyst in the intersubjective space of the treatment situation.

As concerns the Jewish element in countertransference, there is a specific problem in the psychoanalytic movement. All psychoanalysts have themselves been in analysis or still are. The walks that Freud took with Max Eitingon in 1909 are seen as the first training analysis. All subsequent teaching analyses, also called training analyses, are derived from this. As Zaretsky explains:

> Through subsequent training analyses each succeeding generation relived the founding generation's transference to Freud. In the course of all its changes, analysis remained divided between a professional façade and a secret, fantasied, and ambivalent love aimed at Freud (2004, p. 107).

We have previously encountered a similar thought in Thomä and Kächele that was also expressed by the French psychoanalyst Janine

Chasseguet-Smirgel. According to her (1987), every psychoanalyst is of Jewish descent because of his identification with Freud and the psychoanalytic pioneers, who are as it were his forefathers. Logically, this thought can even be extended to everyone who has been in psychoanalysis, but then it becomes too unwieldy. Analysts, in spite of all their disputes and schisms, can say about themselves: *we analysts*. Analysands and ex-analysands cannot say that; they do not have such a bond.

* * *

In the scope of this study, the concepts of transference and countertransference have to be handled with care. First of all, not everything is transference. Psychoanalysts appear in their office and also outside it. That produces reactions, as does every public appearance. Psychoanalysis changes, and psychoanalysts make mistakes and should be contradicted inside and outside the treatment situation. Psychoanalysis is developing. What a psychoanalyst can do and what he thinks are the object of continual debate, just like the entire scientific enterprise. The discussion does not need to be carried on in terms of transference. This means that it is erroneous to trace the opinion of an opponent back to his own conflicts based on the personal relationship of that person to psychoanalysis.

Psychoanalysis is a discussion that fits with its time and has always been the subject of debate. It has changed greatly in the course of time. I cannot think of a reason why at a given moment it would not, like every school of thought, become a movement from the past and die out. Medical practices and lines of thinking evolve, are adapted, rejected, and replaced by new ones. This has real and unreal sides. To make transference, and especially its Jewish aspect, responsible for all the unreal sides of the process is an over-simplification that I am unwilling to accept. However, it is sometimes enlightening to discuss the transferential sense of a situation.

I also want to avoid making anthropomorphic statements about social phenomena. Strictly speaking, groups and organizations are not subject to transference or countertransference. But members of a group have thoughts about another person and also about the psychoanalyst. Those thoughts sometimes have a transferential character, and psychoanalysts react to that. The analyst reacts to whatever hinders or disrupts his work or makes his existence irrelevant—not always with actions but with feelings. These can be considered as a countertransference reaction.

A problem does present itself in my chief principle. Transference and countertransference are terms from the treatment situation, and they cannot simply be transferred to other forms of relationship. Every love or hate of a work of art, a political position, or a social phenomenon could then be traced back to very personal reasons and in this way be made unimportant. Social discourse would become poisoned because it would lead to a continual reduction of every opinion or feeling to an extremely personal level. On the other hand, such irrational elements sometimes creep into social discourse so that you are tempted to think that they must be driven by strong unconscious motivations. That occurs and has occurred when there is a question of the value of psychoanalysis and the relationship between practitioners of psychoanalysis.

* * *

My basic principle presupposes that between the *psychoanalyst* and *society* there is a relationship that can be understood as the treatment situation. The essence of Zarestsky's argument is that psychoanalysis has provided the conceptual structure that made the second industrial revolution possible. In his poem "In Memoriam Freud", W. H. Auden (1940) ascribed the same importance to Freud:

> For one who'd lived among enemies so long:
> if often he was wrong and, at times, absurd,
> to us he is no more a person
> now but a whole climate of opinion
> under whom we conduct our different lives.

Is it a good idea to write about psychoanalysis as the practitioner and society as the sick person? Sometimes there are good grounds for that. Freudian ideas have had influence on society. Psychoanalysis is both an insider and an outsider. It has always lurched between these two alternatives. It can remain faithful to its liberating utopian beginning, or become a part of the bureaucratized welfare state and its repressive forces. Analysts have wanted to become the healers of society.

The practice and theory of psychoanalysis have been the cause and result of a great number of social changes. The less hierarchical relationship of parents and children, of men and women—about whom it is now said aloud that they share the secret of sexuality—would have been unthinkable without psychoanalysis. In the same spirit Zaretsky mentions the growth of personal autonomy and the emancipation of women. He says that democracy has been radicalized by psychoanalysis, which has also made it more complicated. And in the broader culture Freudian thinking helped to expose the combined action between the public and the personal, by bringing to the surface the hidden transferences that connect social movements and social groups to each other.

Zaretsky sees psychoanalysis on the one hand as the companion to the second industrial revolution and on the other hand as the theory that cleared the way for a movement against the ideal of the Enlightenment by making space for the irrational, which it did not have before. Feminism, which would later turn fiercely away from psychoanalysis, is its offspring. The courageous discovery by Freud of his own *feminine side* in his relationship to Fliess is the basis of a public acceptance of homosexuality. Until the advent of psychoanalysis, the psychiatrist treated illnesses of the brain, and subsequently human diseases became his terrain—until that extreme position also had to be abandoned and both approaches gained validity. The consequences of Freud's thoughts have contributed significantly to the secularization of Western Europe. And finally, the work of Benjamin Spock, who was a psychoanalyst but became known as a paediatrician, set the tone for understanding instead of hierarchical parenting. Zaretsky calls him a *closet psychoanalyst*. He started his professional life as an analyst, but he never mentioned it.

* * *

Now I still have to make clear what is a Jew according to me. Being Jewish is a socio-cultural, historical, and religious concept. Memmi tries to describe this exhaustively in his extremely personal and also very important cultural and historical work (2003, pp. 17, 29). He distinguishes three concepts, each of which conveys an aspect of what being Jewish entails. He calls them *judéité, judaïsme*, and *judaïcité*. For him being Jewish (*judéité*) means that someone is Jewish and how and in what way; Judaism (*judaïsme*) means all Jewish doctrines and institutions; and Jewish community (*judaïcité*) includes all Jewish individuals. Less formally he says that all Jews are oppressed and hold the same position as slaves, proletarians, colonized peoples, natives in the colonies, and women.

Ido Abram, a philosopher and professor of Holocaust education, is pragmatic. In his systematic analysis of the concept of Judaism, he points out that the so-called Jewish identity is a mixture of descent, the history of the group, the person's own history, religion, and culture. Anti-Semitism also has an influence on Jews. After 1945, the Shoah and the establishment of the state of Israel were added. Abram (2003) emphasizes that the ingredients of Jewish identity have something to do with each other but are present in varying quantities: in one person, primarily the Shoah and Israel; in another, religion; in a third, the social environment; and in a fourth, birth and upbringing. In the course of the individual stages of life of a Jew, the emphasis can vary because of inner development and life events. Identity can take on more or less meaning.

Abram's flexible approach is very useful. Jews differ from one another in their relation to Judaism. The importance of the Jewish identity differs by individual and by group. In its most significant form it can be found in the beginning of the book of Jonah in the Bible. When the boat on which Jonah sailed was in danger of being wrecked, the sailors drew lots to determine on whose account the tempest had been caused—and the lot pointed to Jonah as the one guilty of the disaster—the following classic dialogue took place between him and his fellow sailors:

> "Tell us, you who have brought this misfortune upon us, what is your business? Where have you come from? What is your country, and of what people are you?" "I am a Hebrew," he replied. "I worship the Lord, the God of Heaven, who made both sea and land" (Jewish Publication Society, Hebrew-English Tanakh, 2000, p. 1333).

Here is a convergence of people, nationality, religion, and individual identity. The fact that he is a Jew is for him the central value. It is a core identity, a concept that shows the importance of the first years of a human life. At that time a feeling originates: I am this, and I belong there. This identity is formed by voices, accents, the way that a young child is treated.

A detail to which Freud and many analysts after him have paid a lot of attention is the circumcision. On the eighth day of his life it establishes the Jewish man's identity according to those who raise him. In the most superficial form of experiencing being Jewish there remains only the thought that one, two, three, or four parents or grandparents were Jewish.

* * *

The anti-Semite is inseparably connected to the Jew. The Centre for Information and Documentation on Israel (CIDI), a Dutch organization that does annual research about anti-Semitic incidents and disseminates information about Israel and Jews, has developed the following definition of anti-Semitism: *Treating Jews differently as a person or as a group from other people or population groups, in particular in adopting a hostile position in relation to Jews because of prejudices.* Freud himself had a favourite quote from Ludwig Börne who said:

> It is quite amazing. I have experienced it a thousand times, and it always remains new. One person blames me for being Jewish, the other forgives me for it, and the third one even values me for it, but they all think about it. As if they are bewitched by the magic circle of Jews from which none can escape.[6]

The German communications scholar Bernd Sösemann has noticed that anti-Semites emphasize six themes in scholarly literature.

> Anti-Semitism promotes the following six topics: to document the general validity of anti-Semitism, to show the unity and the oneness of Jewish society, to indicate the difference of this group, to note their differing social status (class), to stress their inferior value, and to look for the soul and intellect of the Jews (n.d.).

Sösemann thinks that these characteristics are always present in various degrees.

The manifestation of anti-Semitism changes with place and time: "In every phase of modern history, anti-Semitism has a different face" (Sösemann, n.d.). Pieter van der Horst, a classicist and professor of the New Testament, Hellenism, and early Judaism at the University of Utrecht, mentions several archaic hallmarks of this in his retirement lecture (2006). He dates the first anti-Jewish writing from the third century before Christ, but he dates the first virulent form of hostility toward Jews from the first century. He sees misanthropy, wickedness, and lack of education as sources of the charges.

The tale that Jews fatten up people and children in order to eat them at Passover was first told by the sophist Apion, who lived from 20 BCE until 45 CE. A leitmotif in that story—hence the title of Van der Horst's lecture—is that Jews supposedly engage in cannibalism. That fits the tradition in which civilizations that consider themselves superior accuse the lesser ones of consuming human flesh. In Christianity, the accusation of deicide is added: the Jews killed Jesus. They were also accused of causing the Black Death (the plague in 1348) in Europe, which led to a pogrom: a passionate massacre of Jews. Passionate because it promoted good and fought evil. This passion was very clear during Nazism. Van der Horst then continues:

> It is after all sufficiently known that in Nazi propaganda Jews as a people were demonized and dehumanized to such an extent that in the end a majority of Germans, Austrians, Poles, etc., could no longer see the Jews as anything but dirty vermin that had to be exterminated. The mass murderers in the concentration camps could go home at the end of every day with the good feeling that they had served humanity by exterminating dangerous vermin (2006, pp. 18–19).

This speech was not allowed to be delivered in its entirety, among other reasons because of the following sentence: "With this we encounter a great and worldwide problem, to wit that the Islamic world has taken over the torch of mindless anti-Semitism from the Nazis and continues carrying it with enthusiasm and fervour".

* * *

This is the psychotic version of the hatred of Jews, which was not called anti-Semitism until the publications of Marr, who unashamedly called himself an anti-Semite (1879 a, b). In this book we will sometimes have to deal with this, but usually with derived forms that show Jews as slightly odd, as not belonging to the sort of ordinary people who are smilingly called *our kind*. This kind of vague feeling, which cannot be called hate but certainly aversion, leads to all sorts of exclusion mechanisms that affect psychoanalysis itself and Jews in psychoanalysis in its wake. Then there emerges a mechanism to keep psychoanalysis untainted by Jews, and Jews sometimes participate in what has come to be called *Jewish self-hate*. This runs from a psychotic form (Weininger, 1903) through accommodations that Jews consider necessary in order to become a respected member of the community—including the psychoanalytic one—to great discomfort with and a forceful renouncement of their origins. In its mildest form it can be considered an accommodation to the existing majority. In a more intense form there is a question of identification with the aggressor as has been described extensively by Bettelheim (as described definitively in Anna Freud, 1936).

* * *

Even in official definitions of "Jew" one encounters anti-Semitic biases. The Marxist historian Deutscher looked in the *Oxford English Dictionary* and reported the following:

> ... the accepted meaning of the term "Jew": firstly, it is a "person of the Hebrew race"; secondly—this is the colloquial use—an "extortionate usurer, driver of hard bargains". "Rich as a Jew" says the proverb. Colloquially the word is also used as a transitive verb: to jew, the Oxford English Dictionary tells us, means to "cheat, overreach" (1986, p. 38).

The Dutch *Van Dale* dictionary (1992) also falls apart when it deals with Jews. After an introduction to the concept of Jew, it is responsible for an untruth when it states that "in the past [the word] was used as an invective or an insult". Why "in the past", I wonder. Anyone who wants to hear the word "Jew" as an insult should go to an away game of the Ajax soccer team. And if more convenient, a corner bar will do.

The linguist Ewoud Sanders has written three newspaper columns (2004a, b, c) about the history of compound words with the word "Jew" as described in the unabridged *Van Dale*. In 1924 it had 40 compound words with "Jew"; in 1950 there were 57. Between 1950 and 1999, 35 of these compound words disappeared: this was triggered by criticism of rather offensive descriptions. A fierce controversy was carried on in the newspaper. One of the dictionary editors states: "You can't make a dictionary responsible for the fact that the word 'Jew' is sometimes used as a term of abuse or in a racist way. A dictionary is a list of meanings of words and of linguistic facts". Ewoud Sanders then quotes Henk Verkuyl, a professor at the University of Utrecht. Verkuyl stated that there were "vestiges of anti-Semitism" in the *Van Dale*. Sanders says about this: "He [Verkuyl] even accused Hans Heestermans, one of Verkuyl's successors, of using 'bullshit' by hiding behind the argument that by deleting meanings and words you do harm to the language". I agree with Sanders when he ends his series of articles as follows:

> I think that these deletions are ill-advised for another reason. Our lexicon says a lot about the history of Dutch Jews and the history of anti-Semitism in the Netherlands. *Van Dale*, the oldest edition of which was made by two Jewish brothers-in-law, is in this respect an important and interesting source. In the latest edition this is no longer the case.

Later we will encounter statements by analysts who, according to me, react rather irrationally against Jews as a group and as individuals, and against Israel as a Jewish state. At that time I will also raise the question as to whether that is a normal political attitude. Sometimes I think that choosing a position in this way is also related to their ostentatious *disidentification*, especially as analysts, vis-à-vis the Jewish state.

The scholar of German language and literature Sander Gilman has shown himself to be an authority on anti-Semitism. In book after book (1991, 1993, 1994) he shows with painful precision how Jews, because of the inherently pathological nature attributed to them in the 19th century and earlier, were considered unsuited to carry out scholarship. Jews were thought to be sick, degenerate, superficial, and incestuous. He shows again and again how the Jewish foot, voice, nose, and mind were of inferior quality. It is a scholarly version of ordinary Christian prejudices. Gilman's recurring theme is that science was defined in such a way that a Jew could never be a good scientist or physician.

Oxaal, a sociologist and social historian, points out that in the 19th century being Jewish as such had a low status (1988, p. 44). In this light it is not surprising that in that century hundreds of Jews had themselves baptized every year. Reform Judaism with its more lenient laws emerged at that time; it combined a striving to remain Jewish with the wish to be accepted as a member of Western culture.

There is another, different way of thinking about the phenomenon of "Jew". The previously quoted authors Frosh and Ostow both make a connection between the Jewish tradition and the objectives of psychoanalysis. According to Frosh, the central characteristic of Judaism is the use of Talmudic patterns in reasoning and exegesis. In his view, that leads to a typically Jewish way of thinking. There is the unrestricted shaping of thoughts, starting from a strictly preserved framework, but also a fascination with words, with learning and evaluating, the option to see things differently. All this originates in the Jewish social position, which is eccentric, and in the central place that learning has traditionally held in Jewish culture in which learning the Talmud in particular is an exercise in subtle reasoning. In the mythology of psychoanalysis, the Jewish character of its founders caused them and their successors to stand outside the orthodoxies of their time. That gave them the opportunity to develop a radical perspective on society that was independent from tradition (Frosh, 2003).

Ostow reminds the reader that the Orthodox Jew prays three times a day for knowledge, insight, and sound judgment; and that does not differ much from insight into oneself, which is the central objective of psychoanalysis. The exact understanding of biblical and rabbinic writings that is central in Jewish *lernen* is parallel to the attempts the analyst makes to read the text of the patient as accurately as possible. The argument against declaring psychoanalysis to be Jewish is that any activity based on science strives for knowledge, insight, judgment, and precision. But for Jews as well as for analysts there is a certain measure of ritualizing in obtaining this knowledge. Their common goal is "deducing the hidden meaning of a manifest text by the application of set methods" (Ostow, 1982).

According to Gay, the combination of atheist and Jew was necessary for the invention of psychoanalysis (1987). Deutscher (1968) places Freud in the lineage of Spinoza, Heine, Marx, Rosa Luxemburg, and Trotsky, who viewed the universe as regulated by laws. When people live between two cultures, they think dialectically and see society dynamically. The patient who is analysed by Freud is not German, British, Russian, or Jewish, but a human being in his universality, with all his wishes, scruples, inhibitions, fears, and troubles.

* * *

Although in the second half of the 19th century and the early part of the 20th century the professions were fairly open, Jews were not yet welcome. We must not forget that Freud had left his original profession as neurologist and was busy founding a school, a core of what would become a profession, or indeed an identity. Freud invented the word *psychoanalyst* and the profession. He was the first to practise the profession and the only one for ten years. He felt isolated, locked in his own circle. He needed something else: followers, people who also wanted to call themselves psychoanalysts, academics who wanted to conduct a practice similar to his. In short, the emerging profession of psychoanalyst needed practitioners, and the Jews wanted entry into the professions. They saw psychoanalysis as an academic profession without too many social entrance barriers. In the heroic beginnings being Jewish was even an advantage. Freud got along better with Jews than with non-Jews, and the slowly expanding circle around him recruited members from its own network. In addition to the attraction of the psychoanalytic movement for Jews, there was from the beginning a distance between the psychoanalytic and the Jewish identity. The concept of identity must not be considered lightly here. According to Erikson (1956), it has become a "cornerstone" in the existence [of the psychoanalyst] as a human being, as practitioner of a profession, and as a citizen. An elegant, clear definition. The increased awareness of the complexity of life has led to identity being seen as more interactive, as shifting from one role to the other (Simon, 2004).

The psychoanalytic identity can also be used to make oppressive demands of the analyst. A quote from Freud describes this problem:

> Psycho-analytic activity is arduous and exacting; it cannot well be handled like a pair of glasses that one puts on for reading and takes off when one goes for a walk. As a rule psycho-analysis possesses a doctor either entirely or not at all (1933, pp. 152–153).

This quote can also be used to differentiate the analyst from the psychiatrist, the psychologist, and the psychotherapist. In this reasoning the psychoanalytic identity cannot coincide with any other. It is not stated explicitly, but there is a strong differentiation between the psychoanalyst and the Jew: a useful and necessary distinction. Later authors (for example Wille, 2005) use this text to say: all in all you belong completely to psychoanalysis or not at all.

The Jewish analyst wants to be seen as an analyst and not as a Jew. Ostow expresses this as follows: "Many Jews resented not only the culture that excluded them but also the culture that was excluded" (1982, p. 15). This same author noticed that in the monumental standard work of the Jewish analyst Fenichel, *Psychoanalytic Theory of Neurosis*, there are three mentions of Christian Science. The word Jew does not occur once. From this inferior position as Jew in combination with his sovereign position in carrying out his profession, the analyst in transference must dare to say the unspeakable and not be afraid to be considered as an outsider.

* * *

The nature of the Judaism of Freud and the others in the founding generation differed from each other, as did the later generations of psychoanalysts with regard to their possible Jewish origin. For me it is important to show what it means to be seen as a Jew. The Jew has always served as *the other*, hated and admired, especially as the often too close *outsider*. This is how it was when psychoanalysis began. I believe I can show that psychoanalysis has been treated as the Jew among sciences and that it has tried to escape that stigma by defence and self-cleansing.

This book is a search for the moments when the supposed Jewish character of psychoanalysis is under discussion. I will not be silent about what this means for the behaviour of non-analysts, especially for the opponents of psychoanalysis. I am increasingly intrigued by the movements within the psychoanalytic world itself to escape its Jewish background, to break free from it. In my research I found more examples of this than I had expected. That was an unpleasant surprise.

Notes

1. Blumenberg has written about the relationship between psychoanalysis and Judaism and about the question of the meaning of anti-Semitism for the analytic identity. See: Blumenberg (1995, 1996, 1997, 2006).

2. I am referring to the circumcision of the male Jewish baby on the eighth day of life by a *mohel* trained to perform this ritual.
3. This is a form of therapy that uses psychoanalytic concepts. There are differences in practice. In psychoanalysis the therapist sits and the patient lies down. The frequency of treatment is three, four, or five times a week. In psychotherapy the therapist and the patient both sit, and the frequency of therapy is less than three times a week.
4. For this fragment about transference and countertransference I have used as a guide Earl Hopper, *Theoretical and Conceptual Notes Concerning Transference and Countertransference Process in Psychoanalysis, Psychoanalytic Therapy, Psychoanalytic Group Therapy and Group Analysis*, which he sent to me as a personal communication, and Laplanche and Pontalis (1967).
5. Freud, S. (1915). Observations on Transference Love (Further Recommendations on the Technique of Psycho-Analysis III). The Standard Edition of the Complete Works of Sigmund Freud, Volume XII.
6. Felix de Mendelsohn got his quote from Freud (1960) p. 421.

CHAPTER TWO

Freud: a Jew in Europe

> I felt young and healthy, and my short visit to the new world encouraged my self-respect in every way. In Europe I felt as though I were despised; but over there I found myself received by the foremost men as an equal.
>
> (Sigmund Freud, *An Autobiographical Study*, 1925a, p. 52).

I consider Freud's relationship to his Jewish origins and—as always—the relationship of others to this background in three ways. I start with his scientific-political manoeuvres, and thereby think of the Freud-Jung-Abraham triangle. The conflict there is between Freud's loyalty to psychoanalysis and to the Jews surrounding him. He could barely stand the Jewish analysts around him, but he was very loyal to B'nai B'rith, the elite Jewish organization, in which he even accepted a board position. In chapter three, I discuss his friendship with Pfister and in particular how each of them separately and together handled the contents of Freud's book *The Future of an Illusion*. Chapter four deals with Freud's last magnum opus, *Moses and Monotheism: 3 Essays*. In this book, Freud's relationship to Judaism, both open and concealed, is visible. *Moses and Monotheism* is about their Moses, the one of the Egyptians, and our Moses, the one of the Jews, and *The Man Freud*, as Ehrlich (2003) calls him. Mortimer Ostow, a Freud expert, psychoanalyst, and Talmud scholar, calls Freud the prototype of the Diaspora Jew and argues that Freud shows these three aspects of himself (1999). As Ostow sees it, it is the task of the Diaspora Jew to obtain a position in the country where he lives and in the Jewish community to which he belongs. The author uses the word *host community*, as if you always live in rented rooms as a Jew.

* * *

In 1908 Freud was 52 years old. That gave him the right to adopt a fatherly attitude towards his colleagues. His reputation was growing, as was his authority in his own circle. This circle became larger, but in polite society just the mention of his name made people laugh or sometimes caused repugnance. Freud was quite certain that it was his theory that caused this. According to him, people could not bear the thought that even young children have libidinous *sexual* wishes. Jones (1972–1974) was of the same opinion. The latter was very penetrating in his comment that around that time the sexual stigma (odium sexium) had replaced the religious stigma (odium theologicum), which was in turn replaced by the political stigma (odium politicum). Freud and the psychoanalysts have, depending on the spirit of the times, suffered from all three. His followers and he were considered sexual perverts, compulsive and paranoid psychopaths, atheists, and political radicals who wanted to overthrow society. From each of these points of view psychoanalysis was painted as a danger to humanity.

In the summer of 1908, the second edition of *The Interpretation of Dreams* was in preparation, eight years after the first one. Freud wrote a new introduction for it. The disappointment in the lack of recognition for what he considered his masterpiece is evident in the foreword (p. XXV):

> If within ten years of the publication of this book (which is very far from being an easy one to read) a second edition is called for, this is not due to the interest taken in it by the professional circles to whom my original preface was addressed. My psychiatric colleagues seem to have taken no trouble to overcome the initial bewilderment created by my new approach to dreams.

> The professional philosophers have become accustomed to polishing off the problems of dream-life (which they treat as a mere appendix to conscious states) in a few sentences—and usually in the same ones; and they have evidently failed to notice that we have something here from which a number of inferences can be drawn that are bound to transform our psychological theories.

In the previous year he had met Jung for the first time. By that time, they had been corresponding for two years, exchanged comments about the other's writings, referred patients to each other, discussed treatments and exchanged opinions about colleagues. All this with a growing affection, certainly from Freud's side, although the many compliments to Jung clearly have a seductive function. Freud recognized in Jung someone who could think, had imagination, and could be very useful for what was central in his life, *the Cause (die Sache)*;[1] this involved the development, dissemination, and defence of the body of analytic ideas, winning followers, and forming an organizational structure that should be part of it. Such an organizational structure would encompass municipal, national, and transnational professional associations and training, the creation of journals, publishers, and the organization of conferences.

He let Jung know how limited he felt by the reception of his work and the qualities of his colleagues: this in spite of the fact that his years of intellectual isolation were past. His letters are from a provincial jail to an inhabitant of the greater world. They are attempts to escape the feeling of being rejected. That feeling remained, although no longer completely supported by the facts. Freud's attention was primarily taken up by diplomacy, which was needed to keep the Psychoanalytic Movement going. He looked for leaders, scholars, publicists, clinicians, financiers, and organizers. At the same time he wanted to make sure that there would be more psychoanalysts, train them, and make them into associates. For this he needed to start a school and establish an organization because he thought he had discovered a new truth and he wanted to convince the world of it. A careful education took place with all its consequences. For Freud it was essential that this schooling be connected to the greater non-Jewish world. His mission succeeded fairly well. The movement flowered and the newly acquired followers were enthusiastic about the new insights. In Budapest, Berlin, and

Vienna psychoanalysts were starting to practise their profession and to develop their contacts. An important step to professionalization, internationalization, and institutionalization was made with the First Psychoanalytic Congress on April 26, 1908 in Salzburg, Austria. There were 42 participants who called themselves *Friends of Psychoanalysis*, nine of whom, among them Jung and Abraham, gave presentations. From Freud himself they heard the case that later became a classic as the story of the *Rat Man* (1909b).

In 1910 Freud saw for the first time an opportunity for an expansion of the psychoanalytic movement. Psychoanalysts were no longer only in Vienna. Their number was expanding in Europe and even in the world. Jung who lived in Switzerland became an active member; the Welshman Jones lived in London; Abraham had a substantial practice in Berlin and was busy establishing an institute there; Ferenczi carried out his profession in Budapest. Abraham Brill and Morton Prince lived and worked in the United States. They were the pioneers of the second wave: during a congress in Nuremburg, the International Psychoanalytical Association, the IPA,[2] was established. The Swiss minister's son Jung was named as President for Life. Ferenczi delivered an address welcoming him and in it characterized the initial period of psychoanalysis as a heroic time when Freud stood all alone. He did not mention Freud's original comrades-in-arms, the Viennese. Without actually calling it such, they had founded the first psychoanalytic organization. The informal "waiting room group", which had started in 1902 with four men at Freud's invitation, had developed its own dynamics. In 1908 there were 20 members, and with Freud's encouragement they took steps toward autonomy. The existence of the group became formalized; they were called the Vienna Psychoanalytic Association. In this organization there started to be such things as entrance requirements, membership dues, and squabbling about admission and non-qualification. As a group the Viennese analysts felt passed-over by the appointment of Jung and disowned by Ferenczi's address. They saw themselves as faithful companions of Freud from the beginning of psychoanalysis. When Freud found out, something happened that seldom occurred: he burst out in a uncontrolled fit of anger against his Viennese followers. Freud's first biographer, Wittels, describes the scene as follows:

> I had never seen him so excited. He said: "Most of you are Jews and therefore incompetent to win friends for the new teaching.

We are all in danger". He grabbed his coat at the lapels and said: "They won't even let me keep the clothes on my body. The Swiss will save us, and all of you as well" (2003, p. 140).

Actually Freud was here working out in practice what he had written in a more thoughtful manner to Abraham when the latter was close to being in conflict with Jung. He wrote Abraham a few sentences that are never absent in discussions about psychoanalysis, or about Freud and Jung, and that I want to include here with the footnote that the editor of the Freud-Abraham correspondence has added.

> I nurse a suspicion that the suppressed anti-Semitism of the Swiss that spares me is deflected in reinforced form upon you. But I think that we as Jews, if we wish to join in anywhere, must develop a bit of masochism, be ready to suffer some wrong. Otherwise there is no hitting it off. Rest assured that if my name were Oberhuber,[3] in spite of everything my innovations would have met with far less resistance (Falzeder, 2002, pp. 53–54).

The incident described by Wittels is confirmed by the memories of the Viennese analyst Isidor Sadger[4] who was a member of the "waiting room group". He was the one who could, after Freud, call himself the first psychoanalyst. He did not really fit well in this group. The biographical note that Andrea Hupke and Michael Schröter added to republication of his work had as its title "Approach to a non-loved analyst". He lived from 1867 until 1942, when he was murdered in the concentration camp Theresienstadt. He has escaped oblivion because very talented and devoted bibliographers found his personal memories of Freud, dating from 1927, in the library of Keio University in Japan and in the National Hebrew Library in Jerusalem and edited and published them. They had remained hidden because Sadger wanted to publish them himself after Freud's death. But at that point their publication was opposed by Jones among others. About Freud's attitude towards his own Jewish group he wrote: "It remains a fact that any Christian follower was dearer to Freud than ten Jewish ones". He describes the same scene as Wittels and lets it end with Freud's exclamation: "Jews have to settle for being culture carriers. I have to join science" (Sadger, 2006, p. 74).

Freud's intimate non-relationship with Schnitzler and Herzl, two representatives of the Jewish elite whose paths he did not cross or barely crossed, was of a very different nature. He himself declared that he did not dare to contact Schnitzler. Freud wrote him as follows:

> I have plagued myself over the question how it comes about that in all these years I have never sought your company and enjoyed a conversation with you (assuming that it would not have been unwelcome to you). The answer is this much too intimate confession. I think I have avoided you from a kind of awe of meeting my "double" (Jones, 1972–1974, vol. 3, p. 474).

There was also a careful attempt to approach Herzl. Freud wrote him a flattering note with a compliment about his play *Das neue Ghetto* and asked him to review the *Interpretation of Dreams* for the *Neue Freie Presse*. And he added: "I beg you to keep this book as a token of the esteem in which I—like many others—hold you as poet and fighter for our people" (Loewenberg, 1971, p. 367). However, he never spoke to Herzl, although they lived in the same neighbourhood.

After seeing Herzl's *Das neue Ghetto*, Freud's dream "My myopic son" emerges. About this he says:

> The Jewish problem, concern about the future of one's children, to whom one cannot give a country of their own, concern about educating them in such a way that they can move freely, across frontiers—all of this was easily recognizable among the relevant dream-thoughts (1900, p. 442).

As a result of this explanation, given by Freud himself, but not only because of this, I concur with remarks by the Freud scholar Yerushalmi and the psychiatrist Emmanuel Rice who state that Freud was more familiar with Zionistic ideas than he let on (Loewenberg, 1971; Rice, 1990; Yerushalmi, 1991). The thought that for Jews there is no place to give their children a safe shelter is a Zionistic one. However, *Das neue Ghetto* was not a play about persecution but instead about Christian-Jewish reconciliation. The content of Freud's dream refers to the basic document of Zionism, *Der Judenstaat* by Herzl (1896)—written four years after the play when, as a result of the Dreyfus affair, the hope for a Jewish state had evaporated. It is the dream in which occur the ironic greetings *auf Geseres* and *auf Ungeseres*, expressions coined by Freud.[5] In the dream he lets a boy ("clearly my oldest") say "auf Geseres" instead of a goodbye kiss.

"Auf Ungeseres" is said to "both of us", one of whom is the dreamer. Freud writes about this: "According to information I have received from philologists, *'Geseres'* is a genuine Hebrew word derived from the verb *'goiser'*, and is best translated by 'imposed sufferings' or 'doom'". Its opposite means "unsalted", but in Freud's association it becomes "unleavened". Freud then relates the abbreviated Passover story about the exodus from Egypt in order to explain the meaning of the dream. It was about the liberation from slavery, just as he must also have dreamed about the liberation from anti-Semitic Vienna. Freud must have known the Pesach story well because his father recited it every year at Passover.

At the level of explicit content of the dream, it is striking that the inversion *auf Ungeseres* must rest on the understanding of the expression *auf Geseres*, an intimate melancholy Yiddish greeting. For the initiated listener, "auf Ungeseres" is also an allusion to Passover where unleavened bread replaces leavened bread in reality and in symbolism. The text fragment by Freud ("according to information I have received from philologists") is too detached in relation to what Freud must have known. In my discussion of *Moses and Monotheism* I will return to this subject.

Avner Falk, the Israeli authority on psychoanalysis, interprets the dream as if it were Freud's father addressing his son:

> You are myopic: you do not see the two sides of yourself, the masculine and the feminine, the paternal and the maternal, the Jewish and the universal. *You are indeed shortsighted* and one-sided, *for you are trying to overlook your own fierce attraction to Jewish nationalism, and to me,* and your *preference* for *"Auf Ungeseres"*—the unleavened bread *your* people eat at *Passover* (1978, p. 283).

Falk concludes that the conflict between the Jewish and the universal bothered Freud to the end of his days. An ironic footnote: Freud's name does not appear in Herzl's diary that counted over 18,000 words (Ellenberger, 1970, p. 558).

* * *

In his personal life Freud was always fully aware that he was Jewish and acted as such. As is evident from the incident with his Viennese followers, he understood quite well that what was normal and fairly uncomplicated for him could be a reason for exclusion from his non-Jewish surroundings. He did not want to be thwarted by his Judaism. He saw religion as an obsessional neurosis. At home he could allow himself to forbid various domestic ceremonies connected to Judaism. He forbade his wife Martha—from a family of rabbis—to light Shabbat candles on Friday evening. Although Freud had his own developing relationship with his Jewish origins, his wife remained in her heart the traditional Jewish housewife. To demonstrate this she initiated what the Freud biographer Gay called "a standing joke, repeated for half a century for the benefit of sympathetic visitors".

It is Friday afternoon. Freud has already fled to England, and a young scholar from Oxford is paying a visit. They are talking about psychoanalysis and about developments in Austria after the *Anschluss*. At five o'clock Martha intervenes in the conversation and says:

> "You must know that on Friday evenings good Jewish women light candles for the approach of the Sabbath. But this monster—*Unmensch*—will not allow this, because he says that religion is a superstition". Freud gravely nodded and agreed: "Yes," he said, "it *is* a superstition," to which the Frau Professor, addressing her visitor, rejoined: "You *see*?" (Gay, 1987, pp. 152–153).

Freud did have a *chuppa* (the canopy for the Jewish wedding ceremony), but that was because in Austria a religious ceremony in addition to a civil ceremony was required. On that occasion he even considered becoming Protestant, but Breuer prevented him from doing this.

There is no difference of opinion about the Jewish holidays being celebrated at the Freuds—they were not. There are contradictory reports about the question whether they participated in non-Jewish customs. Their son Martin remembers: "Our holidays were Christmas with presents under a tree lit by candles and Easter with nicely painted Easter eggs". The Canadian professor and Freud biographer Paul Roazen interviewed a non-Jewish neighbour of the Freud family, a Mrs. Ochsner. She told him that members of the Freud family visited her at home to see her Christmas tree because Sigmund and Martha were not familiar with it from their families. To make things more complicated—their daughter Anna remembers that as a child she would go to Hebrew lessons in a liberal synagogue on Saturday mornings (Rice, 1990, pp. 121–122).

There is uncertainty about the question whether Freud let his sons be circumcised. Their circumcision or lack of it is not mentioned in the biographies that I have consulted (Breger, 2000; Clark, 1982; Gay, 1989; Jones, 1972–1974; Sulloway, 1979). This caused the authors Maciejewski (2002) and De Klerk (2003) to ask the Jewish community of Vienna whether Freud's sons were circumcised. The answer to that question was that they did not appear in a circumcision register. Both authors concluded that they were not circumcised. I posed the same question to the same authority and it resulted in the following email:

> Some communities have no Sefer Brith Mila [circumcision book], the Mohel [the person who performs the circumcision] often has his own book. The absence of an entry is no proof that the children have not been circumcised. Best regards. Chief Rabbi Chaim Eisenberg.

For me no conclusion can be reached from all this. No candles on Friday evening but a circumcision? That happens. On the other hand, Freud participated intensely in Jewish life. His children married Jews. Not being circumcised is an exception to the rule for Jewish boys and awkward in the dressing room of an athletic club or youth centre, just as being circumcised makes them exceptional in non-Jewish surroundings. Freud's repeated statement that he and his family were Jewish seems a concealed reference to the circumcision of the boys:

> On the other hand I have always had a strong feeling of solidarity with my fellow-people, and have always encouraged it in my children as well. We have all remained in the Jewish denomination (1925b, p. 291).

It is also hard to imagine that Freud did not have his sons circumcised. In all the fuss about the "*aliquis* dream" that he recounts in *The Psychopathology of Everyday Life*, he takes as an example "… a certain young man of academic background. I soon found that he was familiar with some of my psychological publications. We had fallen into conversation—how I have now forgotten—about the social status of the race to which we both belonged". This man fears that his girlfriend is pregnant. The denouement comes in a circuitous way. The man who is uncertain about having children with his girlfriend says to himself:

> Have you really so keen a wish for descendants? That is not so. How embarrassed you would be if you were to get news just now that you were to expect descendants from the quarter you know of. No: no descendants—*however much we need them for vengeance* [author's italics] (1901, pp. 8–14).

The report of this thought presents two possibilities. For me the most obvious one is that this was Freud's own dream and his own thought. He analysed numerous dreams in *The Interpretation of Dreams* in the same way. It is also possible that it is really someone else's dream; from Freud's obvious understanding of the dreamer it seems that for Freud vengeance is also a comprehensible motivation. Freud valued the continued existence of the Jewish people and understood the feelings of vengeance for what has been done to the Jews through the ages.

What is shown above all in the letters to Jung and to Abraham is that Freud was on his way to recognition but felt that he was not getting it; he feels like an outsider who scratches at the doors of respectability (Falzeder, 2002; McGuire, 1974). What the sociologist Elias observes in the relationship between the middle class and the court nobility at the end of the 18th century, applies to Freud. Elias quotes from Goethe's *Werther*:

> What irritates me most of all, is our odious bourgeois situation. To be sure, I know as well as any other how necessary class differences are, how many advantages I owe to them myself, only they should not stand directly in my way (1939).

At the same time Elias places this in the perspective of his ideas about the development of groups and professions in society by stating:

> Nothing better characterizes middle-class consciousness than this statement. The doors below must remain shut. Those

above must open. And like any other middle class, this one was imprisoned in a peculiarly middle-class way: it could not think of breaking down the walls that blocked the way up, for fear that those separating it from the lower strata might also give way in the assault (1939).

This comment could also apply to Freud and the rising bourgeoisie. And it applies as well to the striving for emancipation by Jews and physicians and by Jewish physicians and the admittance of the psychosocial to the medical; the thinking and feeling that first becomes the concern of the physician and later, as urged by Freud, also the province of the non-physician (1926). In the later development of the psychoanalytic profession, the door to upstairs is wide open.

Suitable physicians as well as laypersons were recruited. Freud was generous towards the latter. He wanted to have followers who would help the cause so that the circle of analysts would grow. Contrary to Freud's wishes, there was also a tendency to let only physicians practise the profession. Especially the American leaders did not want to admit non-psychiatrists into the profession. Wallerstein (1998) has written a fascinating description of this fight. The analytic profession has made sure that very strict criteria were employed in all stages of analytic training, from admittance to training and to recognition as analyst. The legitimate rationale behind this was to protect the patient against bungling. However, in the light of the quote from Elias, the motivation to keep the door tightly closed behind oneself is also perceptible.

Freud stated that he wanted to have academic recognition for psychoanalysis in the form of a professorship, but Gicklhorn and Gicklhorn (1960), who want to protect the reputation of the University of Vienna, deny this. They say that Freud did not carry out his bureaucratic obligations, that he gave too few lectures, that he had no real interest in academic life and did not spend enough money socially as was necessary in order to obtain a professorship, and that he behaved in a querulous manner. From the conclusion of their argument it follows that he should have waited his turn because it always took decades before you were appointed as acting professor at the University of Vienna. He would never become a full professor: for that a conversion to Christianity was necessary.

Eissler, the guardian of Freud's reputation, does not accept this (1966). He gets to the bottom of the question: no lecture given by Freud, no tea visit with a professor, is overlooked. He believes that Freud's appointment as professor most certainly was thwarted. He finds it odd that Freud was not appointed as professor, even as acting professor, until 17 years after his "habilitation" examination. After much research, Eissler shows that in the period from 1885 to 1900, 35 lecturers were given that honour within one to five years after the same examination, 24 after six to ten years, and 18 after 11 to 15 years. Four, of whom Freud was one, had to wait 16 to 20 years, and one received the title after 28 years. Or, as D. B. Klein remarked in his study:

> Seldom were Jews appointed to full professorships (in 1894, two of the 53 Jews teaching at the University of Vienna reached the highest rank). Classes taught by Jewish professors were boycotted at the university. Efforts were made to limit the Jewish enrolment in gymnasia as well (1985, p. II).

Freud was dissatisfied with the social influence of his Viennese Jewish colleagues. He had doubts about them and felt confined by them. He was honest about his preferences and did not hide his Jewish cultural prejudices. He wrote as follows about the wife of a patient whom he referred to Jung: "One of the few Teutonic women I've ever liked". But the warning he expressed to Jung about the publications that his Viennese colleagues were preparing is clear:

> You see how petty one becomes when one is reduced to such company as I am here in the Vienna Society. Last Wednesday it was again brought home to me how much of the most elementary educational work remains to be done (McGuire, 1974, p. 451).

When he wanted to deepen his friendship with Jung, he did that by slipping him stories about others—for example, he expressed more a feeling than a considered opinion about Jones. Rephrasing Caesar's funeral oration, he writes: "Jones is undoubtedly a very interesting and worthy man". Yet in the next breath he adds: "[B]ut he gives me a feeling of, I was almost going to say racial strangeness. He is a fanatic and doesn't eat enough" (McGuire, 1974, p. 145).

Freud suspects something that has been touched on briefly: Jones did not care too much for Jews even though he associated a lot and very well with them and was married to a Jewish woman for over 30 years. Gay calls him an honorary Jew, always telling Jewish jokes; a man who after 1908 joined Freud and therefore the circle around him, but not completely (Jones, 1972–1974, pp. 184ff.). Freud's friendship with him was not exactly uncalculated. On June 8, 1913, Freud writes to Ferenczi, a friend whom he trusted: "I am very pleased that Jones is acquitting himself well. Be strict and tender with him. He is a very good person. Feed the pupa so that a queen can be made out of it" (Brabant, 1993, Letter 402). In addition, Jones was the one who somewhat understood the position of the Jews. Writing about Freud's initial enthusiasm when Jung wanted to join the movement and the close Viennese Jewish circle around Freud that was very hesitant about it, Jones states: "Their attitude was accentuated by their Jewish suspicion of Gentiles in general with its rarely failing expectation of anti-Semitism" (Jones, 1972–1974, vol. II, pp. 48–49). The explanation that Jones gives for the predictive faculty of the circle around Freud surprises in an unfavourable sense: "The Germans have a good saying about this: *'Hate produces sharp eyesight.'* I would have said: *'Being hated produces sharp eyesight.'*"

Jones is not just anyone in the psychoanalytic world. He played a dominant role in the introduction, design, and internationalization of the movement. He was the one who was instrumental in establishing the IPA in 1910 and the American Psychoanalytic Association (APsaA) in 1911. In 1913 he was at the beginning of the British Psychoanalytical Society. In 1919 he was the founder of the Institute of Psychoanalysis in London, and in 1920 he established the International Journal of Psychoanalysis where he remained the editor-in-chief until 1939. He was the president of the International Psychoanalytical Association from 1919 until 1924 and from 1932 until 1949. Until the 1950s he was the greatest organizer that the analytic movement had produced. In particular, he had to see to it that analysis made it through the Second World War as undamaged as possible (more about this in chapter five).

As concerns the Jewish element in psychoanalysis, according to Klein, Jones saw it as his task not to highlight it too much (Klein, 1985, p. XII). Jones had a hard time tolerating the Jewish bonds of the early analysts because he saw those as an impurity and an obstacle in the psychoanalytic search for truth. According to Klein, Jones deleted the expression of thankfulness to "those of our faith" in the publication of a letter from 1884 that Freud wrote to his wife Martha (1985, p. XII). Because of his behaviour during the Nazi era, Frosh calls Jones "a villain and a hero" (2003, p. 1320). Breger calls him a flatterer (2000, p. 19).

Personal experience and the study of sources led to Jones's best-known work: the first scholarly biography of Freud (1972–1974). He thereby painted the definitive portrait of Freud and, because of his thoroughness, his role in the process of recognition and the professionalizing of psychoanalysis, and the access he had to the first three generations of psychoanalysts, his book is indispensable for anyone who studies the life and works of Freud.

Freud was fairly close to Abraham, the leader of psychoanalysis in Berlin, even though their letters to each other give a rather businesslike impression. Freud was friendly, and on August 22, 1910, after they had corresponded for three years, he addressed Abraham for the first time as "dear friend". Abraham continued addressing him as "Professor". I find this correspondence awkward to read: too much about work and disagreements about it, too little affection on equal terms. Sometimes there is an interruption when they fall back on both their Jewish backgrounds, even when it is an incomplete quote of Heine who after his baptism knew himself to be *hated by Christians and by Jews*. The fragment that appealed to me is from a letter written on December 10, 1917 by Freud to Abraham:

> I am at daggers drawn with writing, as with many other things. Included among them is your dear German fatherland. I can hardly imagine myself ever going there again, even when it becomes physically possible again. In the struggle between the Entente and the Quadruple Alliance I have definitely adopted the viewpoint of Heine's Donna Bianca in the disputation in Toledo: All I can say is … (Falzeder, 2002, p. 364).

What Freud leaves out but what they both know are the classic final lines of this poem (in Falzeder's note the lines have been translated):

> I don't know which one is right,
> But all I can say is,

That the Rabbi and the Monk,
That both of them stink.

In the correspondence Abraham remains the junior who develops into someone, but not completely. Freud is the master, although Abraham starts to hold important positions. The relationship is mostly one between two bureaucrats who are very useful to each other. Abraham sometimes dares to see things specifically about Jewish affairs that Freud prefers to pass over. During his training at the Burghölzli clinic in Switzerland, Abraham was greeted with characteristic aloofness. Abraham saw Jung's anti-Semitism even when Freud still wanted to make him his successor and wrote: "Our Aryan comrades are really quite indispensable to us, otherwise psychoanalysis would fall victim to anti-Semitism" (Diller, 1991, p. 183).

Although Abraham's excellent intelligence, organizational capacity, and loyalty to psychoanalysis were appreciated by Freud, he was repeatedly the least important in several triangles around Freud; first with Jung, then with Rank and Ferenczi. Abraham disappeared into the background and then returned to the centre of Freud's interest with his logical analysis, but sometimes very far-fetched ideas (Cremerius, 1997). We should not forget that Abraham was an ordinary, although prominent, analyst and Jung the first president of the IPA. In 1910 Jung was chosen for the first time, and in 1913 he stood again for election. Abraham saw that the friendship between Freud and Jung was ending and that Jung was moving away from psychoanalysis. Abraham conducted a campaign to urge others not to vote in that second election. Twenty-two of the 52 voters did so. Jung was re-elected. In 1914 he resigned his chairmanship, and at Freud's urging Abraham became interim chairman. Abraham was president during the First World War when there was no congress.

Freud was profoundly disloyal to Abraham when he wrote to Jung that he was aware that a break seemed imminent between Jung and Abraham. He asks Jung to heal the rift because there are so few analysts. But Freud writes in advance that his loyalty will be to Jung:

I regard him [Abraham] as a man of great worth and I should not like to be obliged to give him up, though there can be no question of his replacing you in my eyes (McGuire, 1974, p. 145).

That same day he writes Abraham about the same question. First he starts with an interpretation: "Now, I consider a rivalry between the two of you to be inevitable".[6] Then he agrees with him in his conflict with Jung and explains that Jung's sensitivity is caused by his sensitivity to criticism and his doubts about the value of analysis. He asks Abraham to send his proposed publication to Jung and to take his objections seriously:

> Do not take the little victory over yourself too hard. Be tolerant, and do not forget that really it is easier for you to follow my thoughts than it is for Jung, since to begin with you are completely independent, and then you are closer to my intellectual constitution through racial kinship, while he as a Christian and a pastor's son finds his way to me only against great inner resistances. His association with us is therefore all the more valuable. I was almost going to say that it was only by his emergence on the scene that psychoanalysis was removed from the danger of becoming a Jewish national affair (Falzeder, 2002, p. 38).[7]

On May 11, 1908 Abraham writes that he has followed Freud's advice, and he stresses the Jewish connection between them:

> I freely admit that I find it easier than Jung does to go along with you. I, too, have always felt this intellectual kinship. After all, the Talmudic way of thinking cannot disappear in us just like that. Some days ago a small paragraph in *Jokes* strangely attracted me. When I looked at it more closely, I found that, in the technique of apposition and in its whole structure, it was completely Talmudic. In Zurich, incidentally, I was always pleased that Bleuler and Jung overcame the resistances based on their different constitutions so successfully. All the more painful is the change! (Falzeder, 2002, p. 40).[8]

Abraham also keeps a close eye on the Cause. He reports a striking omission that Bleuler made by not mentioning Freud in a lecture about psychoanalysis. Abraham himself had not mentioned Jung and Bleuler in his own discussion about sexuality "because they are turning away from the theory of sexuality". This sounds like a bunch of ambitious scholars. What is more interesting is that Abraham already noticed signals that things would go wrong between Freud and Jung while the friendship between the two was still intact. But on July 11, in a letter to Abraham, Freud remains painfully neutral in the developing conflict between Abraham and Jung.

> I am afraid that there is a lack of desire for a satisfactory harmony on both sides, although, to be sure, with the exception of what you did recently to please me. I must reconcile you for the sake of the cause; you are both too valuable to me (Falzeder, 2002, p. 49).

This sentence seems to be fuelled by a letter of May 7 from Jung that starts in a businesslike manner (McGuire, 1974, p. 148). Jung discusses his activities for the yearbook that will be published. He thinks that Abraham is a suitable candidate to make the abstracts, but then he adds:

> You will see from this suggestion that my objective judgment of A. is not in the least impaired. For that very reason I have an undisguised contempt for some of colleague A.'s idiosyncrasies. In spite of his estimable qualities and sundry virtues he is simply not a *gentleman* (McGuire, 1974, p. 149).

He then characterizes an article by Abraham as plagiarism, but he adds reassuringly:

> You can rest assured that so long as A. behaves himself decently everything will remain the same on my side. But if he goes too far, an explosion will be unavoidable. I hope very much that A. will be mindful of how far one may go. A break would be a great pity and not in the interests of our cause. He can avoid this eventuality *very easily* by a *little bit* of decency.

The question of plagiarism is important because according to Haynal and Falzeder the opposite was true (Falzeder, 2002, p. XXVI). Jung and Freud had a difference of opinion about the cause of schizophrenia. Abraham supported Freud's point of view in this matter, but he quite properly mentioned Jung's theory. If Abraham had plagiarized anyone—but according to the authors it was a matter of quoting—it would have been Freud.

Freud was not angry, on the contrary. But Jung was—because Abraham did not share his opinion. In this whole spectacle of contempt and power Jung says in fact about Abraham that he does not belong to "our kind of people". He says this about the person whom Jones called "the most normal of the group". That was not so bad, but all the power was in Jung's hands: Not only as Freud's favourite at that moment, but also because he spoke on behalf of Burghölzli, the first psychiatric clinic that had taken psychoanalysis seriously starting in 1903 (Gay, 1989, p. 180). Courses were given at Burghölzli, and in addition to Jung, people like Eitingon, Abraham, Binswanger, Maeder, Bleuler, and Brill worked there in different capacities and at different times. Haynal and Falzeder give a very long and, according to them, incomplete list of staff members, which is even so quite impressive.[9] According to Zaretsky, except for Jones and the Viennese, every analyst who turned to Freud during these years came from Burghölzli. For an ambitious young analyst in the making it was therefore of vital importance to be accepted to that clinic.

Jung's contempt concerns the man who after Burghölzli established himself as the first and only analyst in Berlin, founded a psychoanalytic institute there in 1920, and was its director until his death in 1925. During that time he expanded the institute into a centre of psychoanalytic knowledge, and within that institute he came to be regarded as a highly sought-after training analyst.

I have written that Freud always looked out for the interest of the Cause. That is true, but it is not the whole truth. There is an obviously amicable, perhaps even homoerotic tone in his correspondence with Jung. According to Gay, Jung had three qualities that were irresistible for Freud: not Viennese, not old, and, best of all, not Jewish (1989, p. 202). The correspondence started on April 11, 1906 with a letter from Freud to Jung with the salutation "Geehrter Herr Kollege" (Esteemed colleague) in which he thanks Jung for sending him his *Diagnostische Assoziationstudien*. After a short period of "Lieber Freund und Kollege" (Dear friend and colleague), which started with a letter from November 15, 1907, it became "Lieber Freund" (Dear friend). Jung continued to write "Hochgeehrter Herr Professor" (Highly esteemed professor), which he changed on October 21, 1908, into "Lieber Herr Professor" (Dear professor).

The correspondence with Abraham also began with a letter from Freud, this time about a lecture that Abraham had sent him. The date was June 1907. The change from "Lieber Kollege" (Dear colleague) into "Lieber Freund" (Dear friend) took 92 letters, until August 1910. On July 16, 1908, Abraham complained about his difference of opinion with Jung and about the entire attitude at Burghölzli towards psychoanalysis (Falzeder, 2002, p. 49). The warm welcome that psychoanalysis received initially became gradually cooler. Freudian evenings were stopped, and the traditional psychiatric line was carried out more forcefully. According to Abraham there was more behind it. Obviously he not only recognized Jung's later anti-Semitism long before it started to play a role in society, but he was also annoyed at Jung's spiritualistic tendencies.

On July 23, Freud sends Abraham his comments on a manuscript and writes:

> "I value the resolute tone and clarity of your writings" and continues, "[M]ay I say that it is consanguineous Jewish traits that attract me to them? We understand each other, don't we?" He does not appreciate Abraham's open conflict with Jung and writes to Abraham: "You certainly had every justification for writing in that way, but it would have shown greater delicacy of feeling not to have made use of it" (Falzeder, 2002, p. 53).

In *On the History of the Psycho-Analytic Movement* (1914c), Freud discusses various problems at the reception of psychoanalysis, but its alleged Jewish character gets only a footnote mention. The motto of the document could not only apply to psychoanalysis but also to the Jews of his time. For this motto he takes the legend of the coat of arms of the city of Paris: *FLUCTUAT NEC MERGITUR* (He floats but does not drown).

A small part of Freud's argument is devoted to resistance to the psychoanalytic movement. He mentions that psychoanalysis brings out the worst in the opponent; how people curse him out. Then he comes to the Parisian opponent Pierre Janet who reproaches psychoanalysis for being "Viennese" because it maintains that "one can trace neuroses to disturbances in sexual life". Freud makes fun of this, although he is rather serious at first:

> We have all heard of the interesting attempt to explain psychoanalysis as a product of the Vienna milieu. As recently as in

> 1913 Janet was not ashamed to use this argument, although he himself is no doubt proud of being a Parisian, and Paris can scarcely claim to be a city of stricter morals than Vienna. The suggestion is that psycho-analysis, and in particular its assertion that the neuroses are traceable to disturbances in sexual life, could only have originated in a town like Vienna—in an atmosphere of sensuality and immorality foreign to other cities [...].

And he concludes as follows: "The Viennese are no more abstinent and no more neurotic than the inhabitants of any other capital city".

What he leaves out is that Janet's allegations of pansexuality and his, Freud's, lack of clarity have an anti-Semitic undertone. In the continuation of this passage Freud states that "the city of Vienna has done everything to deny its part in the creation of psychoanalysis", and he speaks about the hostility and indifference of the learned and skilled classes towards the analysts. Again a reproach by Freud, and again no allusion to the alleged Jewish character of psychoanalysis in anti-Semitic Vienna (1914c, pp. 39–40).

Freud does not dare to call the thing by its name, as Roudinesco did in 1982: Janet was simply an anti-Semite and did not mind saying so. His prejudices are exactly the prejudices that are prevalent about Jews: they are money-hungry; they stick together; they are sensual; and above all they ruin good morals and manners. Roudinesco places him and his rejection of psychoanalysis in the context of an anti-Semitic tendency of Jung, Gobineau, Le Bon, and Daudet. She writes:

> Jung's unconscious is of the same nature as the unconscious "à la française"—i.e., the one of Le Bon, and Léon Daudet, but also that of Janet. It is the dark unconscious of the silent masses. It is psychological automatism. It is the people's soul. It is that collective "thing", occult and demonic, which causes man to remain a sleepwalker. This explains why Jung let himself be caught in the trap of Nazi doctrine.

Roudinesco is also clear about seeing this *unconscious à la française* as racist and again shows its anti-Semitism. She quotes Wilhelm Marr, who coined the word "anti-Semite", and who wrote a pamphlet with the title "The Conquest of Judaism over the Germanic", and writes:

> With anti-Semitism the French bourgeoisie of the end of the 19th century finally found the word that was lacking to gain the nobility that the old aristocracy had taken away. An unheard-of revenge on the revolution of 1789; against the nobility of blood, the bourgeoisie proclaimed the equality of peoples, men, and nations. In the name of science, [the bourgeoisie] now takes back its due by proclaiming its worship of a chosen and superior race, the French people (1982, pp. 178ff.).

Notes

1. The standard translation of *die Sache* into English is *the Cause*, but I think that Freud, a worldly man, would have had no objection to translating it as *the Business*.
2. Originally the organization was the Internationale Psychoanalytische Vereinigung, the IPV in German, which was the official language. The official language was changed to English at the 16th Psychoanalytic Congress in Zurich in 1949.
3. An obviously non-Jewish name.
4. His name was Izaak, which he changed to Isidor, a name that sounds less Jewish in German. This information and the following quotes are all from Sadger (2006).
5. *Auf Geseres* can be translated as "until the next misery".
6. He means the rivalry for the love of Father Freud (author's note).
7. "Jewish national affair" is probably an ironic reference to the Jewish National Fund which was founded in Vienna in 1901.
8. Abraham here alludes to Jung's distancing himself from psychoanalysis.
9. Roberto Greco Assagioli, Ludwig Binswanger, Trigant Burrow, Abraham Arden Brill, Charles Macfie Campbell, Imre Décsi, Max Eitingon, Sándor Ferenczi, Johann Jako Honegger, Smith Eli Jelliffe, Ernest Jones, Alphonse Maeder, Herman Nunberg, Johan H. W. van Ophuizen, Nikolai J. Ossipow, Franz Riklin, Hermann Rohrschach, Tatiana Rosenthal, Leonhard Seif, Eugenie Sokolnicka, Sabina Spielrein, Philipp Stein, Wolf Stockmayer, Johannes Irgens Stromme, Jaroslav Stuchlik, G. Alexander Young, and Karl Abraham.

CHAPTER THREE

Pfister and Freud, a friendship

The friendship between Freud and Pfister is known to be sincere. This is evident from their correspondence (Meng & E. L. Freud, 1963). Of course the Cause was of importance, and of course Freud was looking for talented students, and of course it was equally interesting for a young, still unknown pastor to come into contact with a 17-year-older author of worldwide renown. For Freud it was useful to have an opportunity to spread the psychoanalytic body of thought to Switzerland and to expand it to pastoral work with the aid of this energetic and prolific writer. Freud gave sympathetic criticism of the other's growing body of work, and he sometimes wrote a foreword for one of Pfister's books. In their letters there is much fuss about the publication of books and journals, the quality of translations, and the establishment of a psychoanalytic publishing house.

In addition to these business concerns there was also a sincere and friendly relationship between the two men. From their lively correspondence it is clear that they saw each other primarily as authors. In his letters Freud was the same elegant writer that he was in his work that was intended for publication. His plaudits were inventive. On November 21, 1926, upon receiving a complimentary copy of a book by Pfister, he wrote: "Let me congratulate you. I shall gladly set aside a special shelf for the translations of your books if you send me them". Pfister also knew how to give compliments. Two months earlier, on September 10, 1926, he wrote:

> I read through your kind gift at one sitting and with great admiration. You have never before written in such a readily comprehensible fashion, yet everything springs from the depths.

The two letter writers also showed a true interest in each other's well-being. Freud kept a certain distance, but Pfister wrote about his unhappy marriage and about the worries over his son.[1] What is not in them is surprising: the whole political situation in the turbulent Weimar republic, the dangerous developments in the Third Reich, Freud's involvement with the Berlin Psychoanalytic Institute that was "de-Judaized" in 1936 (more about this in chapter 5). Both men lived their own lives and did not let themselves get sidetracked by the outside world.

Freud's growing worries about society were expressed in the correspondence with Arnold Zweig that began in the last decade of Freud's life. In it there are no evident business interests and it shows a freer and more intimate Freud who is sometimes playful but makes no secret of his suffering from his cancer of the jaw. We also get to know him directly and intimately from a preserved speech to B'nai B'rith, as if Freud shed his caution and fear with Jews who were not colleagues (Meghnagi, 1993). But it is as if he cannot show his worries and fears to Pfister because between the two of them pleasure should not be marred by reality. This correspondence also started with an article sent to Freud. It ended on December 12, 1939, with a letter of condolence from Pfister to Mrs. Freud. Because Freud, at Pfister's request, destroyed quite a bit of the latter's correspondence, the major part of the published correspondence, especially for the first few years, consists of Freud's letters. For this reader there is the usual annoyance that the editors also deleted parts from the preserved letters. (It seems that these were primarily from Pfister. However, what has been published from Pfister is sufficient to give an adequate picture of what occupied him.)

Their relationship remained the same for many years: Freud was filled with ideas and was eager to explain them. He took on the role of an unbelieving Jew and sometimes called himself a heathen. He showed himself as a child of the Enlightenment. Pfister remained who he was: a moderate, believing Christian, a pastor, psychoanalyst, educator, thinker, and publicist, a nice, kind man who knew what he wanted and expressed it. About Freud's rationalism he said what a pastor should say: "Your surrogate religion is in essence the 18th century thinking of the Enlightenment, dressed in proud, modern clothing". He was the originator of the application of psychoanalytic ideas in education and an author himself. On November 8, 1934, he proudly announced to Freud that his *Psycho-analysis in the Service of Education* had been published in German, French, English, Italian, Polish, Greek, and just recently in Danish. He was also a believer in psychoanalysis, although Freud was sometimes afraid that he did not give *sexuality* a sufficiently central place. Sexuality functioned as a shibboleth in the emergence of analysis. Paying insufficient attention to sexuality could be an indication of migration to the camp of Adler or Jung. Pfister described, according to him, successful analyses of several weeks or months. That and the fact that he was not a psychiatrist, as well as his therapeutic optimism, would eventually bring him into conflict with the International Psychoanalytical Association.

In his contacts with the Freud family, Pfister made a good impression on Freud's two children, who have written about him. Anna wrote an introduction to the published correspondence in which she gives a brief description of Pfister. After writing how strange it was for the non-religious Freud family to see a man dressed and acting like a pastor in their household, she gives her personal impression:

> [...] his human warmth and enthusiasm, his capacity for taking a lively part in the minor events of the day, enchanted the children [...]. To them, as Freud remarked, he was not a holy man, but a kind of Pied Piper of Hamelin, who had only to play on his pipe to gather a whole host of willing young followers behind him (Meng & E. L. Freud, 1963, p. 11).

The same admiring and surprised tone is also present when Freud's oldest son Martin recounts how Pfister sat at the table with the Freuds when Martin came home with a cut that he had sustained in an anti-Semitic riot.

> I apologized for my appearance and father threw me a sympathetic glance. The clergyman, however, got up and approached me to shake hands warmly, congratulating me on being wounded in so just and noble a cause. This sympathy and kindliness from a dignified leader of the Christian Church heartened me considerably, making me feel less like a battered ruffian (M. Freud, 1957, p. 166).

This incident is told in the context of Martin's membership in the Viennese Zionist student club *Kadima*, the Jewish organization that refused to put up any longer with Jews being beaten up by Austrian students for no reason.

In his correspondence with Pfister, Freud himself shows that he shares his family's opinion. He writes the same about him and to him as did Martin and Anna; he praises Pfister's enthusiasm, gratitude, and trust in people. He states: "No visitor since Jung has so much impressed the children and done me so much good" (Meng & E. L. Freud, 1963, p. 27).

Freud's children thought that Pfister was an exciting man: a mountain climber, honest, sports loving. The opinions of Gay and Jones about Pfister are confirmed by these descriptions. They see him as a nice man of great value, a true friend to Freud. Vitz (1988) remarks that Freud, Jung, and Adler, who did not agree with one another about everything, all separately valued Pfister's character and contributions to the profession. Pfister did not want only to reflect on his work theologically, but—just like his father before him—he took his task as a pastor who studied medicine in order to be "a doctor for body and soul" very seriously.

The essence of what occupied these correspondents can be found in a letter from Freud to Pfister of October 9, 1918, that seemingly concerns being religious. It starts with Freud's respectful but also confrontational opening:

> As for the possibility of sublimation to religion, therapeutically I can only envy you. But the beauty of religion certainly does not belong to psycho-analysis. It is natural that at this point in therapy our ways should part, and so it can remain. Incidentally, why was it that none of all the pious ever discovered psychoanalysis? Why did it have to wait for a completely godless Jew?

Pfister answers 20 days later:

> Finally you ask why psycho-analysis was not discovered by any of the pious, but by an atheist Jew. The answer obviously is that piety is not the same as genius for discovery and that most of the pious did not have it in them to make such discoveries. Moreover, in the first place you are no Jew, which to me, in view of my unbounded admiration for Amos, Isaiah, Jeremiah, and the author of Job and Ecclesiastes, is a matter of profound regret, and in the second place you are not godless, for he who lives the truth lives in God, and he who strives for the freeing of love "dwelleth in God" (First Epistle of John, IV, 16). If you raised to your consciousness and fully felt your place in the great design, which to me is as necessary as the synthesis of the notes is to a Beethoven symphony, I should say of you: A better Christian there never was.

This looks at first glance like a charming quip, but it is not. Yerushalmi notes that it is a reference to Lessing's play *Nathan der Weise* (Nathan the Wise)—evidence of the friendship between Lessing and Moses Mendelssohn (Yerushalmi, 1991, p. 8). Mendelssohn was the great scholar who was unanimously nominated as a member of the Prussian Academy of Science. King Frederick II refused to accept him twice, whereupon the president of the Academy, the French mathematician Pierre-Louis Moreau de Maupertuis noted that the only thing that Mendelssohn lacked was a foreskin. According to Elon, the Israeli historian and journalist from whom I have borrowed this anecdote, Mendelssohn was the first Jew since Spinoza who came out of Jewish isolation and appeared prominently in the dominant culture of Germany and Europe (1984, p. 104). Freud became the second one. In a historical and personal context, Pfister's comment was a compliment from a superior position to someone in a lower situation. That was not nice or complimentary. Pfister showed himself to be a worthy pupil of Jung who, as Freud noted over a year later, did not reject him but wanted to make him *zimmerrein* (Meng & E. L. Freud, 1963, p. 73).[2]

The letter is insulting for two reasons. "You are no Jew" is very odd. Freud not a Jew—Pfister would like that. The Jew is idealized, and the Christian even more. In Pfister's eyes, being a normal flesh and blood person—and a pioneering scientist—is not in store for the Jew. When someone does something valuable, he "lives in God". In the background the "replacement theology" smiles along with Pfister. In it Christianity is the better, the more developed religion, the theology that asks itself whether Judaism after Jesus has remained a legitimate religion. God has replaced his covenant with the Jews by a covenant with the Christians. In this story baptism serves as a civilizing ritual, as an entry into the civilized world. It is what can be seen in the less veiled medieval and late medieval paintings: the slightly dirty, stained, and begrimed *Synagogue* is replaced by a *Church* irradiated by divine light. It is no wonder then that Gay found in Jones's manuscripts information indicating that Anna Freud found this letter incomprehensible. She writes: "What in the world does Pfister mean here, and why does he want to dispute the fact that my father is Jewish instead of accepting it?" (1989, p. 192). At least as interesting is the fact that Gay found this sentence in a letter from Anna Freud to Ernest Jones and that Jones did not use it in his own description of Freud's relationship to Pfister.

The correspondence is also of importance here because of the complicated way in which Freud and Pfister preserved their friendship around *The Future of an Illusion* (1927, pp. 3–57). Freud's announcement comes first:

> In the next few weeks a pamphlet of mine will be appearing which has a great deal to do with you. I had been wanting to write it for a long time, and postponed it out of regard for you, but the impulse became too strong. The subject-matter—as you will easily guess—is my completely negative attitude to religion, in any form and however attenuated, and, though there can be nothing new to you in this, I feared, and still fear, that such a public profession of my attitude will be painful to you. When you have read it you must let me know what measure of toleration and understanding you are able to preserve for the hopeless pagan.

The close was more effusive than ever: "Always your cordially devoted Freud". And Pfister answered:

> As for your anti-religious pamphlet, there is nothing new to me in your rejection of religion. I look forward to it with

pleasurable anticipation. A powerful-minded opponent of religion is certainly of more service to it than a thousand useless supporters. In music, philosophy, and religion I go different ways from you. I have been unable to imagine that a public profession of what you believe could be painful to me; I have always believed that every man should state his honest opinion aloud and plainly. You have always been tolerant towards me, and am I to be intolerant of your atheism? If I frankly air my differences from you, you will certainly not take it amiss. Meanwhile my attitude is one of eager curiosity (Meng & E. L. Freud, 1963, pp. 109–110).

When reading *The Future of an Illusion*, we get a picture different from the one the combatants present to us, but also one that is different from the one Freud gives of himself. It is not a triumphant, anti-religious pamphlet but a study of the function of culture and religion as Freud sees it. The book is written as if there were a dialogue between supporters and opponents of religion. That gives Freud the opportunity to discuss the meaning of religion seriously. The book is interesting because it shows an author who with his imagination wants to give his view of the relationships between and among people but also a view of what they create and have created: civilization. He sees civilization as a restraint on nature, "to elicit life's necessities from it". Civilization is based on forced labour and controlled drives. The gratification that is given by participation in civilization is of a narcissistic nature. One civilization compares itself to the other and regards it with contempt. You can reconcile this with your own modest place within your own culture.

No doubt one is a wretched plebeian, harassed by debts and military service; but, to make up for it, one is a Roman citizen, one has one's share in the task of ruling other nations and dictating their laws. [...]. No mention has yet been made of what is perhaps the most important item in the psychical inventory of a civilization. This consists in its religious ideas in the widest sense—in other words (which will be justified later) in its illusions (Freud, 1927, pp. 13–14).

In contrast to the omnipotence of nature, which can be controlled only partially by civilization, man desires comfort. It is the comfort and protection that the child wants from his father. Comfort that he later wants from God (or Gods) against the cruelty of nature, death, and the suffering that people cause one another. We give this God various characteristics and let him conquer death. We attribute ultimate justice and mercy to him. People want to be God's only child or be members of "The Chosen People" or later live in "God's own country". This conception of God and this relationship to God is promoted to the most cherished cultural idea.

Then follows a fairly long elaboration of the above: the difference from and similarity to his hypothesis from *Totem and Taboo*. The truth and untruth of religion whereby he pronounces the following:

> "There is no appeal to a court above that of reason" but religion has an important organizing function in life. The doctrines of religion are not a subject one can quibble about like any other. Our civilization is built up on them, and the maintenance of human society is based on the majority of men's believing in the truth of those doctrines. [...] An illusion is not the same thing as an error; nor is it necessarily an error [...]. Religion has clearly performed great services for human civilization. It has contributed much towards the taming of the asocial instincts. [...] If it had succeeded in making the majority of mankind happy in comforting them, in reconciling them to life and in making them into vehicles of civilization, no one would dream of attempting to alter the existing conditions. But I wonder whether it is wise to base our cultural demands on it. If the sole reason why you must not kill your neighbour is because God has forbidden it and will severely punish you for it in this or the next life—then, when you learn there is no God and you will not fear His punishment, you will certainly kill you neighbour without hesitation, and you can only be prevented from doing so by mundane force. Religion implies enforced limitations. Those should be replaced by the results of scientific endeavour. This also means that certain precepts will remain and others will disappear (1927, pp. 20, 27, 28, 30, 34, 39).

Freud is also a man who knows his Tenach (Bible). According to Ascher and Wilgowicz (2002, p. 874), Freud, without letting us know, used more than 400 quotes from the Bible in his *Collected Works*.

He places the consolation of religion in perspective in an impressive way when he states:

> Thus I must contradict you when you go on to argue that men are completely unable to do without the consolation of the religious illusion, that without it they could not bear the troubles of life and the cruelties of reality. That is true, certainly, of the men into whom you have instilled the sweet—or bitter-sweet—poison from childhood onwards. But what of the other men, who have been sensibly brought up? Perhaps those who do not suffer from the neurosis will need no intoxicant to deaden it. They will, it is true, find themselves in a difficult situation. They will have to admit to themselves the full extent of their helplessness and their insignificance in the machinery of the universe; they can no longer be the centre of creation, no longer the object of tender care on the part of a beneficent Providence. They will be in the same position as a child who has left the parental house where he was so warm and comfortable. But surely infantilism is destined to be surmounted. Men cannot remain children for ever; they must in the end go out into "hostile life" (1927, p. 49).

When Freud and Pfister debate this text, it is very important to them to preserve their friendship. But they act oddly. Even though Freud calls religion an illusion, he does it with the following reasoning:

> Thus we call a belief an illusion when a wish-fulfilment is a prominent factor in its motivation, and in doing so we disregard its relations to reality, just as the illusion itself sets no store by verification (1927, p. 31).

An illusion is therefore not the same as an error. An illusion is an interpretation by people, based on their imagined wishes. That says nothing about the existence of what is desired. Freud, a detached observer of people, says simple things like:

> We have heard the admission that religion no longer has the same influence on people that it used to. (We are here concerned with European Christian civilization.) And this is not because

its promises have grown less but because people find that less credible (1927, p. 38).

His conclusion is inevitable:

> In the long run nothing can withstand reason and experience, and the contradiction which religion offers to both is all too palpable. [...] No doubt if they confine themselves to a higher belief in a higher spiritual being, whose qualities are indefinable and whose purposes cannot be discerned, they will be proof against the challenge of science; but then they will also lose their hold of human interest (1927, p. 54).

Pfister gives a very insignificant response to that essay by Freud, which is argument, analysis, quip, and lament at the same time. He is insufficiently precise when he writes on November 24, 1927, that Freud completely rejects philosophy and approaches art in a very different way. He drags in all kinds of authorities, like "my friend Albert Schweitzer", who believe in God. But he does not touch the essence of Freud's problem, and that is that man has created a God according to his need, and he can only trust science and himself to keep the world bearable.

Then Pfister comes up with this looming spectre: "A world without temples, the fine arts, poetry, religion, would in my view be a devil's island to which men could have been banished, not by blind chance, but only by Satan". His own psychoanalysis is based on "moral and social hygiene, and is in accordance with the nature of mankind and the world" (Meng & E. L. Freud, 1963, p. 116). He leaves these concepts rather undefined and with them implicitly creates a difference between himself and Freud—and without either he or Freud wishing to notice, he uses the same stereotypes as Freud's opponents.

Freud asks him to publish his objections in the journal *Imago* and emphasizes that the opinions expressed in *The Future of an Illusion* are his own and not those of psychoanalysis—such awkwardness and so unnecessary. A confrontation with the religion that in his youth had given him shelter and intimidation and that now clashes with his self-image as a *geistiger Naturforscher*, an intellectual researcher of human nature, fits in Freud's biography. Gay found a letter to

Romain Rolland in which Freud describes himself as a "destroyer of illusions who had spent a great part of his life destroying his own illusions and those of mankind". This relationship to religion gave him even during his life a number of Freudian interpretations. Gay mentions several and I copy a few.

Meissner, a Jesuit and psychoanalyst, states:

> It seems clear that Freud's religious views, perhaps more than any other aspect of his work and his psychology, reflect underlying and unresolved ambivalences and conflicts stemming from the earliest psychic strata. Behind the Freudian argument about religion stands Freud the man and behind Freud the man, with his prejudices, beliefs, and convictions, lurks the shadow of Freud the child.

And then there is Zilboorg, an analyst (he started as an Orthodox Jew, then became a Quaker, and finally a Roman Catholic) who sees in Freud's religious points of view above all his dealing with the loss of his Roman Catholic nanny who was sent away after some small thefts when Freud was three years old. Vague and unspecific opinions (Gay, 1987, pp. 56–57).

On a personal level, Freud lets himself be fobbed off by a friend who does not go into what he says but only mumbles that what he asserts cannot and must not be true. The *Imago* answer by Pfister (1928) is also inconsequential and does not touch the main points of Freud's argument. He starts with a personal letter to Freud in which he makes much of the close bond between him and Freud. He tells the reader of their walks "in Beethoven's tracks" in the Viennese hills where they discussed the themes from the book. Subsequently he changes Freud "according to evangelical standards" into a *faithful servant of the Lord* because he strives with such heroism for truth and for liberation through love. And by creating psychoanalysis he made available the instrument that breaks the chains of suffering souls and opens their dungeon so that they can rush into the bright land of a life-giving belief that is not far from the Kingdom of God. Pfister applies the New Testament comparison of the two sons to Freud, where the one says that he will obey his father when the latter charges him to go to the vineyard and to labour there and does not go, while the other son says he does not want to go but then regrets it and goes anyway. In Jesus's eyes, the second was of greater value. Pfister compares Freud to the second son who says he does not want God but serves God as the developer of psychoanalysis.

Pfister shows himself here as a proselytizing pastor. Practically anyone who is worthy has joined the Christian religion. Except (psychoanalysis can certainly be a wonderful thing!) the person involved does not know it yet. Elsewhere in the document Pfister does not address Freud's argument in a substantive and interesting way. His thoughts about "religion as a neurotic obsession" are striking. His most important argument is that "real Christianity removes the neurotic obsession". He does not hide the contrast with his image of Judaism to which he attributes "obsessive neurotic legalism, literalness, and attachment to ceremony". He contrasts all this with Jesus's "command to love", the "great act of redemption". *The Future of an Illusion* appears here as a settlement of accounts with the primitive Jewish religion in order to flower fully in Christianity. Pfister, as is obvious in one of his later publications (1934), Christianizes psychoanalysis by equating it with Protestantism. Gay sums up Pfister's position as follows:

> Both [psychoanalysis and Protestantism] work to reduce guilt, which they recognize as a kind of punishment for defying authority, both aim to replace a stern with a kindly father. What is more, both utilize regression as a method of healing: it is no accident that in pastoral care, as in psychoanalysis, the patient becomes as a little child. Most important of all, both Freud's psychoanalysis and Pfister's theology place love at the core of life.

A line of thinking that will be followed by many theologians. Gay notes correctly that the technique here is to praise psychoanalysis while removing its fangs. I, too, think that psychoanalysis is not about these lovely things. It continues to search for an ever-changing truth and is not sugary sweet, even though Gay manages to find in a letter to Jung that Freud feels that psychoanalysis is a "matter of love". But Freud does not say what kind of love or for whom. Gay summarizes this as follows: "It is an intriguing and startling picture: Jesus, not Freud, the first psychoanalyst" (1987, pp. 82–85).

It could not have been pleasant for Freud to be treated like that by Pfister. The *Imago* article was written with the handbrake on in order not to lose the friendship. It is one of the moments when it is pointed out to Freud, surrounded by a smokescreen of praise, that his deepest conviction is alas based on insufficient knowledge of the subject.

In the correspondence between Freud and Pfister, this dispute is touched on several times. Freud is irritated and forcefully rejects religion as a remedy. He says there is no value in the *Imitatio Christi* and points to Mark's story of Jesus's healing of the lame son and looks at the statement "Thy sins are forgiven thee; arise and walk". There he adds the question: "How knowest thou that his sins are forgiven?" He invents the answer: "I, the Son of God, forgive thee". Freud calls this an appeal for unbridled attention. And he proposes the following analogy: "I, Professor Sigmund Freud, forgive thee thy sins," and concludes that this would make him look like a fool. He turns Jesus's healing into healing by suggestion and not one that combats illness. Pfister pays no attention to it. But he does pay attention to Freud's comment:

> I do not know if you have detected the secret link between the *Lay Analysis* and the *Illusion*. In the former I wish to protect analysis from the doctors and in the latter from the priests. I should like to hand it over to a profession which does not yet exist, a profession of *lay* curers of souls who need not be doctors and should not be priests.

Pfister then answers: "If no priest should analyse, neither should any Christian or any religious or morally deep-thinking individual, and you yourself emphasize that analysis is independent of philosophy of life". His feeling of moral superiority is clear in the following sentence: "Disbelief is after all nothing but a negative belief". Freud places a comment next to the entire discussion and writes: "For the present I put up with doctors, so why not priests too?" However, he maintains that "[I]t rests on the general scientific outlook, with which the religious outlook is incompatible". And he again invents the counter-argument against his own assertion when he praises Charles Darwin who "used to go regularly to church on Sundays" (Meng & E. L. Freud, 1963, pp. 125–129).

In conclusion it can be said that the much-praised friendship between Freud and Pfister manages to exist by the grace of politeness. Their areas of fundamental disagreement were sometimes indicated but mainly left aside untouched. The need for political gain was too great on both sides. It is painful that Pfister's reactions differed in tone but not in tendency from the opinion of the versatile biologist and chemist Emil Aberhalden who was known as an anti-Semite and who deplored the spectacle of "a Jew" venturing, wholly unauthorized as he was, "to offer a judgment on the Christian faith" (Gay, 1989, p. 537).

Pfister was extremely friendly and made no overt attempts to convert Freud to the True Religion. You could say that the friendship intensified because he dared to contradict the master. In this view the statements fit very well in that time and in his profession. However, I find that explanation too kind because I chiefly see masked aggression in Pfister. In Freud I see the use of his full diplomatic skills, of someone who is used to continue smiling if it suits him. To Arnold Zweig Freud showed what he really thought of such careful attempts at conversion (E. L. Freud, 1970, p. 48). In 1932 he gives Zweig a book and comments:

> They are the letters of an uncle of my wife's who was a famous classical scholar and, it appears, an outstanding personality. His attitude toward the Jewish and Christian faiths is worthy of attention.

Yerushalmi has taken the trouble to find out what the book really is about. He says:

> The uncle of Freud's wife was Jacob Bernays [...]. A son of the Haham [chief rabbi] of Hamburg, Jacob Bernays remained a scrupulously observant Jew throughout his life. When his brother Michael accepted baptism to obtain a professorship, Jacob went through the traditional ritual of mourning for his dead (1991, p. 47).

According to Yerushalmi, Freud identified particularly with the "exchange of letters in 1892 between Bernays and his good friend Christian von Bunsen who at the time was the Prussian ambassador in London". The latter told Bernays that for him, as a Jew, no matter how diligently he tried, there were absolutely no prospects for an academic career in Prussia. Bunsen, who was a religious Christian, urged Bernays to convert, not because it was useful, for he knew that this would be below Bernays's dignity, but as a way of perfecting his Judaism. An additional argument was that this "would also put him in the mainstream of world history". Bernays was not convinced.

Notes

1. This information is from Gay (1986). The source for Gay's characterization of Pfister ("with all his warmth and goodness" Pfister "skirts the ridiculous") is the private correspondence between Freud and Eitingon (Schröter, 2004).
2. The word *zimmerrein* is the Austrian variant of the German *stubenrein*, toilet-trained or house-broken. Meng turns it into "fit for polite society" and clarifies that it means "house trained" like a dog. In the English translation it seems a reference to a conversation of or a writing by Jung. I consulted the Freud authority Walter Schönau who sees it as follows: "The word 'zimmerrein' is not between quotation marks because it is a quote from Jung; Freud chose the word himself in order to reflect Jung's meaning—not in the letter but in the spirit. It refers to the objectionable aspects of the sexual subject matter". Understanding the text is difficult because the English translator skipped the following phrase from the original: "*Wobei ich allerdings diesen guten Sinn aus Eigenenm ergänzt habe*" (whereby I added this good intention in my own words). However, I think that in the relationship of Jung and Freud the sexual subject matter was overshadowed by the Jewish one.

CHAPTER FOUR

Freud and the man Moses, the man Moses and Freud

Freud's self-willed, obstinate, and potentially atheist Judaism is fully expressed in his next-to-last book. It is one of his two testaments. In *An Outline of Psycho-Analysis* (1940a) he treats the essence of psychoanalysis once more, and in *Moses and Monotheism* (1939) he gives his view of the origin of the Jewish people. The title and the phrase from it in the original German (*The Man Moses and the Monotheistic Religion*) refer majestically and proudly to his leadership and are also a direct quote from the Bible (Exodus 11: 3 and 32. Freud was 83 years old when the book was completed and had suffered from cancer of the jaw for 17 years. In addition, attacks of angina accompanied his old age. He started his first draft of the book in 1933/34, a year after the Nazi takeover. It was also the year that his former friend Jung fired off one of his many anti-Semitic arrows at psychoanalysis. I quote Clark:

> In the *Zentralblatt für Psychotherapie* of January 1934 [Jung] wrote: "The Aryan unconsciousness has a higher potential than the Jewish; that is the advantage and the disadvantage of a youthfulness not yet fully escaped from barbarism. In my opinion it has been a great mistake of all previous medical psychology to

apply Jewish categories which are not even binding for all Jews, indiscriminately to Christians, Germans or Slavs. In so doing, medical psychology has declared that most precious secret of the Germanic people—the creatively prophetic depth of the soul—to be a childishly banal morass, while for decades my warning voice has been suspected of anti-Semitism. The source of this suspicion is Freud. He did not know the Germanic soul any more than did all the Germanic imitators .... Has the mighty apparition of National Socialism which the whole world watches with astonished eyes taught them something better?" (1982, p. 493).

A month later, Jung wondered to Wolfgang Kranefeldt, one of the founders of the Berlin Psychoanalytic Institute, whether the government should not do something against the spreading of the Jewish gospel by that institute. In 1939 *Moses and Monotheism* had to be published by Allert de Lange in the still neutral Netherlands. Freud was close to death and Nazism was in power. What would happen to psychoanalysis, and to the Jews? This question must have been at the back of his mind when he wrote the book. In *Freud's Study of Moses as a Daydream: a biographical essay*, the German Freud scholar and editor Ilse Grubrich-Simitis makes it clear that Moses appears three times in Freud's work—every time as a reaction to a supposed repetition of an earlier traumatic event. The earlier traumatic event concerned the death of his brother Julius when Freud was still a small child, and the later separation from his beloved nanny who with her loving devotion must have replaced his depressed mother. In 1902 we encounter Moses for the first time in Freud when he became preoccupied with Michelangelo's Moses. The second time was in 1914, when he wrote about Michelangelo's Moses figure. This was when the separation from Jung dominated Freud's life. He worked on *Moses and Monotheism* from 1934 until 1939. This was the period of Hitler's takeover. Freud could not completely realize what was awaiting the Jews. He wondered whether psychoanalysis would survive Nazism.

It is the work of an old man. In the book and in the correspondence around it, he complains that he is losing his strength. Yet Freud the politician who always has to defend the Cause is still strikingly present in the text. At the same time he is also the psychoanalyst, the conquistador who once more puts his intelligence, mental power, and imagination to work in order to present, apply, and expand his theories; and, to understand what is going on—as befits an analyst—he involves the present, the subconscious motives, and the genesis in his interpretation, even though this time it involves a whole people and its history. What is especially intriguing is the transference-countertransference constellation, which is extra complicated here because analyst and analysand coincide, but not quite. Freud analyzes the lot of the Jewish people and is part of it. What Freud wonders about is above all: who was Moses; where do the Jews come from; how have they survived so much history? It is generally accepted that the rise of Nazism left deep marks in the book. The book is certainly not a submission to the Nazi doctrine to prevent worse. It is the testimony of a man who shouts out his truth, even though it is probably not welcomed by Jews and Christians. It is a complicated triumphal procession for which the author needs a double murder of Moses.

It is also the work in which he presents himself most explicitly, although ambiguously, as a Jew. He distances himself from traditional Jewish history in order to develop his own subject. He does this not in a hostile but in a detached manner. Moses is his starting point. Freud starts with a wistful expression of regret:

> To deprive a people of the man whom they take pride in as the greatest of their sons is not a thing to be gladly or carelessly undertaken, least of all by someone who is himself one of them.

Thus begins the first essay about *The Man Moses*. Freud finds it difficult to rob his people of their greatest son, but he feels he has no choice:

> We cannot allow any such reflection to induce us to put the truth aside in favour of what are supposed to be national interests; and, moreover, the clarification of a set of facts may be expected to bring us a gain in knowledge.

In 1934 Freud started the first of three essays that would lead to *Moses and Monotheism*. He finished it in 1936—for him a very long production time. He worked on the second essay, published in 1937, in Vienna, which was then still relatively calm. He saw all the signs of the misery that the Second World War would cause. He forcefully condemned the excesses of a totalitarian regime in view of what he knew about the practices of communism in Russia and the emerging fascism in Italy. In something that with hindsight can be seen as a denial of reality, he hoped for protection by the Catholic Church, although he did not care much for it. He thought that Vienna, where "psycho-analysis was born and grew up" would perhaps offer a last shield against the emerging violence. Even though he wrote in the same sentence that "psycho-analysis still possesses no home". But for how long would this fantasized safety still hold up?

> We are living here in a Catholic country under the protection of that Church, uncertain how long that protection will hold out. But so long as it lasts, we naturally hesitate to do anything that would be bound to arouse the Church's hostility.
>
> This is not cowardice, but prudence. The new enemy, to whom we want to avoid being of service, is more dangerous than the old one with whom we have already learnt to come to terms.

Freud wrote this in the first Prefatory Note for volume 3. It was before the Anschluss of March 1938, and the context makes it clear that he meant "we, psychoanalysts" and also, but not mentioned "we, Jews".

In the second Prefatory Note that he wrote as an exile in London in June of 1938, Freud had to admit that his first estimate had been too optimistic. At the time he was afraid that he would, through the publication of this iconoclastic work, lose the protection of the Catholic Church. But after the Anschluss and "Catholicism proved, to use the words of the Bible, *a broken reed*", there was now the additional fear of being persecuted as a Jew. He expressed this as follows:

> In the certainty that I should now be persecuted not only for my line of thought but also for my "race"—accompanied by many of my friends, I left the city which, from my early childhood, had been my home for seventy-eight years (1939, pp. 7, 54–59).

Freud chose as his topic the puzzle of the origin and the continued existence of the Jewish religion and the Jewish people. As the point of departure he takes the life of Moses. No less important is the question of why the Jews have managed to arouse an unremitting universal, primarily Christian, hatred. It is striking that it lacks Freud's usual elegance in writing. This is one of the reasons why the book is difficult to read. It consists of two magazine articles and a summing-up that is sometimes the principal argument. The construction is complicated. In Grubrich-Simitis's opinion, the manuscript is noticeably messier than the other handwritten work from his estate (1997, p. 54). Unlike Freud's other works, it has no foreword. However, as Freud himself says, there are two introductory remarks to the third part that sometimes are contradictory. Part two is four times longer than part one, and part three is ten times longer. The argument of the book is weak, and the basic hypothesis is extremely speculative. Repetitions and irrelevant digressions mar the text. There are passages that can be found literally in previous writings. But it is a fascinating and successful work that invites strong arguments.

It is important here to give an extremely short summary of the apparent chaos. The first thesis is that Moses was an Egyptian of noble birth, actually the son of the princess who found him in the reed basket according to the Bible story. The historian Yerushalmi,[1] who has written the standard work about *Moses and Monotheism*, starts his book with a joke about the subject that he encountered in Freud's own writings. According to Theodor Reik, Freud told him the following in 1908:

> The boy Itzig is asked in grammar school: "Who was Moses?" and answers, "Moses was the son of an Egyptian princess". "That's not true," says the teacher. "Moses was the son of a Hebrew mother. The Egyptian princess found the baby in a casket". But Itzig answers: "Says she!" (Yerushalmi, 1991, p. 1. See also Freud, 1917, p. 161 for a slightly different version of the joke.)

According to Freud's view in *Moses and Monotheism*, Moses becomes a noble Egyptian who has chosen the Jewish people to spread his Aton religion.

The second thesis is that Moses was murdered by the Jewish people. According to Freud, he gave them the Aton religion, which had been introduced by the pharaoh Akhenaton. This religion was not accepted by the Egyptian priestly caste and hence had almost become extinct. It had become spiritualized, without images and statues. The central values of this religion were truth and justice. Sorcery and mysticism were rejected; the emphasis was on spiritualization and sublimation. It was a radical break with the reigning polytheism. Moses took over this stern and imperative doctrine and imposed it on the Jewish people. The Jewish people, just as the Egyptians before them, were unable to meet these demands and killed Moses in an angry revolt.[2] The religion introduced by Moses is abandoned and then returns after two generations. At that point the identity of Moses originates again, but this time in the guise of a new Moses. Moses is then deconstructed into two figures: the Egyptian royal child and the son-in-law of the Midianite Jethro. Eight centuries later, Moses's legislation is codified in the laws of the prophets Ezra and Nehemiah in a "retrograde development" and survives until today as the monotheistic Jewish religion. In Gay's understanding of Freud, the latter thinks that the Jews have to carry with them a harsh, obsessive, self-chastising religion as penance for the murder that they have committed (Gay, 1987, p. 133).

In *Totem and Taboo*, Freud saw the prehistory of a people and its primitive religion. In the beginning there was the archetypal father who was murdered by his sons and then was made into a totem. It is a link in the succession of fraternal clan, matriarchy, exogamy, and totemism. Finally this father is completely forgotten, and his memory is repressed. In essence, monotheism represented the return of the long latent memory of the father, in the form of the One Almighty God, next to whom there is no other.

In short: there was a Jewish people that under the leadership of Moses the Egyptian left the land of Egypt. Later, in the desert, this leader gave his people the Aton religion. This Aton religion was unacceptable to the people. Moses was killed, and under a second Moses, who led the people two generations or a century later, people and religion came together. The killing of the first Moses was forgotten, and its consequences come back in the history of the Jewish people.

In addition to the concept of the murder of the father, this theory is supported by what Freud saw as a parallel in the development of a people and its religion and the development of neurosis in the individual. Both postulate the hypothesis of the return of the suppressed. On this basis Freud showed himself to be a Lamarckian, the doctrine that considers the ontogenesis of an individual dependent on the phylogenesis of a people, in such a strong measure that an individual's characteristics acquired through a life's history become hereditary in the people to which he belongs.

Yerushalmi is surprised at the extent to which Freud's reconstruction remains faithful to the Bible text concerning the chosen position of the Jewish people. The Jews did not create their religion, but the religion created the Jews. Monotheism has as its obvious consequence the concept of the *Chosen People*. If a people chooses one God, the God chooses one people. For Freud the Jews are chosen twice, because Moses literally chose them and, at a deeper level, because what had been suppressed came back only to the Jews. That is but one step removed from the thought that makes Moses into God. In thinking this way, Freud and Spinoza share a heretical Judaism (Yerushalmi, 1991, pp. 34ff.).

In Christianity, this foundation myth is repeated by the crucifixion of Jesus and his resurrection. Freud connects the Christian "original sin" to the feeling of guilt about the murder of Moses: "It was a crime against God and could only be atoned for by death". However, Christ was a son and Moses a father. This is why Freud argues that "Judaism had been a religion of the father; Christianity became a religion of the son". In Christianity the son became God and took the place of the father. This is how Freud understands Christianity's allegiance to anti-Semitism. He says:

> I venture to assert that jealousy of the people which declared itself the first-born favourite child of God the Father, has not yet been surmounted among other peoples even today; it is as though they had thought there was truth in the claim (1939, p. 91).

As an additional factor he mentions the fear of circumcision, which in itself makes "a sinister impression" and also evokes memories of prehistoric times. In Freud's view, circumcision is a sign of the choice by God and because of that a source of jealous anti-Semitism. By their existence the Jews remind others that they came late to monotheism.

> They [the Christians] have not got over a grudge against the new religion which was imposed on them; but they have displaced the grudge on to the source from which Christianity reached them. The fact that the Gospels tell a story which is set among Jews, and in fact deals only with Jews, has made this displacement easy for them. Their hatred of Jews is at bottom a hatred of Christians, and we need not be surprised that in the German National-Socialist revolution this intimate relation between the two monotheist religions finds such a clear expression in the hostile treatment of both of them (Freud, 1939, pp. 91–92).[3]

Erlich turns this story around. He views it as "Freud's last and most telling attack on Jewish narcissism".

> It aims to resolve once and for all the riddle of the internal and external "specialness" of the Jews. The Chosen (and therefore persecuted) People is transformed into the tragically Guilty People, forever atoning for their crime, but at the same time internalizing and transforming mere carnage into spirituality and valued spiritual possessions for all mankind (2003, p. 3).

On the same page Erlich states:

> Freud's effort to understand *geistigkeit* is connected with another struggle: his attempt to integrate his parochial Jewish identity with his allegiance to the prevailing non-Jewish (not to say anti-Jewish) Central European culture and scientific universalism.

This is an apparent contradiction, but the effort to combine a restricted social life with universal values and dignity can be seen as a universal Jewish problem. It certainly was Freud's problem.

There is another peculiar complication in *Moses and Monotheism*. Freud asserts that the Jews killed Moses and did not admit it and have carried this burden for centuries. This point of view contradicts the historical truth. The Romans killed Jesus. In this context the French-Dutch historian Solange Leibovici wonders:

> What do we make of this incomprehensible mistake that Freud makes here? Does it perhaps indicate a wish for reconciliation

with the Christian religion, prompted by the ever-present fear that psychoanalysis will be labelled as the Jewish Science? (n.d.).

The draft title of Freud's book was *Der Mann Moses: Ein historischer Roman* (The Man Moses: a historical novel). I think that it is better to consider it as such. Freud also felt that the book did not go beyond being a very bold speculation. Old Testament scholars do not take it seriously. Freud was neither historian, nor archaeologist, nor Hebrew scholar. Freud is irrelevant in these branches of scholarship. Freud got his information from secondary sources, among them the "Bible" entry in the *Encyclopaedia Britannica*. There is no proof for these sweeping speculations. The essence of the story, the killing of Moses and the subsequent forgetting of the act, does not fit in the Bible story. Yerushalmi remarks that the Bible leaves no misdeed of the people Israel unrecorded. Neither repressing nor forgetting belongs in so much openness.

For our purpose this does not matter. The work is to be understood as a study about Jews and Judaism in the Christian world. Quoting from a letter of Freud to Arnold Zweig, Yerushalmi makes it into a pure and simple declaration of love to being Jewish and to Judaism by Freud. Freud writes: "One's fate in being Jewish was determined long ago by the Fathers, and that often what one feels most deeply and obscurely is a trilling wire in the blood". Freud also writes to Zweig about the land of Israel (then still Palestine):

> and we hail from there [...] our forebears lived there for perhaps a whole millennium [...] and it is impossible to say what heritage from this land we have taken over into our blood and nerves (Yerushalmi, 1991, p. 31).

Grubrich-Simitis sees *Moses and Monotheism* as "a kind of *daydream* generated under dramatic conditions of extreme distress" (1997, p. 60). It has the function of a wish fulfilment, based on childhood impressions where censorship was less severe. The author imagined a better time now that reality had become unbearable. That fits well in the dream theory: the dream based on the past, placed in the present, oriented to the future. Freud's great worry and fear at that time was the uncertainty about the lot of psychiatry and its future.

Psychoanalysis was his child. The psychoanalysts had become his family. The interpretation of *Totem and Taboo*—the murdered and eaten archetypal father and the survival of the clan—is a fear-filled look into the future of psychoanalysis. The fear was lessened by the hope that truth—of Freud, of psychoanalysis, and if need be of Judaism—would reappear after the murder that still was to be carried out. When you continue this speculation, you see how Freud—afraid that he would be murdered by the Nazis—imagined a possibility of survival. For this fantasy he uses the concepts from *Totem and Taboo* and images from Biblical history.

In the entire history of Freud as a Jew there is in this connection also a question about his total ignorance of the Hebrew language, a myth that he maintains repeatedly (1925b, 1930). In the introduction to the Hebrew publication of *Totem and Taboo*, he calls himself someone "who is ignorant of the language of holy writ". The question is whether this presentation of himself corresponds to the private truth. Freud must have known the original text of the Biblical Moses story and the exodus from his Jewish education. Austrian law required five hours of religious education per week for elementary school and high school (*gymnasium*)—that means for a period of 12 years (Stroeken, 1991, p. 326). Freud had lessons from his father and from his honoured teacher Samuel Hammerschlag in the Hebrew language, Jewish traditions, customs, and history, and Freud was always an excellent student. Freud named his youngest daughter Anna after Hammerschlag's daughter, who later became one of his patients (Gilman, 1993, p. 102). It is known that Freud's father Jakob—as is usual at the Seder, at the start of the Jewish Passover—told the story of the exodus from Egypt in Hebrew. Father Freud knew this whole text by heart. When he gave his son the old, newly rebound, leather Philippsohn family Bible for his 35th birthday, he wrote in it a declaration of love to the Torah (Pentateuch):

> Go, read in my Book that I have written and there will burst open for you the wellsprings of understanding, knowledge and wisdom. Behold, it is the Book of Books, from which sages have excavated and lawmakers learned knowledge and judgement. [...] And I have presented it to you as a memorial and

as a reminder of love from your father, who loves you with everlasting love.

Jakob Son of R. Shelomoh Freid [sic]
In the capital city Vienna 29 Nisan [5]651 6 May [1]891
(Yerushalmi, 1991, p. 71).[4]

The question is whether Jakob Freud, who in his old age tried to strengthen the contact with his son about this sensitive subject, would actually have sent him a long letter filled with love and regret, consisting of Bible quotes in Hebrew, if he knew that his son could not read a word of it. And it is even less likely that he would have done this without saying a word about it. Gay turns Freud's father, who read Hebrew as well as he read German, into a completely unreligious Jew and explains the text in the family Bible as an expression of regret about the fact that he gave his son an insufficient Jewish education (1987, p. 125). A study of that copy of the Bible by Emmanuel Rice brought to light that Freud decorated the inscription with red, blue, and green pencils in a way that was characteristic for him and that he also did in other texts (1990, p. 39). These pencils were found among his effects after his death.

Grubrich-Simitis also emphasizes that Freud considered the analysts as his people and his family (1997, p. 72). She indicates the point in time when Freud's first Moses study, *The Moses of Michelangelo*, originated. It was when the break with Jung became unavoidable and Freud feared that psychoanalysis would be ruined. Freud supposedly identified with Moses to such an extent that it makes plausible Grubrich-Simitis's thesis, that *Moses and Monotheism* should be considered as a resumption of Freud's self-analysis. Freud-Moses the stranger, the leader of the analytic-Jewish people, is not allowed to enter the promised land of acceptance of the truth of analysis.

The double question about the hate around him and about the reason for the hate of Jews assured an unsympathetic reception by both Jews and non-Jews—certainly when he rewrote in passing the history of the origin of the Jews. According to Jones, Freud was rather indifferent to the disapproval that he could expect from Jewish circles.

Freud's fear of its publication also had to do with the fact that he had not only written his own version of the history of the Jews, but also that of the origin of religion: Christianity. With real conviction he answered René Laforgue, who tried in 1937 to convince him that it would be wise if he left Vienna: "The Nazis? I am not afraid of them. Help me rather to combat my true enemy. [...] religion, the Roman Catholic Church" (Clark, 1982, p. 491). That was in sharp contrast to the quote given above from Prefatory Note I. This is what happens when you abandon politics and try to speak the truth.

In particular he was afraid of Professor Wilhelm Schmidt—priest, confidant of the Pope, professor of ethnology—who considered psychoanalysis and Bolshevism to be destroyers of the family. Schmidt urged the Vatican to make sure that the fascist government would be in charge of choosing a leader of the Italian Psychoanalytic Movement. In 1935 the Vatican—according to Freud, at Schmidt's urging—had ordered the publication of the *Rivista Italiana di Psicanalisi* to be stopped. There are different opinions about this. According to Vitz, Schmidt was a great scholar (1988, p. 198).[5] Schmidt wrote the 12-volume *Der Ursprung der Gottesidee* (The Origin of the Idea of God), an encyclopaedia about religious and ethnic beliefs of primitive societies in the world. In the margin of this study he forcefully rejected Freud's theory from *Totem and Taboo* about the totemic origin of religion. Vitz considered Schmidt's *Rasse und Volk* (1935) to be one of the strongest attacks on the Nazis' racial doctrine. Schmidt had to flee Austria in June of 1938; he found shelter in Switzerland.

Freud was afraid that psychoanalysis would not survive fascism and National Socialism. Psychoanalysts—and Jews—were unsure about where to find protection. Freud had first placed his hope in the Church, but it also came to be considered a threat. In 1936 Freud even tried Mussolini who was known as an enemy of the Church. He sent him a copy of *Thoughts for the Times on War and Death*; thoughts expressed by Freud during the First World War.

Freud never did understand the true extent of the danger of Nazism. Marie Bonaparte and Ernest Jones were his protectors in Vienna. A whole group of others,[6] rather than Freud himself, was the driving force behind his departure on June 4, 1938, from Vienna to London. When the Nazis burned his books, Freud said, smiling: "What an improvement: in the Middle Ages they would have burned me; now they are satisfied with burning my books". According to Gay, this was Freud's least prescient witticism ever (1989, pp. 592–593).

Moses and Monotheism is a book about fear and persecution, but it is not a fearful book. However, it was considered highly speculative by its author, "like a dancer balancing on the tip of one toe" (Freud, 1939, p. 58). When the Nazis tried to destroy the Jews as a people, Freud showed boldly that the Jews have a very long and meaningful history. The desire to preserve the Jewish identity was so stubborn that Freud sought an explanation for it. He argues that Moses, through his life and death, created the Jewish people. The book can even be called nationalistic.

According to Freud's theory, as developed in *Totem and Taboo*, primitive peoples have to go through a stage of patricide and fraternal bonding in order to become a people; the Jews are a people that still exists and to whom this theory applies. In the dispute about the question whether the Jews are a race, adherents of a religion, or a people, he takes the position that the Jews are a people. They have killed the archetypal father, have united, and can now marry outside the tribe. Freud continued to believe in the theory of *Totem and Taboo*. This despite the 1920 judgment by the American ethnologist Kroeber: "*Totem and Taboo* has been disproved ethnologically". Freud, however, made the *Totem and Taboo* theory and the Oedipus complex into a central part of his thinking about the millennia-long process of the creation of peoples. The greater spiritual freedom of Jews claimed by Freud is, from this point of view, based on carrying out the murder of Moses.

Moses and Monotheism is the work of someone who is deeply convinced of the truth of the psychoanalysis that he has devised himself. It is also sufficiently Jewish that it had to be published in Amsterdam after Freud's departure from Vienna. On March 13, 1938, in his last address to the Vienna Psychoanalytic Society, Freud says:

> After the destruction of the Temple in Jerusalem by Titus, Rabbi Yochanan ben Zakkai asked for permission to open a school at Jabneh for the study of the Torah. We are going to do the same. We are after all, used to persecution by our history, tradition and some of us by personal experience (Jones, 1974, vol. III, p. 236).

Despite fear and uneasiness, it is a highly speculative work that does not hesitate to give free rein to the imagination. And also because of its aim at the time, to give a history of the uniqueness of the Jewish people, it is very brave and frank. Yerushalmi shows quite a few examples of Jewish chauvinism in the book (Yerushalmi, 1991, pp. 52ff.). He also sees this in a letter from Freud to Sabina Spielrein, the Jewish analyst who at the end of the Thirties was murdered by the Nazis or the Russians in circumstances that remain unclear. The letter dates from 1913, when Jung was distancing himself from Freud. The break between Spielrein and Jung (Spielrein had been Jung's patient and also his lover) was final by then. When Freud wrote her, Spielrein was pregnant by her Jewish husband. Freud's expressions are outspokenly ethnocentrically Jewish, this time not diluted by diplomatic considerations or manoeuvres:

> I am, as you know, cured of the last shred of my predilection for the Aryan cause, and would like to take it that if the child turned out to be a boy he will develop into a stalwart Zionist. He or she must be dark in any case, no more towheads. Let us banish all these will-o'-the wisps! I shall not present my compliments to Jung in Munich, as you know perfectly well. [...] We are and remain Jews. The others will only exploit us and will never understand and appreciate us (Yerushalmi, 1991, p. 134, quoting Carotenuto, 1982, p. 120).

This is Freud's authentic voice—the man who says of himself that he is a descendant of "an unbroken line of infidel Jews" (Yerushalmi, 1991, p. 134). A proud man who often had to restrain himself and did so—his expressions of pride in being Jewish sometimes go beyond shame. A part of this self-confidence was being able to trust in the intimacy with others. From his point of view Freud was right to bestow trust in moderation. The story with Jung, Jones, and the Stracheys were signs for him—as if he needed them—that with his non-Jewish followers there was much hidden, not repressed, anti-Semitic aggression that could come to the surface under the right circumstances. Freud, with his expansiveness and his biting humour, was very seldom relaxed. He was always watchful. Psychoanalysis, which he was developing, could easily be ridiculed and dismissed because of the origin of its developer—that was his great fear.

Notes

1. The late Professor Yerushalmi was, emeritus Salo Wittmayer Baron Professor of Jewish History, Culture, and Society at Columbia University.
2. This is a hypothesis put forward by Selin, and Freud refers to it pointedly. However, Selin rejected it himself even before the publication of *Der Mann Moses*.
3. Freud (1939), pp. 86, 88, 91, 91–92.
4. The transcription of father Freud's incorrectly spelled last name and the subsequent information is by Yerushalmi.
5. In this book Vitz argues that Freud's nanny remained central in his life. She was sent away because of theft when Freud was three years old. According to Vitz, the real reason for her dismissal was that she took young Sigismund with her to mass from time to time—his mother disapproved of this.
6. This group consisted of Bullitt, then the US ambassador in Moscow, who made sure that Wiley was appointed consul-general in Vienna with as his special task the protection of Freud; Pichler, the oral surgeon who took care of Freud's oral cancer; Pötzl, a professor of psychiatry in Vienna; and Sauerwald, who had been appointed as Nazi commissioner for the *Psychoanalytischer Verlag* and had become impressed by Freud's work. The only analyst in this group was Eduardo Weiss, an Italian who had access to Mussolini. There was a reasonable hope that the latter, under the influence of Weiss, would defend Freud (Diller, 1991, p. 206).

CHAPTER FIVE

Jerusalem and Hamburg: two congresses

Every other year psychoanalysts from the world over come together for the IPA Congress. These congresses are carefully prepared. The lectures are published before they are presented on the stage of the large auditorium. People meet one another in formal and informal working groups. In addition there is an extensive social programme. It is a festive reunion with colleagues, and people also network with friends and relations.

The place where the analysts get together tells us quite a bit about the expansion of their world. Until 1927, these events took place around Vienna and other places where the pioneers lived. They visited cities like Budapest, Munich, Bad Homburg, Berlin, and The Hague. In 1929 they went to Oxford, and for a long time the location remained in Europe, with Edinburgh as its farthest outpost. There were no congresses between 1938 and 1949, nor were there between 1913 and 1918. It was not until 1977 that they left Europe for a congress in Jerusalem. From 1987 on, the biennial congresses have taken place alternately in Europe and America.

The congress in Jerusalem had a special flavour. Paul Schwaber, who participated, has described it vividly (1978). He saw an exuberant group of representatives dance not only the Israeli *hora* but also sing the refrain of *Tum Balalayka*, "that Yiddish song of shy and teasing courtship". In his article he writes how complicated it had been to get the psychoanalysts to go to Israel. The decision to do so had been made in 1957, but they had managed to postpone implementing the decision for 20 years. Various parties, European Jewish analysts above all, were against it or were hesitant. In addition, the high costs of travel, the hot summers, and the Israelis' lack of experience in organizing large events were used as arguments. When the decision was finally made, only the French were against it.

A speech by Anna Freud was announced. She was 82 years old at the time (1978) and had never been to Israel. She begged off this time as well. Her friend Arthur Valenstein read what she had written. The reason for her speech and what she said were both notable. The reason was the establishment of the Sigmund Freud Chair for Psychoanalysis at the Hebrew University in Jerusalem, the first of its kind. The lecture was mostly conventional. It recounts the history of the ideas of psychoanalysis and does not go beyond 1920. Because it concerns the first academic chair in psychoanalysis, she explains how difficult it was to get a connection to the academic world. And then comes the last minute of the speech—Schwaber's article is still cited because he understood its importance. She let her spokesman say:

> During the era of its existence, psychoanalysis has entered into connection with various academic institutions, not always with satisfactory results. It has also, repeatedly, experienced rejection by them, been criticized for its methods being imprecise, its findings not open to proof by experiment, for being unscientific, even for being a "Jewish science". However the other derogatory comments may be evaluated, it is, I believe, the last-mentioned connotation which, under present circumstances, can serve as a Title of Honour.

Schwaber says about this:

> People hesitated, turned, wondered: a Jewish science! It came from nowhere in the speech. Yet under the auspices of the Hebrew University—title of honour. Maintaining her reserve but emphatically at the climax, Anna Freud faced down the old issue, unexpectedly, transvaluing values. The very quality of

unencumbered statement suggests that the tension has not been resolved but dealt with differently. Nonetheless, with proximate distance still, she bespoke a changed attitude. A historical moment.

For the Jews among the analysts the congress in Jerusalem served to celebrate their survival after near-annihilation. It was also a part of the struggle to legitimize the state of Israel, because then, just as beforehand and afterwards, there were very powerful voices for making the existence of Israel itself a problem. Anna Freud's intervention was also meant to make the Jewishness of psychoanalysis normal. She made Jewish history a part of psychoanalytic history and in passing made psychoanalysis a part of Jewish history. Jewish not as a religion, not as a doctrine, but as a culture by birth: a part of the history and the present of psychoanalysis. A completely unexpected step for a woman who had presented herself all her life as a psychoanalyst and had never taken a position as a Jew. Here she came forward as the ambassador of her father: Sigmund Freud, the Jewish atheist.

* * *

As I have written before, the Jew is indissolubly connected to the anti-Semite. The height of anti-Semitism has for the moment been reached by the Shoah. Before the Nazi period, 80 per cent of the analysts in Germany were Jewish. After 1945 not one was left. Much has been written by others about the attitude of the psychoanalytic movement during the Second World War. I will limit myself to a concise account. Antonovsky, Berman, Brecht, Chasseguet-Smirgel, Freedman, Heenen-Wolff, Lockot, Lothane, Nitzschke, and Wallerstein have studied that history. The research by the historian Cocks was indispensable. Frosh, a psychologist, is an authority on history and on psychology; I have found his work useful. Goggin and Brockman Goggin, usually called Goggin and Goggin, are psychologists who have intensively studied the history and have also tried to understand it psychologically. Brecht and others have told the history by placing many manuscripts by psychoanalysts in accompanying texts in the historical framework.[1]

Cocks has described how the non-Jewish analysts "cleansed" analysis in Germany and took it over. Lothane and Nitzschke express their indignation about what they see as the disloyalty of the IPA and Freud himself with regard to the Jewish psychoanalysts in Germany. Chasseguet-Smirgel gives a tart reply. Berman criticizes the way the analytic community systematically looked the other way during the rise of the Third Reich. He does not even mention Jung's collaboration, but is especially outraged at Jones' political—and personal— decision not to inconvenience the Nazis so that a number of Aryan psychoanalysts in Berlin could continue to work. By not going into the relevant political and social matters at that time, these analysts strengthened the Nazis' legitimacy and thus left the toxic effects and the racism unchallenged. Freedman, Frosh, and Wallerstein give a synthesis of what others have written about the subject. Starting in 1982, the German analytic journal *Psyche* tried to find out what really happened to psychoanalysis in Germany during the Second World War. It published a special issue with the title *Psychoanalysis in Hitler-Germany: What was it actually like?*[2] In 1985, the catalogue of the Hamburg congress was published, and in 1988, a special issue of *Psychoanalysis and Contemporary Thought*.[3]

The history of psychoanalysis in Germany is a story about an institute, a congress, and organizations. In approximately that order I will tell how my subject *The Danger of the Jewish Legacy* has been treated in these three areas. As the basis for the creation of an institute, I see that the German Psychoanalytic Society was gradually dissolved between 1936 and 1938 and was included in the German Institute for Psychological Research and Psychotherapy where it found a new existence as Working Group A. This was done in cooperation with other schools like the Jungians and the Adlerians. By 1933 the Jewish psychoanalysts had already been removed from leadership positions. They were forced to give up their membership in the German Psychoanalytic Society and were finally driven out of Germany. Max Eitingon, a Jew, who had established and financed the outpatient clinic of the Berlin Psychoanalytic Institute and was chairman of the German Psychoanalytic Society, was forced to give up both functions and hand over his offices to the Aryans Felix Boehm, secretary of the German Psychoanalytic Society, and its treasurer Carl Müller-Braunschweig. In the staff of both organizations there was barely a protest against this. The most important reason given for not protesting was to give the Nazis no reason to abolish the German Psychoanalytic Society or the Institute.

The transformation was completed in 1938 when the German Psychoanalytic Society left the International Psychoanalytical Association (IPA). Soon the revamped institute was popularly called the Göring Institute, after its director Matthias Göring, a cousin of Field Marshal Hermann Göring, second in command of the Third Reich. Its official name was the German Institute for Psychological Research and Psychotherapy. On the surface Matthias appeared to be a friendly and kind man, a competent administrator who made the best of a bad job. But he was a convinced Nazi, *until April 1945*. Professor Bräutigam, who as a 22-year-old psychoanalyst candidate had met Matthias in 1942, remembers him as "the antithesis of a powerful figure; as a slender, rather shy man with a pointed grey beard, wearing a uniform of a high-ranking military physician that was too large for him" (1984, p. 907). He may have appeared that way to people whom he considered more or less as his equals.

The truth is more grim. Matthias G. made reading *Mein Kampf* mandatory for his fellow workers. He refused to use his influence to stop the "euthanasia programs", which at the time meant killing people "who lead a life unworthy of life". This included children with hereditary defects and who were untreatable, homosexuals, and the blind. When asked, he refused to support sparing the lives of epileptic patients and said he would wait until there was definitive proof that they had actually been murdered. The leading analysts Boehm and Kemper, who were officers of the German Psychoanalytic Society, diagnosed incurable forms of battle fatigue and indicated the death penalty as therapy for it (Goggin & Brockman Goggin, 2001, pp. 116ff.).

In Göring's institute the character of psychoanalysis was changed; it became psychotherapy. The insight-giving character of analysis, with its purpose of obtaining inner freedom and independence, was changed into a directive attitude with as its goal becoming a good citizen and in that way supporting the war effort. This is incidentally one of the reasons why psychotherapy has until the present continued to have a bad name in many psychoanalytic circles. In that context psychotherapy is seen not as derived from psychoanalysis but as a perversion of it. Outwardly the institute tried to camouflage the break. Freedman repeats the rumour that two portraits hung in the halls of the Göring Institute, one of Freud and one of Hitler, that stared at each other (1988, p. 102). Frosh points out that Matthias Göring was not an intruder, but that he had been invited by the analysts in order to safeguard the continued existence of the institute. Frosh also cites Cocks who maintains that around 1933 many physicians, especially young ones, supported the National Socialist doctrine, which promised that their economic circumstances would be improved and their field would be rid of women and Jews (2005, p. 110).[4] A good illustration of the upheaval caused by the new institute was the celebration of Freud's 80th birthday on May 6, 1936. The new staff celebrated in formal dress. Jews were forbidden to participate in this ceremony. So they decided to celebrate among themselves with a lecture in one of their homes.

The attitude of the International Psychoanalytical Association (IPA) is a separate subject. At first Jones, who was president at the time, went along with the idea that the Berlin psychoanalytic treatment and training institute would be continued with *Mein Kampf* as basic literature and with Freud's works under lock and key. Recognition by the IPA was sought and obtained, with the promise that the independence of psychoanalysis would be respected. When psychoanalysis was mixed with psychotherapy and the psychoanalytic department was downgraded to Working Group A, the German Psychoanalytic Association (DPV) cancelled its membership of the IPA, as it had already wanted to do in 1936. Ten days after Kristallnacht (November 10, 1938) the German Psychoanalytic Association was dissolved by the Nazis and integrated into the Göring Institute.

Brecht and others have found an interview with Göring. He was asked how it was that psychoanalysis—a very modern branch of science—could have such a destructive effect. His answer was that since Freud psychoanalysis had been the almost exclusive terrain of Jewish physicians. As a Jew, Freud could not understand that the unconscious is not the domain of suppressed sexuality but the "foundation of life", the source of creativity. It was precisely on the terrain of the spirit that Judaism could exercise its influence to its heart's content: "For the Jews, psychotherapy became a business, and the poisoning of mental life a necessity, so that they could then undertake to cure the poison" (Brecht, et al., 1985, p. 151).[5]

The training activities continued during the war, and the entire post-war generation of German analysts was trained by people who were trainers or were trained at the Göring Institute. After the war this resulted in an unrecognized problem in transference. Goggin and Goggin found it described in an essay (1993) by Sammy Speier

(2001, p. 174). The latter pointed out the post-war *collective amnesia* of the German Psychoanalytic Association (DPV). Questions and conversations about the history of the DPV during the war were avoided. When during his training analysis Speier asked a question about the role of analysis during the Third Reich, the answer was: "What are your associations, what are you thinking of?" Speier interpreted it as: "Why in the world do you ask me such a personal question?" In this way the analysis was made impossible and he never got to the process of working through the past because the transference was not determined by the fantasies of the analysand but by the presumed behaviour of the analyst. Analyst and analysand were too much on their guard.

In 1979 Germany was in the process of saying goodbye to that past and was putting its house in order. The German analysts also wanted to leave the Second World War behind. They wanted to be completely accepted into the normal world, and psychoanalytic life was part of that. It is strange that such a huge issue was made of returning to Germany for the psychoanalytic congress. As early as 1971 the analysts had returned to Vienna without much fuss. There, too, Anna Freud provided the opening address. At that time, she set foot on "German" soil for the first time in 30 years. The longing to seeing her birthplace again and the thought that a museum and a psychoanalytic institute would be established at *Berggasse 19* won her over. In a letter to Anna Freud, her friend Anna Maenchen called the visit a "nostalgic trip to the past of psychoanalysis". The biographer Elizabeth Young-Bruehl shows that for Anna Freud the Viennese congress meant the recognition of her Hampstead Clinic and the training for child analysts that she had established (1988, pp. 387–407).

The Germans used their presence in Jerusalem during the congress of 1977 to get a congress in their homeland for the first time after the war. They wanted to organize it for 1981. It came up during the Business Meeting of the IPA for the Jerusalem congress. The Jewish representatives in particular reacted very emotionally, arguing that such a congress at that place was still too soon. Great barriers still had to be overcome to get the analysts back to Germany. That did not happen until later. In 1981, the 34th psychoanalytic congress, which would take place in 1985, was awarded to Hamburg. There was a lot of bickering about the location. The original idea was to let Berlin serve as the congress headquarters, as a curious answer to Jerusalem. When it did not get enough support, suggestions followed each other rapidly. Munich, Frankfurt, and Wiesbaden were nominated and voted down. Berlin was considered too political, Frankfurt too small. Munich was known as the city where the Nazis had their start. Bonn and Wiesbaden were too American for the taste of the representatives. In the end it was Hamburg.[6] It turned out to be an important congress, which can be seen from the flood of publications that came out of it.

Hamburg had the unearned reputation that it had never been very pro-Nazi. It was known as a liberal enclave in conservative Germany. At the time of the congress, Klaus von Dohnanyi was its mayor. He came from a family with unimpeachable conduct. His grandfather was Ernö Dohnányi, the composer and conductor of the Hungarian radio orchestra. In that position he had refused to dismiss his Jewish musicians during the war. His father was Hans von Dohnanyi (he dropped the accent) who was one of the participants in the unsuccessful attempt on Hitler's life in July 1944; in April 1945 he was tortured and then hanged by the Nazis.

Klaus von Dohnanyi turned out to be an excellent choice to open the congress. His opening address, which according to my estimate lasted no more than half an hour, is indelibly stamped on the memories of the congress participants. The other speeches, which were primarily of a clinical nature, lacked the moral urgency and force that were needed for the return to German territory. Von Dohnanyi asserted his power. In an opening address that was meant to be festive, he reminded those present that in 1932, during their Twelfth International Congress in Wiesbaden, the analysts had not underestimated the danger of National Socialism. His stern judgment about their later actions was as follows:

> For fear of losing everything, bit by bit was sacrificed, every step being rational—and yet at the same time always in the wrong direction. Here a compromise concerning persons, there a compromise of principles, but always in the pretended interest of preserving the whole—which in the end was lost (1986).

He dared to show his countrymen the most extreme consequence of the concept of nationalism and identification with the nation:

"Whoever says: our Bach and our Beethoven, must also say: our Hitler". In personal contacts he managed to set the right tone as well. He presented the chair of the programme committee, the French (originally Polish) Jew Janine Chasseguet-Smirgel, with a copy of the first edition of Heinrich Heine's *Romanzero*, Freud's favourite book of poetry. She was clearly touched, "especially when I remember 1942".

Hamburg was a successful congress. That was also due to the thoroughness and caution of the organizing committee. For example, it was a period of airliner hijackings and hostages. That created a need for many extra safety measures, unavoidably with many police. On the initiative of the organization committee, those police officers did not wear uniforms. Their uniform caps, buttons, and boots might be too much for Jews returning to German soil for the first time in 30 or 40 years. The programme and the theme of the congress had been worked out with extreme care. There were quite a few stories around that.

The theme of the congress was *Identification and its Vicissitudes*. It was more pragmatic than had originally been proposed. The chair of the organization in charge of the conference, the German Psychoanalytic Association (DPV), wanted to make *Identification and its Vicissitudes in Relation to the Nazi Phenomenon* the guiding theme. The DPV wanted to pay explicit attention to the return of the psychoanalysts to Germany after 53 years. The programme committee was in favour, but a minority had opposed it. People did not want to offend their hosts. Janine Chasseguet-Smirgel worked out a compromise: a presentation of the results of research about the consequences of Nazism on the children of the victims and the perpetrators, with the inclusion of clinical material (1986, op. cit.). This took place on the second day of the five-day congress. The speakers were Hillel Klein and Ilany Kogan and the previously-mentioned Friedrich-Wilhelm Eickhoff. All four are considered excellent analysts with long records of practice and publications. Klein is a survivor who has managed to transform his own heroic and tragic experiences into a detached passion for his patients. Kogan—an Israeli analyst experienced in treating survivors of the Shoah—and Eickhoff write with clinical precision, and Ostow is deeply immersed in Jewish culture and in psychoanalytic thinking.

Yet a problem remained. Because of the treatment on the programme of second-generation victims, regardless of being children of murdered Jews or of murdering Nazis, they were equated: as victims. However, one trauma is not the same as the other. Here Janine Chasseguet-Smirgel's express wish not to let the congress become an emotional chaos or a tribunal came back to haunt them. By discussing both groups in one session during the congress, what needed to be said was not and could not be expressed: naked anger, naked grief. By reducing what had happened politically to the clinical reality of treatment, suffering got all the attention, and the crime could be passed over. No attention was paid to the essential distinction, as was done by Judith Kestenberg, the New York expert on the consequences of the Shoah. She expresses this in a psychoanalytic way:

> Children of survivors need to rid themselves of the invasion of their superego by the double image of the persecutor and his victim.... Nazis' children need to come to grips with their own conscience, with the guilt of moral self-degradation imposed upon them by their Nazi parents. They are not tied together by the Holocaust (1982, p. 164).

The omission of such a distinction is called the "dedifferentiation of victims" by John Kafka, an American psychoanalyst who emigrated from Germany. He explains (1988) dedifferentiation as a defensive process that according to him stands in the way of contact and communication. This observation comes from a man who is described by Wallerstein (1988) as the person who more than any other German-speaking analyst worked on building a relationship with the new generation of German analysts. It should be mentioned here that he was very wary of an "artificial reconciliation".

For the organizers of the conference, the wish to make the Germans once again part of the analytic movement prevented the political reality from being taken into account in the suffering that had been caused. The masochistic processing of suffering was central, instead of the reality of persecution. The clinic has replaced history. That may sound like a somewhat abstract thought; Rabinbach says it more directly in a controversy about the "inability to mourn", a concept made popular by A. and M. Mitscherlich (1967). He writes about the still existing "contempt for what was and is generally considered an exaggerated emphasis on Jewish victims" (Rabinbach, 1995, 321ff.). He points to the ill will that still exists in Germany [only there? (author)] towards Jews, Communists, and Poles, and he states: "In a certain sense, psychoanalysis helped decriminalize the image of the Nazi past" (ibid.).

There was much ado about what to name the congress. Martin Wangh, a New York analyst born in Germany who was living in Israel at the time, recounts (1988) in a spectrum of reactions that followed the congress how the organizing DPV was determined to avoid a discussion about the Nazi period. He is dissatisfied with the results. In some capacity or other he had suggested another theme to Limentani, the president of the IPA: *Mourning and reconstruction, problematic steps in the psychoanalytic and social process*. Limentani had rejected it with the argument that this theme "would not be elegant on the occasion of our return to Germany". In the same breath, Limentani takes a political step and clears the way for the thought that Israel plays the role of Nazi Germany in the Middle East. He compares the situation in the Middle East to the Shoah, subtly but undeniably. Wangh quotes him from a letter of January 28, 1983:

> I would find it a bit suspicious if someone would use that situation (of a possible congress in Israel) to censure Israel about the recent hostilities in Lebanon [...] I would say that the same is true for a visit to Germany.

Wangh remarks that this is a case of confusing a political discussion with a psychoanalytical one. Ostow lets the historical emotional background come through by remarking that the very going to a congress indicates a choice. Those who stayed away were Germans who were afraid of being condemned and Jews who feared being unable to face the confrontation with Germany. Another group was those Jews who were afraid that they would be too friendly and too forgiving. Their fear was that they would in that way betray their murdered family members (Ostow, 1986, pp. 887–891).

The New York analyst Edith Kurzweil (1986) mentions that the original theme of the congress was *Mourning, Forgiveness, Reconciliation*. It was vetoed by the chair of the programme committee, Chasseguet-Smirgel, who had arguments that concerned specific groups. She felt that the congress should not become a tribunal. She had profound empathy for the Jewish participants. She understood that when your family has been exterminated, reconciliation with that fact is impossible. She added prosaically that no Nazi had ever asked for forgiveness of his own accord.

Yet, the congress remained silent about an important subject. The discussion was about *them* and the processing of their past, which was declared history, but there was practically no attention for *us*: the analysts. When it counted, they had demonstrated their disloyalty at every level. The question of whether they could be trusted again was not posed. The four invited analysts referred to the treatment of children of Jewish war victims and of the perpetrators. There was no attention to the effects of the treatments that had been carried out by Nazi fellow travellers and sympathizers: the majority of the German training analysts as well as other European colleagues. This problem is known about German training analysts and was treated by Brecht among others, but I know too few details about other training analysts who collaborated with fascist regimes in their countries. In the Netherlands this problem also surfaced after the war; Brinkgreve (1984) touches on it. I will return to this subject in chapter six.

* * *

Adam Limentani, the above-mentioned president of the IPA, played a very special role as chairman of the congress. He was a diplomatic man, an Italian Jew who had left Italy in 1938 because of the rise of Fascism. He left for England and there acquired an excellent reputation. That resulted in the presidency of the British Psychoanalytical Society and finally the presidency of the IPA. The authors of his obituary describe him as follows: "Adam came from a well established Roman non-orthodox Jewish family who eschewed ritual. He always affirmed his Jewish identity without being chauvinistic about it" (Glasser, et al., 1995, p. 1031). The absurdity of this sentence becomes obvious if you substitute another biographical fact (man, Italian, black, six-year-old, Roman Catholic, or golfer) for Jew. It reflects, as always, the discomfort and the accompanying stereotyping that overcomes the psychoanalyst when he speaks or writes about his own or someone else's Jewishness.

As Limentani saw his role, he was an ideal figure to clear away any possible obstacles in the contact between the IPA and its German members. This is also clear from the official report of the congress, written by the secretary of the IPA, the American Edward Weinshel. He indicates that although only 25 per cent of the programme was devoted to the Nazi period, the whole congress was dominated by coming to terms with it. The gathering was experienced as moving. For many Jewish participants it was their first visit to Germany after the war. The most important question during the congress was how this return was dealt with. Weinshel (1986) writes that something important had happened in Hamburg: "Our German colleagues were not just our colleagues; they had become our friends".

* * *

Indeed, it had been an ordinary congress with lectures and work groups about various subjects, visits to the homes of colleagues, inspections of clinics and other places of interest. However, there was one subject that overshadowed everything else: the Second World War and its consequences for psychoanalysts and their patients.

An exhibition was set up that showed the history of psychoanalysis in Germany before, around, and 15 years after the war through documents and photos. The catalogue for this exhibition became a significant record (Brecht, et al., 1985). Photos of analysts who did not cooperate with the Nazis or collaborated with them in greater or lesser ways were presented together. In mini-chapters small bits of analytic history are given, illustrative in the way vignettes are traditionally used: short illustrations with case material that have the function in psychoanalytic articles of making dry theory living and comprehensible. Because the authors had access to the archives of the British Psychoanalytical Society, which also contain parts of the IPA files, letters and minutes are shown in facsimile. Nazi articles about psychoanalysis are also printed in the exhibition catalogue that later was published as a book. This work is indispensable as a basic tool for anyone who wants to learn about the history of the psychoanalytic movement in Germany before, during, and after the Second World War.

It was also a political combat text. It was a documented refutation by young psychoanalysts of the legend that psychoanalysts in the Second World War collaborated above-ground and in plain view with the Nazis, but underground managed to preserve the essence of analysis from destruction (Brecht, 1995, p. 291). Until the publication of that catalogue, the psychoanalytic collaboration with the regime was still the great family secret known by everyone but not discussed in public or in private. The two organizers of the exhibition, the German Psychoanalytic Association (DPV) and the *Psychoanalytische Arbeitsgemeinschaft* Hamburg (the Michael Balint Institute) have been unwilling to dismount it, and it can still be seen in a warehouse in Hamburg. It has also been released on a DVD by the DPV.

As regards the attitude of the German psychoanalysts during the Nazi regime, the back-and-forth between the IPA, in the person of the president Ernest Jones, and the German Psychoanalytic Society (DPG) especially draws our attention. Until the Nazi period, the DPG was the official German psychoanalytic organization. One of its leaders was Carl Müller-Braunschweig who had already shown his willingness for accommodation and his shifting to active collaboration in a lecture in 1929. This lecture was first published in the *Zeitschrift für psychoanalytische Pädagogik*, and in 1931 a reprint was published in the *Almanach der Pychoanalyse*. A second version, with the title *Psychoanalyse und Weltanschauung*, appeared in the Nazi journal *Reichswart* of October 22, 1933. In 1983 Dahmer, the professional general editor, published the same article in *Psyche*, but this time accompanied by biting criticism. This caused Dahmer to be the subject of a lawsuit and resulted in the loss of his job as general editor of this journal.

The argument in all these articles was that psychoanalysis should make a distinction between Germanic and Jewish psychology. It is a powerful and effective instrument that had fallen into the hands of a "destructive spirit" (the Jewish one).

However, it now has to act not by dissolving and destroying, "but to turn impotent weaklings into people fit for life, those cut off from life into people able to look reality in the eye, those prey to their impulses into those able to master their drives, those incapable of love into those able to love and to make sacrifices, and those who take no interest in life into those serving life in its entirety. In such a way psychoanalysis carries out a splendid task of education and can meaningfully serve the newly developed traits of a heroic and reality-oriented life goal".

In 1936 Müller-Braunschweig asks the president of the IPA, on behalf of the DPG, for support in recovering grants from analysts who had had to leave Germany in great haste. He mentions that only the Jewish analysts have not yet paid back their grants and argues that the resentment of the Jewish analysts about the events in

Germany and about the fact that the DPG is now pure Aryan, can not be a sufficient reason to indemnify the debtors for their moral obligations. Jones helped to reclaim the money (Nitzschke, 2003, p. 100). After the removal of the Jewish members, the DPG was allowed to remain a member of the IPA. This membership did not end until the DPG was dissolved in 1938.

After the war, the goal of German analysts was to be recognized internationally again as soon as possible. The essence of their argument was that they had been *as good as possible* in bad times. Perhaps other Germans had not been OK, but they had been OK. This struggle was fought in a roundabout way. The subject of the deliberations was not political behaviour during the war but whether the therapy that had been carried out at the Göring Institute during the war and had been developed further after the war would be recognized as psychoanalysis. This was a mixture of psychoanalysis and forms derived from it. According to the therapists working there, the institute was a place where psychoanalysts could continue their salutary work in relative peace. In a less positive way, it could be said that the form of analysis was preserved, but that the essence, the freedom that is created through free association, was destroyed. Anyone who attacked them about this after the war was branded as a member of a "two armed, Marxist inquisition execution machine that threatens the honourable members of the Psychoanalytic Association"—as Dahmer, who was a victim, expressed with self-mockery (1984, p. 928). More soberly it can be remarked that that generation of Germans was very severe in judging the war generation. There was a tendency to be quite idealistic in order to replace the total evil of the war generation by the total good of the post-war generation.

Opponents of the work of the Göring Institute and the accommodating DPG argued that continuing work during the war had produced a whitewashed psychoanalysis, stripped of its Jewish and other difficult to digest elements. Proponents, with Schultz-Hencke as their spokesman, argued that it was a research-based development in psychoanalysis. At any rate, the new therapy, *neo-analysis*, was not recognized as psychoanalysis. It is an important moment in the long history of the exclusion of Schultz-Hencke; it had started when he published his *Introduction to Psychoanalysis* in 1927 and tried to combine the worlds of Freud, Jung, and Adler. As a result, starting in 1929 he was no longer invited for training activities of the Berlin

Psychoanalytic Institute. Nowadays the opinion would be closer to the one expressed by the New York psychoanalyst Zvi Lothane who is interested in history:

> Actually Schultz-Hencke was prescient, for neo-analysis was a logical extension of Freud's own ego psychology [...] and it would influence later derivatives of neo-analysis, e.g., Erich Fromm and Karen Horney (2003, p. 93).

The German psychotherapist Dührssen (1994) used Schultz-Hencke in her *History of Psychoanalysis in Germany* in order to attack the conservatism of psychoanalysis. She was reproached severely about this position—as if she wanted to let Nazism glory once again (see e.g., Blumenberg, 1995 and Eickhoff, 1995).

After the war we see the creation of two psychoanalytic organizations in Germany, separated not by collaboration with or resistance against National Socialist authorities, but based on personal differences and ambitions—officially thrashed out—about the question of who practised the purest analysis. As noted by Brecht, et al.:

> The division made it possible for each side to accuse the other of having had the closer affinity with National Socialism. Both societies' reckoning with the past was such that to this day their deep entanglement with National Socialism was denied and was not integrated into their own identity (1985, p. 214).

The later president of the German Psychoanalytic Association (DPV), Herman Beland, clearly expresses the problem of the German analysts in his reflection (1988) on the congress in Hamburg: "Can they manage to take the step from paranoid to depressive guilt?"[7] The German Psychoanalytic Society (DPG), which had openly collaborated during the Hitler period, was—although with hesitation—excluded from the IPA and was readmitted in 2001 as a Provisional Society. As usual, the Jews were held responsible for this exclusion. They had been unwilling to understand that during the Nazi period Jews had to be dismissed in order to preserve psychoanalysis (Frosh, 2005, p. 134).

The German Psychoanalytic Association (DPV), the successor of the German Psychoanalytic Society (DPG), was accepted by the IPA in 1951. In this case the criterion was not political but

JERUSALEM AND HAMBURG: TWO CONGRESSES 99

analytical purity, concentrated in particular around the attitude toward Schultz-Hencke's *neo-analysis* (Eickhoff, 1995). Its first president was the above-mentioned Carl Müller-Braunschweig, about whom Goggin and Goggin remarked: "Over the years he showed a changing pattern of compromises, collaboration, and resistance". They called him a "fallen analyst" because his actions during and after the Second World War were unacceptable from a moral point of view in general and psychoanalytic ethics in particular. Beland dares to remark that Müller-Braunschweig was at that time a deservedly respected psychoanalyst. Therefore it is easy to identify with him. He concludes as follows: "If I had lived at that time, I would probably have thought and acted the same way" (1988, p. 280).

The second president of the DPV was Scheunert who had been a Nazi much more unequivocally: he was the only psychoanalyst who was a member of the Party (the NSDAP) (Goggin & Brockman Goggin, 2001, pp. 135, 137, 161). Both presidents were accepted as leaders of the German group by the IPA that had appointed them. This made the international organization of psychoanalysts an accessory to the cover-up of the psychoanalytic reality during the war. As part of a very different discussion, the British analyst Hanna Segal, 69 years old at the time, said: "When the Nazi phenomenon stared us in the face, the psychoanalytic community outside Germany was mostly silent" (Freedman, 1988, p. 209). She was right, but she could also have added: and that is how they wanted it to remain.

The German analysts are always held responsible for the collaboration with the regime. Without taking anything away from their part, the role of the IPA should not be underestimated. According to Goggin and Goggin, IPA president Jones wrote in a letter of July 24, 1934, to Boehm who was one of the initiators of the removal of Jews from the German Psychoanalytic Society (DPG):

> You will know, that I myself regard those emotions and ultra-Jewish attitude very unsympathetically, and it is plain to me that you and your colleagues are being made a dumping-ground for much emotion and resentment which belongs elsewhere and has displaced in your direction (2001, p. 101, from Steiner, 1989, p. 51).

Goggin and Goggin show convincingly that the political goal of the IPA was not the de-Nazification of psychoanalysis but the preservation of what was considered psychoanalytical orthodoxy (2001, pp. 157–169.). Beland gives a nice explanation of the attitude of his own German Psychoanalytic Association (DPV) members: "Their complete loyalty to classic psychoanalysis was for them the proof that they, too, were persecuted" (1988, p. 270).

The IPA saw its role above all as protecting psychoanalysis. As such it placed the interest of psychoanalysis above the interest of individual psychoanalysts. Brecht disentangles the lawsuit that the Nazi regime instituted against the Berlin training analyst Edith Jacobson in 1936. Jacobson had had in analysis a Communist member of the resistance, who had been put to death because of acts of resistance. She herself was arrested because of complicity and was condemned to two and a half years in prison. Brecht expresses the exact point of view of the IPA: "On the one hand the collaboration of German psychoanalysts was condemned, on the other hand active participation in the resistance was also condemned" (1988, p. 243).

There was one thing that the analysts did not understand but which was grasped by their colleague Bernard Kamm: there is no such thing as a good analyst in murderous surroundings. In 1934 Kamm, as one of the few non-Jews (just like Martin Grotjahn and Richard Sterba) resigned his membership of the German Psychoanalytic Association and together with his Jewish colleagues left Germany to settle in the United States. In 1980 he explains to Regine Lockot who had evidently invited him to the congress why he took those actions:

> If the environment in which analysis is to be undertaken comes too close to the harshness of the originally threatening environment—or even surpasses it—it is impossible for the poor analysand to make the liberating discovery that the original threats have lost their power—have become null and void (Brecht, et al., 1985, p. 181).

The opening session of the congress in Hamburg was characteristic of the denial of the relevance of the history of psychoanalysis for the movement. President Limentani (1986) praises the role that the Germans played in the development of psychoanalysis, and he mentions that the German Psychoanalytic Association is the largest in Europe at that moment, and the second largest in the world. He addresses himself especially to the Germans who are there.

He repeats for them the psychoanalytic task "to remember and to understand the past". He hopes for them that the congress will contribute to "our colleagues coming to terms with the past". Furthermore he speaks to be sure about *their past*, but the generational change means that it is now possible to speak about the past of the organization of and for psychoanalysis, but not about the participants of the congress as individuals.

He especially welcomed the 85-year-old Bernard Kamm, at that time from Chicago. In this way Kamm, instead of the great exception that he was, became the symbol of the attitude of the psychoanalysts. Limentani leaves out the word collaboration. He also does not mention the struggle to have a congress in Germany. The colleagues who could not come because they did not feel up to it are not mentioned in his address, nor are the analysts who were killed in the Second World War. The greatest worry was not to hurt the feelings of the German colleagues, to accept them again into the world of psychoanalysis, to make them into members of the IPA again. And that goal was amply met.

Rafael Moses and his wife Rena Hrushovski-Moses, two experienced Israeli analysts, have pointed out what was lacking at the congress. In a balanced statement they reported how they left Hamburg slightly depressed after the event. They felt that something was not right at the congress, and they tried to put it into words. They did not wish to give the Germans the feeling that they had to be punished for the actions of their parents, but there was something they had to say against the general direction of their colleagues' opinions. They considered the very title of the day that was devoted to the Second World War, *Identification and the Nazi Phenomenon*, a surprising euphemism. In their eyes that abstract formulation obscured the fact that the Shoah was something that people had done to other people. They also found it inappropriate that the Shoah had become only a part of a congress that, no matter how you look at it, was about the Shoah. They were not reconciled to the fact that the theme of the congress, *Identification and its Vicissitudes*, served as an umbrella for various identifications—themes such as identification and perversions, identification and neuroses, identification and personality disorders, identification and childhood and adolescent pathology. By treating the Shoah as a clinical problem, the subject was watered down.

"Holocaust", the word currently used for Shoah, is commonly used for all kinds of wrongs—for example undesirable behaviour of parents towards children. The word "Nazism" is encountered everywhere, even and especially in Israel. Moses and Hrushovski-Moses (1986) place this under a term that they previously devised: *partial denial*. It indicates dealing with a very unwelcome truth. That mechanism prevents the study of the cause of the Shoah that is past and the prevention of the Shoah and Nazism that can still come. At the same time it serves to deny the unique quantitative and qualitative aspects of the extermination of the Jews. They argue that the congress was not successful because everything had been done to make sure that there would not be an emotional outburst; hence not everything that needed to be said came up for discussion.

* * *

Two years after the congress Janine Chasseguet-Smirgel, using the information that she had collected as chair of the programme committee, wrote an article (1987) about her personal impressions. Its title reflects what moved her to write; its literal translation is "Time's white hair we ruffle: Reflections on the Hamburg Congress". The significance of the first sentence of the title can be found in a footnote:

> Alain Suied (1985) associates this line by Paul Celan with the poem *Aspen Tree*, dedicated to the memory of the poet's mother, who was deported to her death, which begins as follows: "Aspen tree your leaves glance white into the dark. My mother's hair was never white".
>
> It was some time after finishing this article that, one night in Germany, I remembered that the dearest of all the people to whom I had not said goodbye had been gassed on arrival at the camp because his hair had turned white between the time of his arrest and deportation.

She notes that a number of colleagues of the *Société Psychanalytique de Paris* who had lost one or both parents in the German camps told her that when they spoke with other colleagues about their difficulty in crossing the Rhine, they felt them to be embarrassed and irritated. Baffled, she remarks that "[T]he lack of interest on the part of the French psychoanalysts (but they are not the only ones) in the Jewish problem and the events of the Second World War is surprising". In Germany she sees how the analysts try to get a grip on their own history again. Despite the excellent quality of the exhibition at the congress, it left a bitter taste in her mouth. She sees the process of gradually giving in of the psychoanalysts who during the Nazi period *let themselves be brought into line*; that process was common.

Chasseguet-Smirgel forcefully attacks the idea that children of Nazis are victims, meaning victims of their own parents. That saves them the trouble of "the need to search for these rejected fragments of the parental objects", meaning identification of parts of themselves that they would rather not see. German youth eagerly takes on the role of the persecuted, "being gassed [by pollution) and annihilated by […] the nuclear holocaust".

Then Chasseguet-Smirgel switches to modern anti-Semitism, directed at the state of the Jews, Israel. In this she reminds me a lot of the German (originally Polish) journalist and writer Henryk Broder who once said: "The Germans will never forgive the Jews for Auschwitz". She notices how young Germans and even some analysts eagerly take on the position of victim:

> However, this reversal, whereby the absolute executioner becomes the absolute victim and the ally of Satan becomes the champion of Good, can be fully achieved only if yesterday's (actual) victim is identified with the executioner (1987, p. 437).

In this way of thinking Hitler was a Jew and the Russian Communists invented the alliance between the Nazis and the Zionists. She continues this line of thinking to the attack on Freud's attitude to the Nazis in 1935. The latter then would have wanted to save analysis by sacrificing the Jews who were part of it. In this way the Jew is made guilty of the *Judenreinheit* of the German Psychoanalytic Society (DPG).

She presents Rolf Vogt as an example of how ambivalence can be handled. He had written how relieved he felt when the Israeli army failed to prevent the massacres at Sabra and Chatila. He *had* tried to trace the origins of this feeling and had heard a voice inside him say: "The Jews are no better than we are". "I was shocked by how spontaneously this *we* suddenly brought me close to the National Socialists and it dawned on me distressingly that I had a guilt, which had hitherto remained unconscious, connected with Nazism, of which I had felt myself to be discharged by imagining the Jews as murderers".

She concludes: "This piece of self-analysis does credit to its author" (1987, p. 493).

Notes

1. Antonovsky (1988), Berman (2002), Brecht, et al. (1985), Brecht (1988, 1995), Chasseguet-Smirgel (1987, 1988) Cocks (1985), Freedman (1988), Frosh (2005), Goggin & Brockman Goggin (2001), Heenen-Wolff (1987), Lockot (1985), Lothane (2001, 2003), Nitzschke (2003), Wallerstein (1988).
2. It is a special issue of *Psyche* with the title *Stimmen zum Hamburger IPA-Kongreß*. The following contributions were included: the opening address by Von Dohnányi, and in addition papers by Jean Bergeret (Lyon), Janine Chasseguet-Smirgel (Paris), Erich Gumbel (Jerusalem), John S. Kafka (Washington, DC), Hans Keilson (Bussum, Netherlands), Judith Kestenberg (New York), Uri Lowenthal (Jerusalem), Mortimer Ostow (Riverdale, NY), Barbara Vogt-Heyder (Heidelberg), Rolf Vogt (Heidelberg), Martin Wangh (Jerusalem), Eddy de Wind (Amsterdam), and Edith Kurzweil (New York).
3. In the 11th year of its publication, pp. 197–337.
4. According to an estimate by Rebecca Schwoch, who received her PhD in Berlin in 1999 on the thesis *Ärtzliche Standespolitik im Nationalsozialismus. Julius Hadrich und Karl Haedekamp als Beispiele*, there were 32,200 physicians in Germany in 1919, and in 1932 there were 52,520. There was much unemployment among them. In Berlin half of the physicians were Jewish; this was one of the reasons there was a lot of anti-Semitism among German physicians. (Randolf Wörner has provided me with these data, and Rebecca Schwoch confirmed them by email.)
5. This is a paraphrase of the statement by Karl Kraus: "Psychoanalysis is that mental illness for which it regards itself as therapy".
6. Chasseguet-Smirgel (1987), Brecht, et al. (1985), and telephone interview with Volkert Friedrich, co-chair of the Congress in Hamburg, second editor of Brecht, et al.

7. I try to use as little psychoanalytic jargon as possible. This short characterization becomes comprehensible by using Stroeken (2000), who says: "Depressive position: the process that in the same person can call forth hate as well as love. A term from Melanie Klein's ideas [...]. In the paranoid position there are only parts of the problem, divided into good and bad, loved and hated respectively".

CHAPTER SIX

Two incidents in the Netherlands

There are three psychoanalytic associations in the Netherlands. The oldest one was established in 1917 and is called "The Association" (*Nederlandse Vereniging voor Psychoanalyse*—NVPA). In 1947 "The Society" (*Nederlands Psychoanalytisch Genootschap*—NPG) was created as a splinter group from The Association. In 2005 a third group was added: the Dutch Psychoanalytic Group (*Nederlandse PsychoAnalytische Groep*) usually referred to by its initials, NPAG or "The Group". In 2005, during the 44th IPA congress in Rio de Janeiro, it obtained the status of Provisional Society, and in 2007 it was fully recognized by the IPA. Both the Society and the NPAG were created as a consequence of conflicts inside the Association. Those conflicts had personal, business, and ideological causes. Although they took place in totally different periods and also in different contexts, both of them were created because of dissatisfaction with the treatment of Jews inside the Association. The first incident was concerning the Second World War; it had to do with the reception of Jewish colleagues who entered the Netherlands as refugees. The second one started with the "anti-Semitic outbursts" (as he called them himself) of a training analyst and the reactions to them. This incident took place between 2000 and 2005.

The first split prevented good cooperation between the Association and the Society for years. The dispute was settled around 2001, when the Society was recognized as a member of the IPA. The consensus about the second conflict was that keeping it secret was a good thing. In documents about it, one can read repeatedly that it was good that "the press" did not get wind of it. I myself have collected material about it. The split, which is now a fact, also is a split in the collection of facts. Anything that is the "Verhage affair" for one person is the "training committee affair" for another, and for a third person it is the tragedy of loosening psychoanalytic discipline and the requirements for training analysts. The facts depend on the chosen theme.

I had hoped to obtain official access to all the written documents, including the board's documents that are available about these incidents. To that end I first submitted an oral and then a written request to the board of the Dutch Association for Psychoanalysis (NVPA). I received a positive answer that did, however, contain the following stipulation:

> The board wants to claim the right to inspect, but also to correct, prior to eventually making the research results public. These matters will have to be set down in a contract.

I felt that I would not be able to work under these restrictive conditions. Therefore I had to manage with sources of information that were made available to me by Association members who were my friends. In my opinion, I have been able to fill the holes in the written material with the oral explanations of people who were involved. This information, not gathered through official channels, led to me setting up my own archive with letters, minutes, and personal opinions. I think that I would have seen the story in the same way if I had been able to go through the official archive.

The first split: the association and the society

Two initiators established the Society in 1947: A. J. Westerman Holstijn and J. H. van der Hoop. They resigned from the Association for several reasons. Right before the war there was a fierce dispute that led to a first split that was later undone. According to Spanjaard there was, in addition to the continuing conflict about training (meaning admission to becoming a training analyst), also the question of admitting lay people (non-physicians), which should be understood to mean admitting German-Jewish refugees from Nazi Germany. Spanjaard gives as one of the reasons a fear of financial consequences. He writes:

> The discussion reveals great fear that the yield would be spread too thin, but also that many members do not accept the great advantage of finally being able to have experienced training analysts. [...] People are clearly not aware of the tragedy that is developing in Germany and in addition fear being overrun by emigrating colleagues who are admitted too easily, a fear that was often heard at the time (1997, p. 38).

Dr. A. J. Westerman Holstijn—appointed in 1934 as clinical professor at the University of Amsterdam to lecture about psychoanalysis of psychoses and Primitivism—sided with those who resisted taking into the Association the German analysts who had fled to the Netherlands. He resigned from the Association in 1936 when he was outvoted. According to Stroeken, he took it badly when the IPA, which advocated taking in foreigners, interfered in Dutch affairs. Because that organization had a German-Austrian bias, Westerman Holstijn used the expression "narcissistic Nazi similarities" in a letter to Laundauer, a German Jewish analyst who had fled to the Netherlands; Holstijn's opponents then used this expression to refer to him.[1] Stroeken writes: "This is one of the reasons that he was held responsible for the nasty behaviour of most analysts in the 1930s". However, according to Stroeken, Westerman Holstijn was the only one among Dutch analysts who never signed the Aryan declaration; this caused him to be dismissed from his post as clinical professor during the war (1997, p. 61ff.).

The second founder of the Society was Dr. J. H. van der Hoop. He, too, was an unsalaried university lecturer at the University of Amsterdam, and he taught the study of neuroses. He was never trusted because—well before the war—he had gone through one of his analyses with C. G. Jung. This was before the latter had distanced himself from the psychoanalytic movement. In 1947 Van der Hoop resigned from the Society. His anger was caused by the fact that he had not been appointed as training analyst.

Brinkgreve (1984) was the first who did research about the reception of German Jewish analysts by their Dutch colleagues. What she sees above all are exclusion mechanisms. These were used and articulated by members of the upper middle class whose members, clearly not bothered by any shame, gave their opinions. For example, De Monchy writes in May of 1933:

> In no way will I assist in letting German analysts—and Jews to boot—get established in the Netherlands. I think it's a great advantage that our Psychoanalytic Association is not exclusively in Jewish hands (Brinkgreve, 1984, p. 144).

Brinkgreve also quotes a letter that Westerman Holstijn—in his role as chairman of the Association—wrote on July 13, 1935 to Jones who was at the time the president of the International Psychoanalytical Association.

> Moreover, because there was *not a single Jew* among the most eminent analysts in Holland, we were until now shielded from the enmity that you encountered in other countries where *anti-Semitic feelings* of opponents, combined with the *Jewish sticking together* of a number of analysts, disturbed the scientific and social situation (Brinkgreve, op. cit., p. 163).

A short comment should be added here: Brinkgreve discovered that in three countries there were barely any Jews who were members of psychoanalytic associations. She writes:

> Apart from the emigrants, the British Psychoanalytic Association counted only two Jews according to Jones. Roazen also notes that the Swiss analytic association was the only psychoanalytic group that had no Jews [1984, p. 345]. The pre-war Dutch analytic association could have been added here, with the exception of very few like Weijl and Tas Sr.

She does not give a reason for the lack of Jews in the Netherlands, but the simplest way to understand this is that the very restrictive admission procedures of the Dutch association were the cause. Formally, the selection was carried out on the basis of the prospective analyst being "sick or healthy"—or rather whether he is fit to carry out his profession. But in this context it is impossible to separate social and personal criteria, no matter what the pretexts may be. Evidently most Jews were considered unsuitable for the profession. I assume that some were considered suitable. For reasons already mentioned in this book, in many countries psychoanalysis was an attractive profession for Jews. I assume that Dutch Jews were no exception.

Westerman Holstijn tried to prevent the German Jews Reik and Landauer from becoming training analysts in the Netherlands. When this became public, and the Dutch Association for Psychiatry and Neurology (NVPN) wanted to discuss it during an annual meeting, the secretary of the Association reacted in a letter of January 11, 1936. Brinkgreve writes:

> He was sorry that this affair had come up in the general meeting, because those who signed the letter would most likely be suspected of anti-Semitism and such, while our protest also involved other colleagues without a Dutch diploma.

Brinkgreve does not forget to mention that the attitude of the Jewish immigrants—eminent in Germany—does not at all show the gratitude and humility befitting refugees. According to her, the affair ended in a "restrained acceptance of the Jewish analysts from Germany" (op. cit., p. 171).[2]

Stroeken relates that Van Ophuisen, the president of the NVPN at the time, tried to make *favourable arrangements* for the immigrants. This caused him to be the subject of a motion of censure, supported by ten members. The acceptance of this motion led to his resignation as president and finally to his emigration to the United States. After the split the Society and the Association each went their own way. Since the last decade of the 20th century the friction between Society and the Association has faded and has disappeared on the official level. There is now cooperation instead of competition. Within the Dutch Psychoanalytic Institute (NPI), members of the Society and the Association work on a basis of equality. Their training and training analysts are treated alike. That is no small matter because the NPI was originally the training, referral, and treatment institute of the Association. Since the middle of the 1980s it has also carried out these functions for the Society.

Furthermore, in 1995 a scientific journal for psychoanalysis (*Tijdschrift voor Psychoanalyse*) was founded by both these organizations as well as five other, including Flemish, psychoanalytic societies. Since 1997 the Scientific Committee, which among other things organizes scientific evenings for members, has been a joint undertaking of the Association and the Society. The Dutch Association for Psychoanalytic Psychotherapy (NVPP) participates in this committee. The mutual condemnation has become history, with some unexpected offshoots to the present. When it really counts, the smaller Society insists that it is an independent organization, not a "second fiddle to the Association", and the Association has a tendency to fall back on its own majesty especially in considering quality.

In addition there was the conviction that the other party was no good during the war—neither psychoanalytically nor politically. That is true, but not really. The Society did not yet exist, and it is said that the merit of the Association was that it abolished itself during the occupation (Jones, 1972–1974, vol. III, p. 199). Chasseguet-Smirgel seems to adopt this opinion without comment (1987, p. 439). This dissolution was virtual, according to Stroeken: president De Monchy and secretary Blok remained members. "The others left the Association," much against the wishes of the president (1997, pp. 46ff.). In fact the Association continued, but not officially and without Jewish analysts; it even organized a technical seminar. This is why I do not understand why Jones and Chasseguet-Smirgel see that behaviour as correct and even heroic. This view must be a reflection of the long-held view of the heroic and steadfast Dutch attitude during the Second Word War. In the Netherlands people now think about this in more subtle ways.

The second split: the association and the NPAG (Dutch Psychoanalytic Group)

On April 13, 2000, three speakers gave lectures in the auditorium of the University of Amsterdam; these were the so-called Duijker lectures. It was the last tribute in that form to H. C. J. Duijker, a professor of psychology who had retired 20 years earlier. The speakers were Iki Halberstadt-Freud, a psychoanalyst, Martin van Amerongen, a journalist and philosopher, and Jaap van Heerden who later became a professor of general psychology. As far as I know, Halberstadt's lecture was not published. Van Amerongen (2000) gave a moving plea to take Freud seriously and to worry about the quality and the disposition of his opponents. Van Heerden's (2000) lecture was published twice: first in a shortened form in the *NRC* newspaper of April 15, 2000, and later in the *Newsletter* of the Dutch Psychoanalytic Association. In the *NRC* its title was "A child does not like to lose its thumb" and was announced as "the Duiker lecture". In the internal publication it has a more straightforward title: "The controversial legacy of Freud". That was nicer than the symposium organizers had originally planned. They wanted to announce it with the title: "Does Freud still have a past?"

What Halberstadt-Freud and Van Amerongen said does not matter in the context of this book. Van Heerden's presentation settles a score with Freud's dream theory and symbol theory—unfortunately by means of a caricature. It was published in the *Newsletter* at the request of Frans Verhage, a training analyst of the Association and professor emeritus of Methods and Techniques of Psychological Research at Erasmus University. Verhage wanted to react because he had been very annoyed by Van Heerden's lecture. He deals (2000) with the latter in two ways. The first way is that of the analyst who looks more closely at the sickness of not appreciating Freud. He writes "Dear Jaap" and continues, "I was at the Duiker lecture and was surprised that you felt that you had to mock Freud's legacy". Verhage shows himself to be a methodologist, a scientific researcher, and a Freud expert. He asks in a pedantic tone: "How can someone who is so well versed in methodology a) give such a wrong impression of things, b) reflect someone's thinking so inaccurately, and c) mix two things so unnecessarily?" The essence of his critique of Van Heerden is that Freud also gave the real its place in the dream and that he would certainly have agreed with the notion of a thumb as a thumb.

* * *

Even in 2000 this debate was already dated. Psychoanalysis is not a theory of dreams and not a dream-interpretation undertaking—Van Heerden could have known that. However, Verhage is significant for another reason. His argument takes an unexpected turn, and a small digression about the *Newsletter* is needed before continuing. The *Newsletter* is exactly what it promises: a club bulletin in which communications from the board and from the IPA are published; there also appear reports of lectures, book reviews, pre-publications of articles, and sometimes an exchange of views. Manuscripts are delivered electronically and not adjusted to one layout style. People are among colleagues and behave in a fairly free manner. In the columns, the conventions of a scientific journal alternate with those of email and personal letters. In such an atmosphere it is tempting to *say what comes into your mind*—the classic invitation to free-association—even though in psychoanalytic circles it is considered highly undesirable to do this in social contact and scientific discourse.

In his methodological polemic Verhage suddenly slips up and gives a conclusion that he introduces as follows:

> And finally this. I have wondered why an expert like Van Heerden discusses Freud's work in such an irresponsible way. I have found an answer to this question, and I want to present it to you. An answer that has come about in a scientifically extremely sound way. Namely, by accident. It went like this. You know that there is at the moment a discussion about anti-Semitism in [the well-known Dutch author] Ter Braak. Now there is not a news broadcast in which the Commission for Reparations for Jewish War Victims makes an appearance that doesn't cause me to have acute anti-Semitic outbursts. I wanted to find out what Ter Braak's anti-Semitism was about. And as things go, I found something quite different, namely the piece: "Nietzsche versus Freud". And via Ter Braak there comes an explanation of Van Heerden's irritation. I then came to the following supposition: Is Jaap's mocking and irritation perhaps directed not at Freud but at Freud-epigones? Of course this does not explain my surprise, but the psychoanalyst can make his peace with it.

The three and a half page letter is signed with "amicable" greetings (2000, p. 151). Amicably from psychologist to psychologist, and especially from methodologist to methodologist, I suspect. This fragment raises more questions than I can answer. Were the "anti-Semitic outbursts" a slip of the pen of an aging man, or a provocation intended to stimulate an argument? Did the man who was in the process of stopping his analytic practice, had finished his last analysis, and had got rid of the analyst's couch want to let the world know what he really thought of Jews? Is he making a confession while blushing, as one might do in private? Did he want to show that all is housed in the unconscious, even when it is the unconscious of a decent person, and that it is sometimes rather fishy. Or was there a neurological disorder, as was argued later? Or did he in total innocence divulge a private conversation fragment? Is it a demonstration of something I have indicated earlier: confusing the office and the ordinary world?

Even the preamble by way of Ter Braak is curious. Gomperts— a Jew but not very pronounced, more a man of words than of the organization, let alone of the synagogue—has written a book filled with tragedy.[3] It is a long cry of disappointment. This very well-read writer who had a great love for authors in the tradition of humanism and the Enlightenment—from Erasmus and Voltaire to Nietzsche, Ter Braak, Du Perron, André Gide, Paul Valéry, T. S. Eliot, and also Fourier, Proudhon, Marx, and Bakunin—had found in all these writers (and not only in them), in their work and in their letters not just a seemingly charming "salon" anti-Semitism, but the hateful kind, the kind that feels that the world would be better off without Jews.

Gomperts points out that these writers were hooked on telling the hate story. He had personally witnessed anti-Semitic incidents. Ter Braak had discovered Gomperts as a talented writer and they had become friends. After the war Gomperts had defended and developed Ter Braak's ideas, and he had met Du Perron through Ter Braak. Yet he caught them in ordinary, day-to-day anti-Semitism, not necessarily directed at him but at others. As a young man, trying to get ahead, he had pushed it aside as irrelevant, but as he thought about it later in life he started to find it increasingly unbearable. However, Ter Braak had committed suicide in 1940 when the Germans attacked the Netherlands, and Du Perron had suffered a fatal heart attack at that time. Were these people anti-Semites? After not wanting to give it any thought for years, Gomperts realized that it was unthinkable but true. From the time he retired until his death, Gomperts spent his time trying to comprehend their unfathomable hatred and that of other important and esteemed authors. But it never made sense to him. The combination of good, spirited, and reliable in public but anti-Semitic on a personal level had disillusioned him deeply.

Gomperts speaks about the "attachment to anti-Semitism". With his literary education and lay analysis he tries to understand the phenomenon. Gomperts reminds us that before the war the church, the school, and the home did not teach that certain Jews were despicable but that evil was the essence of all those who obeyed Jewish religious precepts. Just as children are told that all trees are made of wood, in the same way they were taught that Jews are made of evil and that the meaning of the word "Jew" is "bad person", the "enemy of God". Gomperts quotes the poet Bloem, one of the greatest Dutch poets of the 20th century, from a letter dated August 14, 1921 to a friend and colleague. Bloem writes that he is "disgusted with the modern world, among other things because of the damned pro-Jewishness that makes almost all Christians a victim of the world Jewish cabal". Bloem recommends "daring to see things as they are and to respect sensible anti-Semitism".

Did the idea that outstanding people can also be outstanding anti-Semites touch a chord in Verhage? Or did he nose around in Ter Braak's writings to find a justification for his own aversion to Jews? I do not know and will not go tracking down the motives of a man who did not express an opinion about it. There is a more obvious hypothesis that seems very natural but is difficult to accept for me, as a fellow-psychoanalyst: analysts are very ordinary people. Europeans, post-Christian, but still caught in the Christian tradition that runs from not anti-Semitic to slightly anti-Semitic and also respectable people, to those suffering from severe anti-Semitism. Perhaps that is why Verhage found it necessary to publicize that anti-Semitism really is ordinary.

There has been much speculation whether Verhage is a "real anti-Semite" or not. That is not a very interesting question. It is the act that counts: there are a number of Jews who act in a way that does not please him, and he expresses a feeling about all Jews. It is as if a feeling is waiting for a reason to be felt and expressed. Whatever is impure and undesirable in the self is attributed to the Jews. That is anti-Semitism.

According to me, anti-Semitism as an attitude is not the worst of sins, but it is a dangerous one. It is the first step in an exclusion mechanism that starts with slight social avoidance and in its extreme form leads to death and destruction. That is why it should be dealt with thoroughly in a public debate. If you are guilty of it in civilized company, then you have to take a clear step back if you want to be able to restore your reputation. When a leader of an organization is caught being anti-Semitic, the organization must make it clear that this was not done on its account. This is true even more for a psychoanalytic organization. Only then can things return to normal.

The odd thing is that this slip of the tongue—or of the mind—resulted in such a barrage of reactions and that it finally tore apart the proud institution, the Association. Of course there were fierce battles before it, and it would be a distortion of the facts to say that the split was caused solely by the Verhage affair.

There was already a strong difference of opinion around the private practice of psychoanalysts, the indication for psychoanalysis, the organization of training, and the NPI as training institute. Inside the Association there have traditionally been tensions between the moderates and the orthodox. The hierarchical structure of association life is a breeding ground for conflicts between training analysts and regular members. The opinions of the innovator Melanie Klein have been on the training blacklist for years. Only the destructive side of the dissident analyst Lacan was seen. A small elite decided what was *good analysis* and what was no good. All this resulted in a very authoritarian structure inside the Association, with a stringent code in the name of good analysis. Underneath this there grew a smouldering hatred that would eventually have to come out.

Verhage's letter caused a stir that was expressed in written form in the next number of the Newsletter. In an open letter, Tilly Citroen-Brat, Paul Citroen, Wouter Gomperts, Christa Widlund-Broer, and Ronet Zeehandelaar reacted as follows to the anti-Semitic outbursts:

> Up to the present we had the illusion that in our association it is at the very least taboo to express such disgusting opinions. Now that this does not seem to be the case, we expect the board to take an unambiguous stand against the above quoted statement by Verhage. Excuses are expected from the person concerned. In expectation of this, we wish to express our indignation. We assume that you share our feelings (2000, 15, p. 192).

Other reactions were also received by the board of the Association. Jos Tuynman, a distinguished member who was not a training analyst, later spoke of senescence in Verhage, increased rigidity, diminished empathic capacity, empathic conflict-solving capacity, and a partial lack of critical judgment in thinking that you could publish such an article in a newsletter that can be read by anyone. He thought that Verhage's training authority should be withdrawn. It was revolutionary in the Association for a member who was not a training analyst to address the training committee and give an opinion about a training analyst. He asked for a decision that could only be made by the training committee and not one that the committee would like to make. This was a breach of the hierarchy and was almost unthinkable until that time. It caused a shock of bewilderment and relief in all sections. The letter from the five (all *regular members*) was also seen as "bewildering". It was considered "acting out against training analysts". The reasoning was (and was later expressed): how do they dare criticize a very experienced training analyst and place it just like that in the Newsletter; they should first have asked Verhage for an explanation. Among many members indignation was great about this step that was considered revolutionary.

The letter from the five was the beginning of more reactions. These were the visible part of much indignation and astonishment. But there were also people who supported Verhage. Nick Treurniet's reaction is notable.[4] In his time Treurniet was chair of the training committee and until that time one of the training analysts with the highest status within the Association. He had received a *Festschrift* on the occasion of his 75th birthday. He felt that one reason for the unstoppable turmoil was that there were fierce tensions in the Association about the admission to training analysis and the status of the training analyst. He reasoned that the acting out about Verhage's statement confuses psychological and social reality. The tensions around training are real, but the conflict about anti-Semitism is just as real. A more correct explanation of his statement seems to me that he wished to trivialize the incident. His reasoning that the acting out about anti-Semitism served to hide other sources of displeasure was meant to take the wind out of their sails and in this way get rid of the disgrace of anti-Semitism. In the same way the possible anti-Semitic character of Verhage's statement was also excluded as a source of agitation.

Seven weeks after the article with the contested passage about anti-Semitic outbursts, after much discussion and many emails, there appeared in the Newsletter, right under the reaction of Citroen-Brat and others, a message form the board:

> In addition to the letter from colleague Citroen and others, the board has received other reactions to the contribution of our colleague Verhage in the Newsletter of May 2000. Members and training candidates of our association take offence at his remark about "violent anti-Semitic outbursts".
>
> The board clearly dissociates itself from these remarks by colleague Verhage. In general, the editorial board of the Newsletter board wishes to censure as little as possible in order to let the discussion be as wide-ranging as possible and to let all opinions be heard. With hindsight however, in this case these remarks should not have been published. Colleague Verhage has clearly apologized to the board about this phrase and has showed his regret that he has offended members with this. We have asked colleague Verhage to give an explanation and more clarification, which he will do. He has promised this for the next Newsletter. Board of the Dutch Association for Psychoanalysis (2000, 15, p. 192).

For the time being, this is the last item in print about the affair. Verhage's explanation never gets into the Newsletter; his draft is there. On the letterhead of "Professor Verhage, Psychoanalyst" he asks the editor to publish the following:

> Reaction of Frans Verhage. In the previous issue of this newsletter the Board announced that I would in this issue give a reaction to the letter of 5 members of the Association as a result of a phrase in an article by me, as well as to the reaction of the Board to that letter.
>
> My reaction is: I am sorry that I have offended members and possibly also applicant-members and candidates with this text. For this I offer my apologies. What I meant was not the statement of an opinion, as the 5 members state in their publication, but a feeling that occurred to me at the conclusion of the negotiations about the return of stolen Jewish assets. I found the conduct of the American Jewish World Congress disgusting. My feelings were shared—as shown in the media—by

many Dutchmen. I think that (Jewish) tyranny is not proper in present-day Dutch relations; in hindsight I regret not conveying these feelings more carefully. Hence my apologies. Written, Hindeloopen, July 20, 2000. F. Verhage.

In addition he is angry at the board. He lets them know this in a letter of July 10, 2000. He addresses them as "Board," and there is no doubt about his anger. He feels treated rudely, but point 4 of his letter jumps out at us:

> 4. It is incorrect not to mention that the whole affair started with name-calling by Jewish members. I have had reports from members that they found this shameful. There is apparently only one shameful thing that happened according to the board: awkward phrasing on my part.

He then ends as follows:

> I don't know whether I am still prepared to discuss this affair with you. You pile insult upon insult on my account. I don't need that. I will take my vacation to reflect about matters. There is barely any basis for trust.
> Your colleague.

Neither letter was published because the board felt that they *had an ambiguity that justified not publishing them because it would have been like throwing oil on a fire* (president of the Association during a membership meeting on November 5, 2000).

On July 5, 2000, Verhage had written to each of the five who had signed the letter:

> Dear colleague,
>
> On June 30, I received the text from a letter to the Newsletter by five members, and you were one of them. I was asked to react to it. I did that right away and offered it for publication in the Newsletter:
>
> "As appears from the letter received from some colleagues, I have offended a number of colleagues with a phrase in my article. For this I offer my apologies. I had not expected such a reaction. The fact is that I did not express an opinion but a

feeling. I regret that this led to another interpretation than I had intended. In addition, I objected to the policy of the board in this matter. They did not listen to me in this matter. Yesterday I was told that my letter would not be published. Yet I still want to offer you my apologies. Hence this letter".

All three documents are interesting. In the letter from Hindeloopen, the mindless anti-Semitism is striking. If it were true that the American Jewish World Congress is a disgusting organization that makes money from suffering, you can of course protest against that as fiercely as you want. If someone experiences anti-Semitic outbursts from this organization's conduct, he shows something that Jewish (and also non-Jewish) supervisors, analysands, students, and colleagues should at least beware of, let alone the patients whose treatment is supervised. This causes the very safety inside the Association to become an issue. Tolerance for anti-Semitic expressions in an organization spoils life for other people in it besides Jews. Hate can strike anyone who is not liked by the hater.

The entire Verhage episode is supported by a demonstration of self-evident superiority that could turn out in the wrong way for the less powerful. The name-calling by Jewish members that is mentioned in the letter cannot be found in any of the documents. What was said, and by whom? Where did it take place? When, how, in what circumstances? Were the letter writers guilty? Were they Jewish? If the name-calling did take place, it must have happened after the "Dear Jaap" letter. The difference between feeling and opinion is artificial—legal hairsplitting to avert disaster. "Anti-Semitism" and "anti-Semitic" describe a feeling, an opinion, a conviction. Moreover, it did not involve just a feeling or an opinion, because writing and publishing were actions. Anti-Semitism is a general view, and as Bernstein says:

> Even the anti-Semite who is a convinced adherent of the theory of inferiority likes therefore to justify himself in concrete cases of anti-Jewish behaviour by an equally concrete, though if need be invented or exaggerated case of Jewish conduct (2009, p. 35).

The letter of apology does not excuse itself for the outburst. It sympathizes with the reaction of the other, as if a surgeon were excusing himself for the pain caused by a successful operation. There is no regret about the deed itself. Verhage's letter of apology probably did him more harm than the original outbursts.

The turmoil in the Association increases. The board wants to terminate Verhage's position as training analyst; certainly after his letter of July 10, which it considers anti-Semitic. It is eager to conclude the affair. Verhage wants it as well. On July 29, 2000 he resigns. "Finished", writes chairman of the board Jaap Ubbels, in large handwritten letters under a note to a fellow board member, not knowing that the affair has now really started. The opponents, who feel that the board had been too severe and should have treated Verhage more cautiously, certainly after he apologized, start to object. Treurniet's letter was in this category.

De Blécourt, another friend of Verhage, also a training analyst and moreover an honorary member of the Association, predicts that "the affair will reverberate for a long time because many members will refuse to accept this. This will have serious consequences for the board". He writes a letter (unaddressed and undated, but from the context the date appears to be August 21, 2000). Its essence is:

> The writers [Verhage's opponents] confuse describing an "anti-Semitic outburst" with having "disgusting opinions that are expressed". This confusion contains the danger that a conclusion will be drawn: this is anti-Semitism. I have two questions for the authors of the letter:
> 1. Did they first contact Verhage himself to ask what he meant by his remark?
> 2. Did they realize what the personal consequences could be for Verhage when they publicized this question in the Newsletter, which can be accessed by everyone inside and outside the Association?
>
> In addition, I have two comments for the writers:
> 1. They belong to, or are very involved with, the Jewish population, and therefore run no risk when they open fire on Verhage because of his anti-Semitic outburst, from which they draw far-reaching conclusions. On the contrary, they couldn't go wrong: call someone an anti-Semite and let him figure out how to get rid of that stigma.

2. The board of the Association is being pressured to share their indignation and to take an unconditional position against Verhage in order to avoid the slightest semblance of anti-Semitic feelings.

He concludes as follows:

 I hesitate to utter the word, but it keeps popping up: it seems as if they have committed character assassination against Frans Verhage. And all this because of one very unfortunate remark. The Board should give an account to the membership of the Association of every step that it has taken in this matter.

In this letter the author seems so angry that he has totally lost sight of the whole. He must have known that Verhage himself published his letter and that he was also the one who called his outbursts "anti-Semitic". Apparently everyone can be offended by this, but Jews or those "very involved with the Jewish population" must let it pass. According to De Blécourt, the unfortunate part of the outburst was that it had painful consequences for Verhage himself. According to me, Jews are threatened by anti-Semitism, and not the other way around. We are witnessing a classic anti-Semitic inversion: the Jews have assassinated Verhage.

Psychoanalytic associations throughout the world have one characteristic in common: the power is in the board, but especially in the training committee, the board of the training analysts. The great conflicts are almost always about training, because it is of direct importance for the members (Kirsner, 2000). The training committee makes decisions at all stages, from application for training to acceptance as member and more—who can continue, who has to wait, who is sent away, and who becomes a training analyst. It decides about the training curriculum and who teaches what. It knows the whole association because everyone has taken courses or has been in selection discussions or in training analysis, or has been supervised by one of the committee members. It decides what is correct and good, in people as well as in their opinions. Its finger showing someone the door is equal to a court order, and the result of its policy towards people can be repaired only in exceptional cases. Half-jokingly the members of this committee are referred to as the demigods of the

Association. Verhage had chaired this committee, as had De Blécourt and Treurniet.

Eugenie Oosterhuis is chair when the outbursts come to the surface and the reactions come in. She includes the letter of De Blécourt along with the documents for the September 14, 2000 meeting of the training analysts. She addresses them to the training analysts and to those members of the Association who are doing a delegated training analysis (a training analysis that is carried out by a non-training analyst with the consent of the training committee) and to the instructors of the theoretical course. She attaches her own written description of the events and organizes the facts in her way and gives it the title *Chronology of the Verhage Question*.

Speaking on behalf of the executive committee of the training committee she states:

> Because the whole course of events is determined so strongly by rigidly held opinions, incomprehension, and insults, while the cause of this question was not an irreparable fault, the executive board feels that an attempt at mediation should still be made between Verhage and the board.

She accuses the chair of "using information from an informal conversation to state that Verhage has anti-Semitic feelings and opinions and expresses them". But that was not official and therefore the chair deserves disciplinary action when he writes to Verhage that "anti-Semitic expressions cannot be tolerated in our Association".

Oosterhuis also does not agree with the board because it distanced itself from Verhage's comments "without first asking him what he meant by this remark". She does not make clear what was not clear.

The letters from Oosterhuis and De Blécourt were not discussed at the meeting. Oosterhuis is informed subtly that the summary of events as described by her is her "personal view". She reacts by stating that both documents reflect the point of view of the executive committee of the training committee. There is increased agitation in the Association. The board receives more than 20 letters about the affair. It formulates the purpose of the general meeting of October 5 as follows: "Report on the course of events and the fundamental responsibility of the board to safeguard the integrity of the emotional climate of the association".

The meeting was confusing. The board explains that it has tried to de-escalate the conflict by not publishing letters from Verhage. Those who feel that the board acted too harshly question if there was sufficient consultation with Verhage. They propose a mediation committee chaired by an ex-politician, but her conclusions are unacceptable by the opposition group. People want to organize a day about discrimination and anti-Semitism, but that does not happen. Only an explosion can clear the air.

A question is developing whether the board of the training committee has gone beyond the limits of its task and authority. The training committee tries to distance itself from its chair's letter of September 14, and especially from the letter of De Blécourt that was sent as the training committee's point of view to the training analysts—all this without wanting to let go of its position of power. Tuynman expresses the growing distrust in the training committee. He writes on February 26, 2001:

> With dismay we, as members of the Dutch Association for Psychoanalysis, observed how the entire executive committee and the training committee and most psychoanalysts reacted in confusion to anti-Semitic writing of a valued former member of the Association. Powerless disclaimer and anger at the observers of the "faux pas" of the above-mentioned ex-member; instead of "containing", understanding and structure. "Structure" in the sense of: of course anti-Semitism has no place in our association. Anyone who thinks differently does not belong in our association. But the truth was interpreted as slander.

The board collapses. The chair, Jaap Ubbels, announces his departure and that of the other board members. The board resigns and an interim board (with two ex-chairs) is chosen on March 18, 2001. This forces the resignation of the executive committee of the training committee.

The Verhage affair has become the training committee affair and then becomes the Newsletter affair. And for the third or perhaps the fourth time a curriculum is drawn up for a partially common theoretical course in the training for Association, Society, and NVPP candidates, at least for the first year. A study day about anti-Semitism is planned but does not take place. Whatever the affair may be called, it seems to be closed.

The interim board does its work and makes sure that it is followed up in a timely manner. Training is restructured and a new training committee is set up. It is most important to restore the democracy of the association. The training committee, which was a state within the state, becomes an ordinary administrative committee. The old board and the old training committee, which had become opposing parties, have both resigned. A new start can be made within the Association, but much damage has been done, especially to reputations and to power structures. The former training committee has lost too much influence to want to continue, but it seems difficult to bring the affair to a conclusion. The process of splitting continues. The whole structure of the psychoanalytic landscape changes, and all bonds of cooperation that had slowly been created are now under tension. The members of the old training committee are unwilling to put up with the minimal latitude they have been given. A split within the organization seems unavoidable.

The group around the old executive committee that used to call itself the Oppositional Group, a number of people who agreed with them, and some analysts who were in training with them—around 20 people—form a new organization: the NPAG. The matter between them and the Association explodes around cooperation with the Dutch Organization for Psychoanalytic Psychotherapy. The official stumbling blocks are the differences in opinion about the partially combined theoretical training of the Association, the Society, and the Organization for Psychoanalytic Psychotherapy and the changes in the institute for training analysts. The Group (NPAG) says that it does not want the trainers of psychoanalytic psychotherapists to get control over training for psychoanalysts. There is a mediation effort, officially called "research", by the IPA that makes the separation final. The IPA recognizes the NPAG very quickly. And why not? The interest of the IPA is to keep psychoanalysts and psychoanalytic candidates on board, and the NPAG defended its interests quite effectively.

Yet there is a detail that demands attention. One of the members of the Association (Michael Chayes) gives his view on the conflict to the chair of the exploratory committee (Anne-Marie Sandler), emphasizing the role that the Verhage affair played. He receives the following official answer from her (letter of April 6, 2005 on behalf of the Exploratory Committee):

When Dr. Gattig [a member of the exploratory committee] and I became acquainted with Dr. Wenniger [president of the NVPA] and heard about the offensive anti-Semitic incident that occurred in your association, we both wondered why your association had not set up your own ethics committee. This kind of anti-Semitic behaviour cannot be tolerated in a psychoanalytic association and should be presented to an ethics committee.

In other words, the NVPA, which does not have such a committee, is blamed, and the NPAG, which harbours members whose behaviour could be investigated by the committee, gets off scot-free.

Now that the split is a fact, it is clear that the Verhage incident was one of the straws that broke the camel's back. Many other business and personal interests, loyalties, and hard feelings, but also differences of opinion, made up the rest of the bundle.

Notes

1. This letter was first quoted by Brinkgreve (1984, p. 286); later it was also in Brecht, et al. (1985, p. 65). What is particularly striking is the patronizingly kind tone.
2. Only Landauer, Levy-Suhl, and Waterman established themselves in the Netherlands. None of the three survived the war.
3. This is H. A. (Hans) Gomperts (1915–1998). His nephew Wouter Gomperts is an analyst who will be mentioned as one of the "five" who signed a significant letter. According to Herman Verhaar in his eulogy (1988) after Gompert's death, Hans Gomperts had several working titles for an extensive study of anti-Semitism in literature. First he wanted to call it "Anti-Semitism of the Right-minded" and then "Hating and Being Afraid". After his death, this almost completed study appeared as "A grain of truth" (2000). The publication of this book caused the discussion in the media that Verhage refers to in his reaction to van Heerden.
4. I mention it earlier than it actually took place. His letter is from September 29, but at that point Treurniet repeats an opinion that he had already expressed orally.

CHAPTER SEVEN

International

The psychoanalytical world is larger than Vienna, London, Zurich, or Amsterdam. It is encompassed by the IPA,[1] the association of all psychoanalytic associations. In every book about the history of psychoanalysis and in every biography of Freud, the IPA is present as the centre of psychoanalytic life.

Locally and nationwide, decisions are made by associations that are connected to training institutes. The local or national organizations determine the professional life of the analyst. The IPA guards the analytic quality of the associations that are affiliated to it. It admits associations and evaluates their training. The shortest definition of a psychoanalyst can simply be someone who is a regular member of the IPA or of one of the affiliated associations. During the conflict that was discussed in the previous chapter, the IPA was a threatening presence in the background because the "group of five" who signed the letter wanted to involve the ethics committee of the IPA to judge whether there was a question of anti-Semitic incidents in the Association (NVPA). The relevant documents had already been translated. The intended complaint was withdrawn when the chairman of the interim board of the Association declared in the *Newsletter* that anti-Semitic expressions had indeed been expressed and that the five had rightly drawn attention to it. On the other hand, the NPAG had discredited their former colleagues by accusing them of diluting the criteria in the training programme.

The history of the IPA has not yet been written. On its website one can see where its congresses have been held and when various topics were under discussion. The speakers and the IPA board members through the years are also mentioned. What really took place in the IPA is concealed in various incidents that writers mention in passing when they tell other stories. In this way I encountered in Wallerstein (1998), Strozier (2001), and Kirsner (2000) several internal conflicts that are related to the issue that I have discussed.

It is not my task to write the missing history of the IPA, not even in the light of my subject. But I do want to investigate—on the basis of a couple of incidents that I think I can examine—how psychoanalytic organizations and individual analysts proceed with respect to Jews. The incidents are local, but each by itself adds to the Jewish/non-Jewish psychoanalytic mosaic that I am trying to create.

First I will briefly recount the wanderings of Masud Khan, whose anti-Semitism contributed to his downfall. In the public settlement of this affair, the anti-Semitic element was pushed into the background. Next I will discuss an incident in Belgium that was the consequence of an interview with Donald Meltzer who expressed himself as anti-Jewish in a Belgian psychoanalytic professional journal. This caused a disturbance that turned out markedly differently from the comparable affair in the Netherlands. Following this, I will examine in detail matters that are connected to each other in time as well as in content. What I refer to is the appearance of Edward Said in London. Or rather, the action of the Freud Museum that concerned Said who was not welcome to hold a lecture about Freud in the Freud Museum in Vienna. The Freud Museum in London let Said be introduced by the analyst Christopher Bollas who made offensive remarks about Israelis and compared them to fascists, which the audience accepted without comment.

Suddenly stereotypes about Jews were transferred to Israel and Israelis. This was also the case during the anti-Semitic confrontations at the United Nations World Conference on Racism, Racial Discrimination, Xenophobia and Related Intolerance and the NGO-forum preceding it in Durban in 2001. The role of the IPA in this and the way it played out are the subject matter of chapter eight.

Masud Khan

Masud Khan (1924–1989), a British analyst of Pakistani origin, was a colourful man. Extremely gifted and dangerously destructive, to himself as well as to others. Attitude and reality were mixed up in him. He probably had no right to the title of Prince that he liked to use. But he did possess extensive estates in Pakistan that enabled him to live in a princely style in Europe. Very soon after he arrived in England from Pakistan as a 22-year-old, he was accepted for psychoanalytic training. He became a well-known psychoanalyst and author of numerous articles and four books that were also translated into French (1974, 1979, 1983, 1988, published in the United States as Khan (1989)). He was an art lover, a Shakespeare scholar, and a renowned bibliophile. A friend characterized him as follows: "He was a good and decent person—provided you were part of his world. He was generous and kind to "his people" and very, very protective" (Hopkins, 2006, p. 218). He was a welcome guest in the capitals of psychoanalysis. In London and outside it he had a rich social life that extended into the art world. A characteristic of his work was that he dared to look at himself and his patients without reserve.

Two biographies have been written about him. Both are worth reading, both written by psychoanalytically trained psychologists, both the result of extensive research of sources (Hopkins, 2006, and Willoughby, 2005). He did not come to a good end. His social success was lost, his relationships were short-lived, and his marriages broke up tragically. In 1977 he was dismissed from his position as training analyst because of transgressive behaviour with patients. His alcoholism shortened his life. Khan's last year was lonely and sad.

His last book, *When Spring Comes* (1989), was published a year before his death from cancer and cirrhosis. Khan's expulsion from the British Psychoanalytical Society (BPAS) resulted from what he tells about himself in this book and a complaint by five members of the psychoanalytic society about gross anti-Semitic insults in it.[2] In 1988 he was expelled from the British Psychoanalytical Society because he "discredited psychoanalysis and the BPAS". The expulsion and the judgment do not directly touch on the openly anti-Semitic character of the writing, although it was a part of the complaint.

When Spring Comes starts with Khan's equating Freud's mildly ironic Zionism at the start of that movement to Jung's active anti-Semitic National Socialism before and during the Shoah. At the end of the introduction he writes:

> But the faith one is born to, one can rarely shed. Carl Jung has acknowledged this publicly and professionally, and Professor Doctor Sigmund Freud only in correspondence, privately.

Then he adds the already quoted sentence from a letter of Freud to Sabina Spielrein: "I … would like to take it that if the child turned out to be a boy he will develop into a stalwart Zionist" (1988, p. IX). Freud as an underhanded whisperer of a no-good secret, versus Jung's open and above-board struggle. The rest of the book contains frenzied anti-Semitic attacks and equally strange violations of the laws and constraints of psychoanalysis.

The content of the book is also surprising in other ways. The discipline of the analytic hour is not respected. Patient and analyst have the right to offend each other. In the treatment of a homosexual man the report of Khan's own words in an argument during an analytic session is striking:

> May I add that Dave [partner of the patient] is safer in his person wrapped neatly round my Mongol Muslim little finger than he ever has been, these many years, wrapped round, and into as well, your dirty Jewish arse.

On the next page, Khan comments on the fact that the patient did not carry out his threat of suicide: "So you didn't carry out your Jewish harikari! […] Now Dave has a long wait for his execution by you, while you wail at the wall" (1988, pp. 94f.).

His own princely splendour is displayed ostentatiously to patients by his home, his clerk, his secretary, and his domestic servant. In this context, the dialogue that Hopkins recounts is particularly shocking. It concerns the same Jewish man who consulted Khan as a last resort because he was having suicidal thoughts. Khan quotes himself as the clinician:

One more personal remark about me, my wife, my staff or my things, and I will throw you out, you accursed nobody Jew. *Find your own people then. Shoals of them drift around, just like you.* Yes, I am anti-Semitic. You know why, *Mr. Luis?* Because I am an Aryan and had thought all of you Jews had perished when Jesus, from sheer dismay—and he was one of you—had flown up to Heaven, leaving you in the scorching care of Hitler, Himmler and the crematoriums. Don't fret, *Mr. Luis;* like the rest of your species, you will survive and continue to harass others, and lament, and bewail yourselves (1988, pp. 92–93, quoted in Hopkins, 2006, p. 364).[3]

The other biographer, Willoughby, describes how Khan had marital fights in his patients' presence. They witnessed how he answered telephone calls in detail during the analysis—often because of his problems with his own analyst Donald Winnicott, for whom he also did editorial work. The list of his improprieties is long: sexual relationships with patients; getting ex-analysands to do his dirty work; pairing patients off with each other. No contamination is avoided. It was not until five colleagues[4] had lodged a complaint about his last book with the central point "that Kahn had cast the profession into disrepute and had been explicitly anti-Semitic", that the ethics commission stated unanimously:

We had a duty to uncompromisingly disassociate psychoanalysis from overt expressions of racism and from indulgence in malicious defamation, especially when it is published for all to see for years to come. So we recommended to our Council that his membership be terminated; this was then carried out (Willoughby, 2005, pp. 234ff.).

Just as happened in the Verhage affair, Khan was too quick for the board and the committee. On July 22, 1988, the committee wrote him that he was expelled. On July 26, 1988, he wrote back triumphantly:

I received your letter of 22 July 1988. I cannot comprehend what was your need to write this unsavoury letter to me, since I resigned from membership of the British Psycho-Analytical

Society as from 13 July 1988, as stated in my letter to the President, Dr E. Brennen [sic], a copy of which is enclosed.[5]

This resignation was not accepted because, even though he was no longer a member of the BPAS, he would still continue to be recognized as a psychoanalyst by the IPA.

I do an injustice to this exceptional man by describing him only as aggressive and anti-Semitic. His first three books are worthwhile and are still used in psychoanalytic training. But his behaviour was so transgressive that it became intolerable. His talent and his behaviour were already apparent in an earlier stage of his life, in 1976. He was proposed as the chief editor of the prestigious *International Journal of Psychoanalysis*, a position that he had barely missed getting earlier. While the appointment was being processed, he provoked a quarrel that eventually involved the police in a well-known restaurant in Paris. The scandal caused by this affair made the appointment impossible (Hopkins, 2006, pp. 280ff.). He disparaged Freud, as described above, but he gave the collected works of Freud as a birthday present to non-analysts. And he went for psychoanalysis to Anna Freud when his life threatened to fall apart.

The report about his expulsion is worth reading, especially for what is not in it. Anne-Marie Sandler, the wife of one of the five complainants, is the author of the report 2004, pp. 27–42). She was the chair of the ethics committee of the British Psychoanalytical Society from 1998 until 2003. She lists all the points of the affair and uses the complaints written up by Wayne Godley (2001, pp. 3–7), an ex-patient of Khan. About *When Spring Comes* she says "that certain passages […] contravened the ethical code of the Society and its rules" (2004, p. 34). However, the core of the complaint about the book was anti-Semitism, and Sandler leaves that out.

Is anti-Semitism not bad enough or too awful? Sandler's report contains another sentence that is worth citing: "Perhaps the most worrying issue for training institutes is the transmission of boundary violations from one analytic generation to the next". The reader may supply his own thoughts about boundary violations. My own imagination goes in the direction of anti-Semitic prejudices, even though these are removed from the text. At any rate, the psychoanalyst Bollas (according to his colleague Eric Rayner) remained grateful to Khan all his life for the training analysis that he received from him

(Willoughby, 2005, p. 177). I will write about Bollas in forthcoming pages.

The history of the expulsion is taken out of the personal sphere by Linda Hopkins, who wrote a detailed analysis:

> Khan had prejudices against many groups in addition to Jews. His targets included Americans, the British, Hindus, feminists, and psychoanalysts in general. Anti-Semitism, however, is so central to his legacy that it warrants separate consideration. [...] Khan's anti-Semitism was of the wounding variety rather than the bone-breaking variety, similar to Eliot's. [...] A friend commented: "Masud's anti-Semitism was a red herring. He was actually very interested in Jews—they were a fascinating subject that he wanted to understand". [...] An analysand remembers that Khan supported the existence of Israel and "often used to maintain that there was nothing more impressive than a cultured Jew". [...] Several anonymous British analysts suggested to me that his anti-Semitism developed in England as an exaggerated mirroring of bigotry that he observed and experienced within the British Psycho-Analytical Society (BPAS). An anonymous Jewish peer said: "The British analysts used Masud to act out their own prejudices. They needed a Satan, and they chose a wonderful actor for their script". And a Protestant analyst told me that anti-Semitism still thrives in Britain and the BPAS: [...] "whatever people may pretend". [...] Rycroft [a Protestant British analyst (author)] recalled: "At Society meetings, which were always terribly crowded, I remember Winnicott [who was Protestant] coming up to me, shaking me vigorously by the hand and saying, "Dr. Livingstone, I presume?" An anti-Semitic joke I think—it's what Stanley said when he met Livingstone in the middle of Africa .... The Society after the war was predominantly Jewish. It wasn't exactly a problem not to be, but you had to be careful. I think that was what he meant. It was a relief to meet a blond Gentile in the woods". [...] So Khan may have spoken in part for colleagues when he expressed anti-Semitism. But even if that is the case, open disrespect for Jews is something that has never been characteristic of any group of British analysts. [...] [Khan's friend] Barrie Cooper [made the comment]: "His anti-Semitism was meant as an

attack on his colleagues and the Institute. It was a 'professional' anti-Semitism" (2006, pp. 367ff.).

Donald Meltzer

The following incident took place in Belgium. Donald Meltzer (1922–2004) was a well-known and, as a writer, a very visible psychoanalyst. He also wrote several books that are worth reading (for example, 1967, 1982, 1988, 1992). According to Frisch and Vermote (2000), who interviewed him, he contributed revolutionary ideas to the metapsychological formulation of theories, in particular the dimensions of psychological functioning and the functions of the dream. In addition, he developed trail-blazing ideas about autism and the "aesthetic conflict". It should not really matter, but it must be said that Meltzer was Jewish. His parents had emigrated from Lithuania to the United States. He went to England at the age of 32 because he was captivated by the theories of Melanie Klein. He went into analysis in England, established himself there, and then became a training analyst. In the early 1980s problems arose between him and the British Psychoanalytical Society, or rather the training committee. Meltzer's qualifications as training analyst were revoked.[6] Meltzer, too, did not let himself be sent away or have his qualifications taken away by a board. He let his membership in the Society lapse by no longer paying dues.

In the interview with Frisch and Vermote we get to know him as a gruff radical with standpoints that were not always tenable. With such opinions he probably did not make himself loved by the powers that be. However, outside England he became a much sought-after speaker and teacher. He gave lectures and organized courses in Italy, France, Spain, and Argentina. In Belgium, too, he had intellectual authority. He was known there as an expert in the application of the ideas of Freud, Klein, and Bion. Therefore it was obvious that two prominent analysts would want to introduce him to the Belgian psychoanalysts in a somewhat more personal way. For this there was a good opportunity: the Belgian psychoanalytic journal, *Revue Belge de Psychanalyse*, had a series "Carrefour Psychanalytique" that consisted of a set of interviews with prominent analysts. Meltzer was invited as the fifth one in 1999. The interviewers were Serge Frisch and Rudi Vermote, from Luxembourg and from the Flemish part of Belgium respectively. The conversation was in English and was published in French. The purpose of their interview was to set down a monument, but it did not turn out to be a very flattering portrait. We see a man who always attracted attention because of his robustness changed into a fragile old man. He lives in beautiful surroundings, in woods—toads jump away from the interviewers' feet. He free-associates when he thinks, with closed eyes, just as he used to teach. The interviewers go along with the music of his story. They barely interrupt him. Later they place fragments of his writings into the texts of the interview, most of it in English and some in French.

The interviewee is obviously still angry about what happened in the British Psychoanalytical Society. He explodes at the very first question:

> I certainly think that there is a crisis—but a crisis in society, not one within psychoanalysis itself. The reason for it seems to be an excessive interest in psychoanalysis by the public; its success with the public is based on Freud's works and is reinforced by what publishers call a publicity offensive, by a personality cult, and all that it involves. It is the same dynamic that was at the origin of Nazi Germany and the Soviet Union—the cult of personality, the illusion that there is a "sage" who knows all the answers.

He continues by saying that the wrong people are attracted to psychoanalysis:

> In a way, psychoanalysis attracts certain people for two inappropriate reasons. On the one hand, there were some candidates who saw the opportunity to earn a lot of money, and on the other hand it attracted those who had already failed in their professional life.

He is also dissatisfied with the admission, selection, and training policies. He believes that in order to get ahead in the world of psychoanalysis the same qualities are needed as in politics. Clearly those are not qualities that he admires:

> This whole selection process has created a system that resembles the one that puts criminals in prison: it is an absurd system

that can only produce hardened criminals because prison is a system that reinforces criminal tendencies.

He sees Socratic training as ideal and thinks that as soon as you start using preconceived selection and training criteria "it is no longer possible to differentiate that system from fascism". The interviewers clarify this fragment with a quote from *Sincerity and Other Works*:

> My own experience has demonstrated that this aspect is loathed by almost everyone, for it places the student in the position of defendant rather than aspirant, the teacher in the position of persecutor rather than colleague, the committee member in the vestments of an elite, and it sets the unnamed concept of heresy hanging in the lovely corridors and rooms of Mansfield House.

Meltzer continues with his construction of the analogy between Moses and Freud.

> Freud was a very complicated man, a kind of Moses. Leading the Hebrew people out of Egypt suited him very well; but the state of mind of the Hebrews at that time has remained firmly fixed in the Jewish people—hence the Shoah, anti-Semitism established as national doctrine and so forth. Moreover, it created an elitist attitude, and psychoanalysis has suffered a lot from this innate elitism.

This leads him to a plea for non-hierarchical psychoanalysis. He strongly resists the "surrender to insurance companies" that are set up like dictators. In his view patients live in a state of *projective identification*, and after some elaborations about his practice, he indicates that for him a successful analysis leads to a lifelong friendship with his ex-patients:

> It becomes difficult to differentiate a good analysis from the divine love discussed by Socrates and Plato. In my experience, a friendship that lasts for life starts at the end of any successful analysis. My best friends, without a doubt, are my ex-patients.

In the next number, the editors of the *Revue Belge de Psychanalyse* disassociate themselves from the interview. They write: "The Editors hereby dissociate themselves from the anti-Semitic statements made by Donald Meltzer who takes entire responsibility for them". The interviewers also apologize for their lack of intervention. They write: "His associative manner and perhaps the whole atmosphere grabbed us in such a way that at the moment itself we did not catch the impact of that sentence about the Holocaust". They let Meltzer say that some reactions reflect the confusion between a social conversation and a psychoanalytic exchange. They make Meltzer responsible for everything that he has said, and they support the statement of the Editors.

Some things in this interview are striking. Meltzer shows above all that he detests everything and everybody. At the age of 78 he looks at his life, and what he sees does not please him. Certainly not his own world, that of a psychoanalyst, a Jew, and a training analyst. He knows that he has been marginalized in these three areas. He makes an effort to understand where anti-Semitism, and the Shoah as its last instance, comes from and does this in a narcissistic manner. Where one would expect "we Jews", he says "they" and this results in the accusing statement that they caused the Shoah themselves. He makes the Jews guilty of the hate towards them and the numerous attempts to annihilate them. He is not alone in this reasoning. The French analyst Anne-Lise Stern, who was originally German, describes how she was told by her analyst that her arrest by the Germans was a consequence of her masochism (2004, p. 194).

It is reasonable to pose the question why exactly the Jews have gone through history in such a striking way for such a long time and have been hated for such a long time. However, that is different from making the Jews guilty of this hate. Meltzer pays for the fact that he does not make a distinction between reflecting publicly and free-associating privately. If only he had read what others had to say about the subjects he broached, then he would have encountered Leon Wieseltier. This literary editor of *The New Republic*, who wrote the much-admired *Kaddish* after the death of his father, is also an active public intellectual. In 2003 he wrote the following that sheds some light on prejudices:

> It is the essence of anti-Semitism, as it is the essence of all prejudice, to call its object its cause. But if you explain anti-Semitism as a response to Jews, and racism as a response to

blacks, and misogyny as a response to women, then you have not understood it. You have reproduced it (2003, p. 4).[7]

Anti-Semitism can be seen as a projection of omnipotence: the Jew as one who is capable of everything, the absolute good as well as the absolute evil, who has access to the unknown and the forbidden and is therefore hated. This projection can change into projective identification that no longer just dominates in the emotional life but also becomes concrete in reality: money dealing is bad and forbidden, so you force the proverbial other—the Jews—to do it. They then become the evildoers and are even more worthy of hate.

As a recipient of this hate, the Jew develops "Jewish narcissism" (Gans, 1994) according to the historian Evelien Gans. It is quite something if you are considered guilty of everything that happens in the world. In this way you rise above the ordinary and that produces a perverse pleasure. You start to see yourself as the centre of a sadistic world that is after you. She does not write it in these exact words, but that is the theoretical basis of her book. Of course Meltzer does not need to agree with one of these modes of thought, but anyone who blames the Jews so one-sidedly for their own lot and therefore points to them as the cause of the Crusades and the Shoah places himself outside social discourse and characterizes himself as a self-hater.

Meltzer also shows his generalized hate when he tells the interviewers about the hierarchization of the training and connects it to the wish of the analyst to be respected. He accounts for this from the fact that Freud and his followers were Jewish. I do not know whether hierarchization is Jewish. Perhaps you could express that idea among friends. Looking at it as a matter of fact, it is a necessary step in the professionalization process. If you start in a new profession—and certainly in health care—then you need to show that the public is well off with you. You make it a full-time business, with qualified people, you wear your best clothes and establish yourself in the best neighbourhoods, and you take care that your training and its criteria are strict and visible. The most obvious matter is that you try to control the instructors and the students as strictly as possible in all phases; analysts always did that, and they still do.

Meltzer also makes a grave blunder when he says that Israel has embraced anti-Semitism as a national doctrine. With this he confuses one of the reasons for the creation of the state with the reality of life in Israel. It is in the same category as statements like: in the United States everything is about the dollar, or, in France eating has become a religion. That is drivel.

I also cannot explain Meltzer's odd lapse in his next statement:

> "Psychoanalysis, considered as a British science, was expelled from Germany and was established in England and the United States".

It is amazing how very well-informed people lose their head in the heat of their argument. According to Meltzer psychoanalysis is not Jewish; that was clear even to the Nazis. Meltzer should clearly have known that its so-called British character was the reason that psychoanalysis was unwelcome in Nazi Germany. A clear-headed Meltzer knows that, while an angry Meltzer acts like an angry adolescent and kicks whoever happens to be in front of him. All in all, the interview got out of hand, and the interviewers should have protected the man they admired too much from himself by shortening, censoring, and being more active in the interview.

The editors are not the only ones who are angry—after the publication several indignant letters appear, among others from Susan Wolff, whose thesis has already been mentioned. Jacqueline Godfrind, a training analyst in the Belgian Association, condemned Meltzer's attack on the training. There is also a defender, someone who had enjoyed his lectures and had not found a trace of anti-Semitism in the interview. For us the question is important because the Belgian colleagues and Meltzer react differently from the Dutch in the Verhage affair. They see their misstep and react effectively. The editors and the interviewers dissociate themselves vigorously from the inadmissible passages. No circle of supporters, asking what he could actually have said or meant, is created around Meltzer; and no "Group of Five" has to spring into action to prevent the affair from being covered up. No "Meltzer affair" comes into being. Meltzer does not completely excuse himself, but he does not accuse anyone else and does not let others do it. This creates a very different outcome than from the Verhage affair. In this way such an affair remains small, and analytical life can continue from where it was.

Yet there remains a psychoanalytically and sociologically interesting question that I prefer not to ask and barely dare to ask—especially because I do not have an answer and the possible answer does not please me. In the editorial offices of newspapers it is assumed that one letter to the editor represents the unexpressed opinion of at least 20 other readers. In group analysis the individual voice of a participant counts as "spokesperson of the group". But when vandals who call themselves supporters of a soccer club commit acts of vandalism, the club managers declare that these people are not "real supporters of our club", or that opponents, or the referee, did the same thing. In this way they manage to condemn and justify bad behaviour in one breath. That is why the question remains: for whom did Meltzer speak, and for whom did Verhage and the others mentioned in chapter six speak, and what club did they not really support? With this unanswered question in the back of my mind I will first go to London and then to Durban.

Edward Said in London

Writing about "Said in London" and "The Battle of Durban" I have to pay very close attention. In the next two parts of this chapter the subject is how psychoanalytic writers and policy makers let themselves get carried along in what the sociologist De Swaan (2005) calls "anti-Israel enthusiasm". Jews and non-Jews agree that this is different from anti-Semitic enthusiasm. To chant "Sharon murderer" is anti-Israel. To shout "Adolf Sharon" is anti-Semitic according to Hirschfield and Van der Sluijs (2005), the anti-Semitic watchdogs of the Netherlands. The first is permitted, the second one not. De Swaan tries to differentiate between Jews and Israelis, between anti-Jewish and anti-Israel, and shows the difference between these last two. With clever ambiguity he writes:

> I will argue that it is not quite "latent" or "unconscious" anti-Semitism that underlies so many critical statements about Israel, but that nevertheless an unspoken message does resonate in much critical discourse. It echoes something quite different, that still may be hard to accept for Jews: it suggests a certain abandon, a kind of enthusiasm in denouncing Israel's actions.

In anti-Israel sentiments, De Swaan sees "the tone of sincere indignation and at the same time feverish exaggeration. In fact, the government of Israel is not doing to the Palestinian nation what Hitler did to the Jewish people and the author must be aware of it". In a compelling argument he shows that despite his carefully treated distinction—almost a taboo—not to let the two overlap, he sees them almost run together:

> Rabbis shout *Sieg Heil*. The fat capitalist with the crooked nose and the dollar signs in his eyes has reappeared: in Arab cartoons and on alternative websites.[8] These rudimentary equations are perfectly congruous with the conspiratorial paranoia of classical anti-Semitism (op. cit., p. 365).

Particularly striking in De Swaan's argument are the efforts that he sees to take the burden of the Shoah off the shoulders of Europeans, to concretize the rejection of anti-imperialism in the rejection of Israel and the steps to equate Israel with South Africa as it was before the abolition of apartheid. He sees enthusiasm for decolonization coincide with the condemnation of the Jewish state. According to him, in world politics Israel occupies the place that Jews always had in the eyes of anti-Semites. The Jewish state is promoted to the source of all the evil in the world.

In its annual report "Anti-Semitic Incidents in the Netherlands", CIDI tries not to make the mistake of confusing anti-Israel behaviour and anti-Semitism, but it does not always succeed in separating the two (Hirschfeld & Van der Sluijs, 2005, op. cit.).[9] According to the authors, a line is crossed when Jews and Israelis are confused with each other. They see a whole series of classic anti-Semitic prejudices creeping into the rejection of Israel. It is realistic to speak of a Jewish lobby, because every interest group has a lobby. It becomes more suspect when there is mention of a Jewish voice. Is there such a thing?

Exaggeration and distortion continue bit by bit by regarding the economic position of Jews as decisive in the political spectrum, and then the way is clear to claiming the existence of so-called Jewish characteristics in discussing world politics. In this kind of discussion it is usual to complain about the Jewish domination of the media and to say that any criticism of Israel is automatically interpreted as anti-Semitism. From here it becomes natural to compare Israel's government with that of the Nazis, to equate the Israeli army with the SS, and to speak of the Palestinian Holocaust and of the genocide carried out by the Israelis. Finally there is the fact that a boycott is being demanded against Israel while that demand has never been made against other countries. In this complex of thoughts and deeds, the line boundary between anti-Semitism and political agitation or action is violated according to Hirschfeld and Van der Sluijs. These authors state that the anti-Semite does not need to satisfy all these requirements. Even one is sufficient according to them—for this they refer to literature.

The above-mentioned criteria seem reasonable to me and also applicable to what I will describe below. In one paragraph, the Israeli author Amos Oz (2002) summarizes trenchantly the complexity and the simplicity of the Israeli-Palestinian conflict.

> Two Palestinian-Israeli wars have erupted in this region. One is the Palestinian nation's war for its freedom from occupation and for its right to independent statehood. Any decent person ought to support this cause. The second war is waged by fanatical Islam, from Iran to Gaza and from Lebanon to Ramallah, to destroy Israel and drive the Jews out of their land. Any decent person ought to abhor this cause. Yasser Arafat and his men are running both wars simultaneously, pretending they are one. The suicide killers evidently make no distinction. Much of the worldwide bafflement about the Middle East, much of the confusion among the Israelis themselves, stem from the overlap between these two wars.[10]

It is a relief to read that he does not justify the existence of Israel through the Shoah or another tragedy from Jewish history but that its existence is natural for him. Israel has to continue to exist because it exists. Israel is the solution for one problem: a people without a country that now have a country. It is the cause of another problem: the Palestinian people have lost part of their land. To understand the Palestinian-Israeli conflict and to try to contribute to the solution is the task of the intellectual who works on this. However, if a prominent psychoanalyst does not recognize the jungle of conflicting interests, desires, and fears as confusing or pursues a disposition of the facts that does not do justice to the conflicting perspectives of the parties and within the parties, but instead sees the Israelis as the source of all evil, then he becomes a racist supporter and makes the institute that accommodates him guilty of old-fashioned anti-Semitic propaganda. I refer to Christopher Bollas and the Freud Museum in London.

But first the facts: one of the most forceful and most effective adversaries that Israel has ever had was Edward Said (1935–2003). He was a professor of English and Comparative Literature at Columbia University in New York, a political activist, recipient of 16 honorary degrees, author of more than 20 books that were translated into more than 36 languages; he spoke fluent English, French, and Arabic, and could get by in Spanish, German, Italian, and Latin. He wrote a lot, and he gave the impression that he was looking for a solution of the Israeli-Palestinian problem that would be fair to both parties. He was an authority with a worldwide reputation and was interviewed in newspapers and on television. The BBC made an impressive documentary about him.

In his public appearances, the fact that he was a prominent literature critic was in the background—his fight for the Palestinian cause was in the forefront. He became well known outside the academic world through his book, *Orientalism* (1979).

Its central thesis is that the study of "the Orient" is in itself a colonial undertaking. We Westerners make the Eastern peoples different, inferior, exotic, irrational, and on a lower rung of civilization. According to him, all this is meant to keep the Oriental in his place and to be able to exploit his riches as we please. This is an extremely simplified account of a book that has served as a spearhead to give the whole vision of "the East" another direction. This book and the autobiographical material that followed it, Said's literary and cultural-historical discussions, and his in-depth knowledge of classical music combined with his great talent as a pianist gave weight to his political activism.

He had an enormous influence on contemporary public opinion, and that has continued after his death. Of course one should not overestimate all this. In 1993 Philip Roth already drew the flip side of this portrait. In *Operation Shylock*, Roth shows how one of the characters, Ziad, is completely exhausted. Said-Ziad appears as a blind hater of Jews and Israel. His anger and suspicions have long ago clouded his view. Of course I cannot confuse reality and fiction, but when I read Roth I had the feeling of having encountered the truth. This was reinforced further by Roth's afterword in which he writes: "Any resemblance to actual events or locales or persons, living or dead, is entirely coincidental. This confession is false".

Said's political pronouncements, his proposals for a solution of the Israeli-Palestinian conflict, were the basis of his moving autobiography as a Palestinian exile. Again and again phrases like the following appear:

> I was born in November 1935, in Talbiyah, then a mostly new and prosperous Arab quarter of Jerusalem. By the end of 1947, just months before Talbiyah fell to Jewish forces, I'd left with my family for Cairo (1992).
>
> I was born in Jerusalem and spent most of my formative years there and after 1948 when my entire family became refugees, in Egypt (1998).
>
> ... my recollections of my early days in Palestine, my youth, the first twelve or thirteen years of my life before I left Palestine (1994).

Yet anyone who examines his life and his work sees quite a few lies. Weiner has made a study of this and has spelled out the central fable: Said describes himself falsely as a destitute Palestinian refugee who fled from the violence of the Israelis (1994).[11] His father was a Palestinian Arab who emigrated to the United States in 1911 and was naturalized. After some time he settled in Cairo. Said himself grew up in a prosperous area of that city. He was born in the house of his father's sister during a family visit in Jerusalem. A few months after his birth the family returned to Cairo where he went to school until he was 15. Claims that he supposedly went to the Anglican St. George's School in Jerusalem turned out to be false. His name does not appear in the books of the school. In later publications Said had to retract the fairy tale he made up. At that point he simply says that he grew up in Cairo—probably because Weiner's publications and the preceding research had come to his attention. Weiner also shows convincingly that the so-called beloved house at 10 Brenner Street in West Jerusalem (Said placed this street in East Jerusalem) was never lived in by Said's parents, but instead by his aunt with her husband and their children.

The second lie that was central to Said's public persona was that he was politically moderate, working for a compromise. That, too, was not the case. He was against the Oslo accords that involved the recognition of both the Palestinian state in the process of formation and the state of Israel. He was uncompromisingly against it. His solution to the conflict was a bi-national state of Palestine that would include all Palestinians and their descendants who had fled the violence of 1947–1949 and all the Jews of the then former state of Israel. Even Arafat understood the unreality of this demand. For Israeli Jews it was taboo because they would once again be a minority in a state hostile to them.

Said's uncompromising attitude remained hidden behind his moderate and cultivated manner—as he wrote:

> Nothing I have said ... must be understood except as an acknowledgment of Palestinian and Jewish history—in fierce conflict with each other for a period of time, but fundamentally reconcilable to each other within a common historical perspective (1979b).

On the other hand, there were anti-Semitic statements like those quoted by Alexander, Popov, and Lange, just to name a few (2003). He expresses his opposition to the war in Iraq as follows (the quote includes the comments of the authors):

> "The Perles and Wolfowitzes" of this country have led America into a war "planned by a docile professionalized staff in [...] Washington and Tel Aviv" and publicly defended by "Ari Fleischer[12] [who I believe is an Israeli citizen]". [A New York Post journalist who attempted to find the source of Said's phony claim about Fleischer located it in the website of the White Aryan Resistance Movement.]

To be perfectly clear, I am not giving my opinion about the war in Iraq, only about Said's discussion.

Said had friendships that matched his worldwide renown. Two will suffice here: Noam Chomsky and Daniel Barenboim, both Jewish, the first a linguist, the second a pianist and conductor. With Barenboim he founded the West-East Divan Orchestra[13], a youth orchestra that had as members Arabs and Jews, Palestinians and Israelis. Said was a complicated puzzle in which love and hate were easy to project onto him and also tumbled together within him.

May 6, 2001, was the 150th anniversary of Freud's birth, and Said had been invited in August 2000 to give the official speech for the Viennese Freudian Association. I have no knowledge of any debates about this invitation within the institute, but the outcome is known. Said accepted the invitation, which then was withdrawn in April 2001. The reason was that a few days earlier Said had let *Agence France Presse* photograph him as he threw a rock at an Israeli guard post. Throwing a rock, even in the direction of Israel, means something more than it might appear on the surface. It was a rock thrown over a gate behind which Israelis were walking—a symbol of the stoning of Satan. Therefore it was a very aggressive act. In the Muslim tradition you throw rocks at despised and despicable people or objects. It is a declaration of impurity and has a symbolic value: the ritual stoning of the unworthy. The *hadj*, which every Muslim has to accomplish once in his life, ends with throwing a rock toward Mina, north of Mecca. Said, a Christian, knew very well what he was doing. In Western eyes it looks like the innocent game of an old man who wants to hit a guard post with a rock; for the Arab masses it is a significant act in which the evil nature of Israel is acted out.

The situation in the Middle East was given as the reason for withdrawing the invitation. In the phrasing of the president of the Viennese Freudian Association, they were afraid of hurting the feelings of the Viennese Jews. In this context he also mentioned the rise of the neo-Nazi candidate for prime minister, Jörg Haider, the Holocaust, and the history of Austrian anti-Semitism.

This action, which conveyed empathy, quickly turned against the Association and in addition against the suspect Jewish machinations behind it. The opponents of the invitation should first have sat on their hands (as young chess players are taught to do) before making their brilliant move. One could say that emotion trumped intellect.

It was as though Said's supporters had been waiting for this step. Said and his circle managed to change this loss into a gain in an instant. In less than no time he changed from an aggressor who joined the opponents of any compromise into an innocent scholar and a victim of Jewish dominance, a comfortable position from which he liked to operate. The repercussion of the rock does not land on him—and not on an Israeli patrol—but on the reputation of the Viennese analysts and in particular on the Jewish members among them. An added advantage was that his appearance now attracted more attention than if his public would have consisted of an audience of 200. Said himself achieved his first victory by saying that he had not thrown a rock but a pebble, that it was a joke, and that he couldn't help it if there happened to be photographers in the area. He proceeded in a rhetorical triumph that immediately reached the world press. He managed to compare himself with Freud—just as in his view the Palestinians are equal to the Jews as victims of oppression: "Freud was driven from Vienna because he was a Jew. Now I am driven away because I am a Palestinian".

Prominent analysts, together with several traditional supporters of the Palestinian cause, immediately came to the aid of Said and left the unworthy comparison for what it was. They wrote a letter to the Viennese Freudian Association, and had it printed in the *London Review of Books* (March 22, 2001):

> The distinguished critic and Professor of English and Comparative Literature at Columbia University, Edward Said, was invited to deliver the annual Freud Memorial Lecture in Vienna on 6 May (the anniversary of Freud's birthday).
>
> The invitation, which Edward Said accepted, has been withdrawn "on account of the political development in the Middle East". We wish to state that we deplore this move and consider it to be contrary to the spirit of psychoanalytic understanding and dialogue.

No intellectual, not to mention an analyst, can put up with that. The Freud Museum in London seized this chance to get the psychoanalytical dialogue going again within its walls and let Said hold his Viennese lecture. There is evidently no doubt about what took place there; there is no question about what psychoanalytic dialogue and the psychoanalytic concept mean, and as far as that is concerned whether Said was the appropriate speaker. The public reputation of analysis was on the line, and in that case measures could not be strict enough. It no longer matters that the argument of the dialogue and the concept is nonsense. The fundamental principle of analysis is that the patient must say what comes into his or her mind. Inside the analytic situation the patient may indeed say and think anything. He may indeed hate and desire his father as well as his mother, his brother, and his sister, and in addition his neighbour and his boss. He may also express the passionate desire to murder all his opponents. In this situation the analyst has another role. He tries to understand and to order *the material* that the patient contributes so that the patient will understand himself better. After the analytic hour the office door opens again, and the rules, laws, and customs that regulate human lives are back in force. The usual difficult rights and duties are back in force; social reality is back in force. It is to be hoped that you will approach it more freely after analysis. However, if you harm, offend, or rebuff someone or his friends or relations, the offended party no longer has the tendency to invite you to his house. In that light Said's invitation was withdrawn. Perhaps clumsy, politically stupid, fearful—a perfect case of cold feet. But the principal tenant of the Viennese analytical house was within his rights, especially since a public discussion and not a psychoanalytic one was to be expected.

That political discussion now takes place in another place and at another moment. This time not only by Said but by his entire entourage. He gives the lecture on the planned date in the Freud Museum in London. He is introduced and followed by two signers of "the Letter": Christopher Bollas, an analyst, takes care of the introductory remarks, and Jacqueline Rose, a literary scholar, closes the evening. The entire event is recorded in a fine small book, *Freud and the Non-European*, published in 2003 by Verso in association with the Freud Museum in London.[14]

Bollas had also read Weiner; hence in his introduction he changes Said's biography so that there are almost no lies. He describes Said's background as follows (p. 4): "His first deep contact with the fate of the exile was in 1948, when his family was driven from Palestine, and he was not to return for 45 years". In English there is no distinction between *nuclear family* and *family*, unless you use this precise terminology. And if I read Weiner correctly, Said's aunt and her family had left long before disturbances broke out in Jerusalem; moreover, there was no fighting in West Jerusalem: details that determine the truth, and Bollas does not want to be confused by them. Bollas leaves the indelible impression that the Jews forced Wadie Said's (Edward's father) family to leave their home:

> Perhaps it was his Aunt Nabiha's energy and determination to address the "desolations of being without a country or a place to return to" that inscribed itself in that gathering momentum that was to become Said the international figure, but he has alluded to the importance of his move to the United States—first to boarding school, and then to Princeton University—which not only widened his horizons, but became an object to be used.

The distortions can barely be counted. Said becomes his Aunt Nabiha who supposedly was a refugee from the Israelis. His departure for study in the United States becomes a flight from Israel. Even after that Bollas gives an incorrect version of the story. He reaches the nadir when he paraphrases Said approvingly and speaks of "negative hallucination", of "not seeing the existence of the other, the intellectual genocide" taking place in the West.

Bollas refers to one of his own terms, the "Fascist State of Mind", that appears in chapter nine of his book *Being a Character* (1992, pp. 193–218). In it he starts his argument with the Turks' slaughter of 800,000 Armenians, which was preceded by the latter's loss of citizenship. He treats the Shoah and its commemoration as a defence against present harm that is being done to the Third World. He writes:

> Although the genocide against the Jewish population in Nazi Germany—the Holocaust—seems an irreplaceable icon to evil in the 20th century mind, we may wonder if its ironic function (the Jew now used once again to serve as a point of projection) is to serve as a continued mental negation of the continuation of genocide. We seem to know this, as citizens of the Western world do try not to eliminate from their thoughts the re-emergence in Cambodia of the Khmer Rouge which put to death millions of people. "Never forget", the cry of the Holocaust victim, seems a tellingly apt injunction: we seem all too able to forget (1992, p. 195).

According to Bollas, the beginning of the "Fascist State of Mind" manifests by taking away human dignity from a future group of victims. With Stalin, the bourgeoisie was the first group to be humiliated and then to be annihilated. Bollas feels that the Fascist State of Mind exists in each one of us, and he quotes Bakunin:

> All the tender feelings of family life, of friendship, love, gratitude, and even honour must be stifled in the revolutionary by a single cold passion for the revolutionary cause.

He also presents a central point from Lifton (1986) about how Nazi doctors had to bring about a splitting within themselves in order to be able to carry out their atrocities; how they had to make themselves into a machine in order to perfect the "total cure", the cleansing cure of killing.

After a detour via Hannah Arendt, Bollas gets to his definition of the Fascist State of Mind:

> Thus something almost banal in its ordinariness—namely, our cohering of life into ideologies or theories—is the seed of the Fascist state of mind when such ideology must (for whatever reason) become total (1992, p. 200).

A moral void is present in the mind of the fascist:

> On the verge of its own moral vacuum, the mind splits off this dead core self and projects it into a victim henceforth identified with the moral void. [...] As the negation of the qualities of the other are destroyed via the annihilation of the other, a delusional grandiosity forms in the Fascistically stated [sic] mind (1992, p. 203).

Bollas seamlessly applies this conceptualization that pertains to the fascist in each of us to "the Israeli refusal to recognize the existence of the Palestinians". For a propagandist, it is good to be so one-sided, but it is far beneath the dignity of Bollas the thinker—and this for various reasons. The transition from individual to state cannot be made just like that, and when the argument makes it necessary then the steps have to be set up explicitly. When that happens and if it is necessary to look at Israel, then something like a part of Israeli reality can be constructed in the same way as is done in individuals.

This kind of argument applies to many peoples, if not all. The more vehemently a people is involved in the struggle for its existence, the greater the chance that one can discover such a fascist core in which the other not only is no good but also does not exist. It is a question of *he or I*. Anyway, if Bollas wants it, let the Fascist State of Mind apply to Israel. Then it becomes clear to the naked eye that in the thoroughly politicized Israeli society a passionate struggle is taking place to undo that very thing. Israel is very complex—and this is happening as noisily as possible.

The facts on which Bollas builds his argument do not tally. He could know that in September of 1993 the PLO received the following letter from the then prime minister of Israel:

> September 9, 1993
>
> Yasser Arafat
> Chairman
> The Palestinian Liberation Organization
>
> Mr. Chairman,
>
> In response to your letter of September 9, 1993, I wish to confirm to you that, in light of the PLO commitments included in your letter, the Government of Israel has decided to recognize the PLO as the representative of the Palestinian people and commence negotiations with the PLO within the Middle East peace process.
>
> *Yitzhak Rabin*
>
> Prime Minister of Israel

Bollas does not mention the fact that until 2001 Israel was the only member of the United Nations that was not allowed to belong to any regional group. This was because the Arab countries refused to accept Israel as a member of the Asian group. As a result it was impossible for Israel to become a member of the Security Council, and it is the only member state that is barred from ever being president of the General Assembly of the United Nations or to become a member of any department of the General Assembly and its most important commissions. It was not until May 2000 that Israel was accepted as a temporary member of the West European and other States Group.

To bring the Second World War as close as possible, Bollas calls suicide terrorists *a part of the resistance*: "The aim of such resistance is not to overcome Israel, it is to return Israel to itself, for better and for worse". The suicide murderer as analyst who in the Freud Museum points out the consequences of his deeds to Israel the patient—hoping for a cure or a civilized retreat from the face of the earth. Then Bollas continues with two pages of praise for the indeed very gifted and much-honoured Said.

Freud and the Non-European (Said, 2003)

It must not have been easy to be present in the audience of Said in the Freud Museum in London on May 6, 2001. It was one of his last lectures, the essence of his next-to-last book. Said had leukaemia and would live less than another year and a half. The 43 pages that he read in about two hours are complicated. What Said writes about Beethoven and Freud's *Moses and Monotheism* also applies to him: the text is an example of the *Spätstil* (late style) of a creative mind: "episodic, fragmentary, unfinished". What he wrote is difficult to fathom and irreconcilable elements are still in the text. In it we are overwhelmed by his profound knowledge of West European literature and by the sharpness of his reasoning. In this knowledge, love of art and culture go hand in hand with the immense anger of the author who feels that everything that is not Western is not seen.

Inner contradictions are confusing for the reader. When Said speaks of his appreciation of the "ancient, venerable faith of the Jews", this appreciation is accompanied by his attempt to make Egyptian what is valuable and original in it. The less complimentary comments that he makes about work from the *Spätstil* period can be applied to his own work:

> Intransigence and a sort of irascible transgressiveness, as if the author was expected to settle down into a harmonious composure, as befits a person at the end of his life, but preferred instead to be difficult, and to bristle with all sorts of new ideas and provocations [...] Above all, late style's effect on the reader or listener is alienating—that is to say, Freud and Beethoven present material that is of pressing concern to them with scant regard for satisfying, much less placating, the reader's need for closure.

Then Said begins his actual argument. He starts with the observation that Freud was a Viennese Jew, scholar, philosopher, and intellectual, "who lived and worked in Austria or in England". Yes, of course. He lived in Austria from 1856 until June 1938, and from that date until the date of his death—in September 1939—he lived in England. Well ... yes. The way it is expressed by Said, the tragedy of the 82-year-old man who has to leave his home and his country becomes the story of a travelling modern scholar or a wandering Jew. Said does not present incorrect facts, but he suggests a totally different life.

Then follows the remark that Freud's view and knowledge of other cultures were shaped by his education in the Judeo-Christian tradition. Said makes a curious exception: "Perhaps not the Egyptian tradition". He attributes to Freud an expertise about ancient Egypt that would have surprised the latter. According to Said, Freud recognized "the other" only through the classics of Greco-Roman and Hebrew antiquity. He did not know the non-European. Said grants him that with a laconic comment: "In any event, I believe it is true to say that Freud's was a Eurocentric view of culture—and why should it not be?"

Franz Fanon is named by Said as Freud's contentious successor; moreover, he turns out to be one of the most important sources of inspiration of Said. According to Said, Fanon's main purpose is to indict Europe for having divided human beings into a hierarchy of races that reduced and dehumanized the subordinates to both the scientific gaze and the will of the superiors.

* * *

Fanon does not limit himself to European colonialism. In his condemnation he also includes European humanism that was unable to look beyond its own borders. Said agrees with Fanon's attack but reproaches him for not offering a way out for breaking through the racial hierarchy. Said himself admires Jane Austin, Thomas Mann, Romain Rolland, Erich Auerbach, and Freud. Said emphasizes their Eurocentric world view, but he feels that these authors are also worthwhile for the non-European, non-Western reader who is inclined to push their work aside as racist, unaware of the other, especially when a non-Western person and his way of life is described. He sees earlier writers about non-Western territories and situations as material for present-day authors who have a view that is not limited by the West. He sees Freud as someone who charted old terrain anew. That makes it possible for his reader to read him again and again and to rearrange and reuse his material.

Said points to Freud's complicated and, according to Said, hopelessly unresolved connection to his own Jewish identity. That offers Said the freedom to do what he wants to with *Moses and Monotheism*. He gives Moses an Egyptian identity, and he has the latter's monotheism derive directly from the Egyptian pharaoh Akhenaton. In the knowledge of unknown history, Freud is given a role that he would have rejected smilingly: a scholar of ancient Egypt. Said writes (p. 33):

> Freud must have known perfectly well that monotheism returned to Egypt first in the form of primitive Christianity (which remains in the Coptic Church of today) and then via Islam, which he does in fact discuss briefly later in the text.

Said gives Jewish circumcision an Egyptian origin. In the game that Freud plays with history, Said comes with a third dimension of unreality: he lets the name of the God of the Jews come from Arabia. He makes Freud's "Historical Novel", "The One-Legged Dancer", "The Guesswork" Freud's last application of the concept that he worked out in the *Abriss* (the outline) one last time, the daydream that Freud had about the Moses story, into an essay that is the result of historical archaeological research. He turns Freud's theoretical game into historical reality.

* * *

Said then jumps to Freud as an opponent of Zionism. That story is also more complicated than Said presents it. As I mentioned earlier, Freud saw the perspective of liberation for the Jews in Zionism. He admired Herzl, whom he saw as his double just as much as Schnitzler (Falk, 1978, p. 360). He refused income from his works that were translated into Hebrew. He was not unsympathetic towards Zionism, but he wondered if its goal was attainable. He himself never considered emigration to Palestine. More than most Zionist supporters he was aware of the Arab presence in Palestine and dared to realize that two claims to the same piece of land could end in a long struggle. In this connection, the following extract from a letter that Freud wrote to Dr. Chaim Koffler on February 26, 1930 is often quoted: "I can raise no sympathy at all for the misdirected piety which turns a Herodian wall into a national relic, thereby offending the feelings of the natives". Every couple of years this letter appears in the press as "Sigmund Freud's secret point of view about the establishment of the State of Israel". However, turning Freud into an anti-Zionist is giving a false impression of matters, and transforming him into an authority on political matters is also incorrect. That is evident from the same letter in which he writes: "I can certainly sympathise with its goals [of Zionism]. I am proud of our University in Jerusalem and am delighted with our settlement's prosperity". All this matters little because Freud was not a political thinker and did not want to be one. If he had any political point of view about the Middle East, it was from a Jewish perspective, with as an underlying idea the practice of moderation.

Said does not only know Yerushalmi, who places Freud so clearly in the Jewish tradition, but also Chemouni (1988) who does not completely agree with Yerushalmi. The latter says that Herzl and Freud have divided the world between each other: Herzl who gives the Jews a specific place in the world, and Freud who gives them the realm of the universal. Freud was fascinated by Rome, Athens, and Jerusalem: Rome as a symbol of the destruction of the Temple followed by exile; Athens as the city where the mind reigns; Jerusalem as fulfilment of the intellectual ascetic ideal, the symbol of Freud's intellectual ambition. He sees the actually existing Jerusalem as a dilution of the ascetic ideal, but also as a loss that can be redeemed by the collective effort of Zionism.

Said sees Freud swing back and forth between two poles. On the one hand he is forced to be part of the Jewish lot, as Yerushalmi portrays it. That is the result of the reality of fascist Europe. On the other hand, he sees the triangle that emphasizes the unsolved problem of exile and belonging nowhere, as depicted by Chemouni.

Said uses *Moses and Monotheism* in a way that violates the text. He writes the following:

> As for the charge of Jews being foreigners (the implied context is, of course European), Freud is dismissive of it, because in

> countries like Germany, where anti-Semitism is pervasive, the Jews have been there longer, having arrived with the Romans. On the accusation that Jews are different from their hosts, Freud backhandedly says that they are not "fundamentally so", since they are not "a foreign Asiatic race, but mostly consist of the remnants of Mediterranean peoples and inherit their culture".

According to Said, Freud says this in order to be able to take cover under the equality and superiority of two Western civilizations and to turn away from the Eastern civilization that the Jews do not share.

However, Freud's words exist in another context. They are from Freud's umpteenth attempt to explain anti-Semitism: according to him the Jews have indeed murdered the Father, and they have amply atoned for that. Then there is his surprise at the vehemence and permanence of anti-Semitism, and he examines the reproaches to the Jews.

This brings Freud to his favourite "Narcissism of Small Differences": the fact that small differences between people and groups can lead to fiercer hate than big differences. The other who behaves as if he is equal to the established class is much more intolerable than the other who wants to remain a stranger or at least remains seen as such. Therefore Freud does not make the Jews equal to the Germans, but similar as well as different. That is not the same as wanting to hide under the protection of the majority. Said deconstructs this. He connects this passage with Freud's emphasis on Moses's being an Egyptian. Said wonders whether Freud is looking for a hiding place in Europe where he lives.

There is a thread that runs through the whole essay. Freud at first designated the Moses book as a historical novel. It is a fantasy, in his eyes a theory about how the Jewish people might have originated. *Totem and Taboo* is the most important theoretical source. The point of departure was the doubt that Freud had felt when as a boy he heard the story of the Egyptian princess who found a baby boy in a basket and adopted it as her own child. That child would supposedly become the leader of the Jewish people.

Freud's doubt about the historical truth of what he had heard as a child, combined with his total belief in his own theory and the delusion of grandeur that many people experience when their life falls apart, produces the fairy tale that is *Moses and Monotheism*. An interesting book, on which I have unleashed my own imagination in chapter four. Said does something different: he turns it into a scholarly work that describes a historical truth and that can be useful to him in rewriting the present so that it gives rise to a reality of which he wants to convince the world. That produces his truth, and this becomes the Truth, which is greater than the facts. In this way, in Said's all too concrete view, circumcision becomes an Egyptian custom, monotheism originated in Egypt, and the Egyptian tradition becomes the cradle of Judaism, Christianity, and Islam. It may be true, but it is not likely. By transforming these hypotheses into facts they become lies.

Said's position is that according to the Nuremberg laws the Jews were "foreign, and therefore expendable" and were turned into non-Europeans. He continues:

> The Holocaust is a ghastly monument, if that is the right word, to that designation and to all the suffering that went with it. Then there is the almost too-perfect literalization that is given the binary opposition Jew-versus-non-European in the climactic chapter of the unfolding narrative of Zionist settlement in Palestine (2003, pp. 40–41).

Said's rhetorical power is in that sentence. He lets us think what he does not say: the Jew as a Westerner sparing nothing and no one and the Palestinian as defenceless Easterner, uprooted and persecuted. The Jew as Nazi, the Palestinian as Jew. At the same time he empathizes about the Shoah, and that empathy can feel genuine. Yet he also says "foreign, and expendable" about the Palestinian in Jewish eyes, and the audience is invited to think that the Israelis are or were busy carrying out a holocaust of the Palestinians. Then he shifts to the political context of his argument, and that is of course about the Israeli-Palestinian conflict. It has as its focus:

> a tiny sliver of land. In this setting, Israel was internationally adopted by the Atlantic West [...] as, in effect, a quasi-European state whose fate, it seemed—in an eerie asseveration of the Fanonist argument, was to hold non-European indigenous peoples at bay as long as possible. [...] Inside Israel, the main

classificatory stipulation was that it was a state for the Jews, whereas non-Jews, absent or present as so many of them were, were juridically made foreigners, despite prior residence there.

In Said's argument Israel, the refuge for Jews, becomes a state with exclusive land rights for Jews. He makes Freud a part of this with the following reproach:

> Israeli legislation countervenes, represses, and even cancels Freud's carefully maintained opening out of Jewish identity towards its non-Jewish background. The complex layers of the past, so to speak, have been eliminated by official Israel.

Again a shower of truths and falsehoods. Is it Moses's or Freud's identity that coincides with present-day Jewish identity? Do non-Jews have no rights in Israel? Was there only non-Jewish emigration from Israel in 1948? And how about Jewish emigration from the Arab countries, which was practically total? Everything is too simple: the West colonizes and the non-West is oppressed. This can get much applause but brings in little truth.

Freud is again used as an authority in an area where he was not one. Freud constructed a history of the Jewish identity in the Diaspora, a reconstruction, but not a command to create a future identity. It would not surprise me if the worldly Israeli variant had pleased him. At any rate his own life was quite worldly and at the same time quite Jewish. His last and least complicated quote from *Moses and Monotheism* illustrates this. In his second introductory chapter he writes gratefully about his reception in London. He mentions the letters of welcome from other newcomers and adds:

> And in addition there arrived, with a frequency surprising to a foreigner, communications of another sort, which were concerned with the state of my soul, which pointed out to me the way of Christ and sought to enlighten me on the future of Israel.
>
> The good people who wrote in this way cannot have known much about me; but I expect that when this work about Moses becomes known, in a translation, among my new compatriots, I shall forfeit enough of the sympathy, which a number of other people as well now feel for me (1939, pp. 57–58).

Freud did not much care for conversion attempts.

Said concludes his remarks by saying that the state of Israel bases its right of existence also on archaeology, carried out with enthusiasm in order to give Israel a centuries-old foundation. Said is pleased that the Palestinian side will start on it too. He states that there are also archaeological finds that are evidence of Palestinian settlement. He wants these two histories to be considered complementary and not conflicting: this in the name of unity of science and, I would add, as a first stage of a bi-national state. Said wants the Jews to be more cosmopolitan and less connected to the land than they are. He wants non-Jewish Jews in Deutscher's sense of the word. He prefers Jews like Spinoza, Marx, Heine, and Freud, about whom he remarks that they have all been excommunicated from Judaism. In reality that was true only for Spinoza. Heine[15] and Freud were, in their own ways, quite Jewish and not Jewish at the same time. Then he mentions, correctly, that the lot of being scattered and uprooted is no longer unique to the Jews:

> In our age of vast population transfers, of refugees, exiles, expatriates and immigrants, it can also be identified in the diasporic, wandering, unresolved, cosmopolitan consciousness of someone who is both inside and outside his or her community.

The literary scholar Jacqueline Rose concludes the book *Freud and the Non-European*. She summarizes the above in words that Said does not use:

> Freud's partial, fragmented, troubled, and at times self-denying relationship to his own Jewishness can provide a model for identity in the modern world.

Then, as a logical sequel, follows what Said leaves to others to think: *Israel represses Freud*, in which *represses* has a double meaning, represses and oppresses. Rose prefers the scattered and uprooted Jews. She is afraid that this interesting variant threatens to be lost in Israel. The "multiple layered character" that she attributes to the Jews is withheld from the Israeli. She changes the title of Said's essay to "Freud *the* Non-European". To this she adds that it is "suggesting that the fixity of identity is something from which it is very hard to escape". According to her, *Moses and Monotheism* "has a great deal to say [about this]. For if it offers an account [...] of identities that know their own provisionality, it also does the opposite". Some texts serve as a Rorschach test; you can read into them what you wish so that the reader is the only one characterized by it.

Why this elaboration about Said? First of all, because he is so incredibly intelligent and seductive, but at the same time very ambiguous about Jews—and all this in the name of psychoanalysis. You see the ruling Israeli in uniform and the uprooted Palestinian. The Israeli as non-Jew, according to the reigning stereotype: not suffering and not human. And the Palestinian as the Jew who does possess these characteristics to a greater extent. Secondly, I have dwelled on Said because Freud as Jew is used as an anti-Israeli weapon. Moreover, this took place in the Freud Museum, the place where Freud died.

Notes

1. Until World War II it was the IPV, *Internationale* Psychoanalytische *Vereinigung*.
2. Later the musician Wayne Godley describes this transgressive behavior during psychoanalysis (2001).
3. She leaves out the phrases I have italicized. In a footnote in this text Linda Hopkins quotes (p. 487) two American analysts indirectly: "Two American psychoanalysts, Harold Searles and Marie Coleman Nelson [private communication, 1996], expressed to me their opinion that critics of Khan's anti-Semitic intervention were drawing conclusions based on a limited reading of their case, and that Khan's intervention was justifiable because it was effective". It is not clear whether Ms. Hopkins showed them her edited version or the one in Khan's own words.
4. Lionel Kreeger, Harold Stewart, Joseph Sandler, Malcolm Pines, and an unidentified fifth (Hopkins, op. cit., pp. 369–370).
5. Please note the incorrect spelling of the name of the president, Dr. Eric Brenman. The destruction of a person's name is the final purpose of the aggressor. The Shoah museum in Israel is called Yad Vashem: "A Memorial and a Name".
6. According to the obituary that appeared in the *International Journal of Psychoanalysis* (Hahn, 2005, p. 177), ideological differences with the psychoanalytic establishment brought about his departure.
7. I also mention Wieseltier (1998).

8. For a quite uncanny collection of anti-Israeli cartoons in the Arab and Western press, cf. Joël & Dan Kotek, *Au Nom de l'antisionisme; L'image des Juifs et d'Israël dans la caricature depuis la seconde Intifada* (2003).
9. CIDI (Centre for Information and Documentation on Israel) publishes this yearly report.
10. As a novelist he has more freedom than as an essayist, and as such he lets the main character in *A Tale of Love and Darkness* (Oz, 2005) and his father talk about Europe and the world: "There, in the big world, they had scratched on all the walls "Yids, go back to Palestine"—so we went back to Palestine, and now the whole world screams at us: "Yids, get out of Palestine"".
11. The facts in these paragraphs are from Weiner. He has made a very thorough study (essentially not refuted) of Said and the story of his life as suggested by him. Weiner's material comes from interviews with friends, acquaintances, classmates, schoolmates, and family members of Said. Weiner's written sources were archives of the Mandate government about Palestine of that time, and also the land registry, archives of the Chamber of Commerce, telephone books, and newspaper files from Jerusalem and Cairo.
12. At that time Perle and Wolfowitz were important officials in the US Department of Defense; Fleisher was the press secretary of the White House.
13. Named after a cycle of poems by Goethe, called the West-Östlicher Diwan.
14. Verso advertises itself as a "Radical Publisher" whose motto is: *Books with a Critical Edge*.
15. Heine was baptized but did not become Christian in the least.

CHAPTER EIGHT

The battle of Durban

In chapter six I reported how difficult it was to get hold of the material about the events described. That was completely different when I wanted to do research about the participation of the IPA in "The United Nations World Conference against Racism, Racial Discrimination, Xenophobia and Related Intolerance" in Durban in 2001. On February 26, 2004, I wrote to the then president, Daniel Widlöcher. The next day I received a response from the general director of the IPA. The president had asked him to cooperate fully with my research, and he did. Within three weeks I was in possession of three folders of relevant records. A year later, when I asked to look at the minutes of the board about this affair, the answer was a polite "yes". And three days later they were in my electronic mailbox. The feeling of relief to be allowed to know what is going on was strengthened when I got in touch with a number of analysts in New York. They let me interview them by telephone and helped me to get access to written material.[1]

In addition, I obtained information by telephone from Henk Jan Dalewijk, the interim director of the NVPA (see chapter six) who was also on the board of the IPA. During the events that will be described, he was a member of the CUN, the IPA Committee on the

United Nations. As far as I could gather from the documents, he was rather peripheral as such. In our conversation, he emphasized the integrity of Afaf Mahfouz as he and others experienced it. I have not attempted to get in touch with her or with Isaac Tylim, the other main character in this story. In my opinion Mahfouz and Tylim both said what they had to say in the documents. My additional information is from numerous newspapers and magazines that appeared during the conference.

The Durban conference was intended to consider injustices in the world: slavery, poverty, neglect, hunger, disease, torture, and avoidable death. It was a large United Nations event. It was for a good reason that Durban had been chosen as the place for the gathering. Post-apartheid South Africa had become a symbol of the new freedom and of throwing off the yoke of racism. As often happens when there is a gathering of power, there were two meetings: an official one for governments that served to make decisions on behalf of the United Nations, and preceding it a forum with NGOs (non-governmental organizations) associated with the UN. The conference took place from September 1 to 7, and the NGO forum was from August 27 until September 2. The NGOs had access to the real conference and were allowed to exert pressure. However, they had no vote.

It is considered difficult for an NGO to be admitted. But the IPA had succeeded in this. How it happened is a story in itself. The original committee consisted primarily of clinicians, analysts with a practice, who approached the United Nations. They wanted to apply analytic concepts on a larger scale than that of their office. This committee was the CUN. Originally its chair, Ruth Lax, was the central person. During the 1997 IPA conference in Barcelona she managed to get the board of the IPA to agree with her attempt to set up an NGO of analysts. Her reasoning was that lawyers, psychologists, and psychiatrists had their own NGOs, so why not analysts. The board of the IPA agreed with this and established an official committee with as its purpose to get access to the United Nations. She filled it primarily with New York analysts.

Through her contacts Lax had heard of a capable lobbyist, the political scientist and lawyer Afaf Mahfouz, who had also completed psychoanalytic training. On behalf of another organization the latter was already in charge of an NGO, the ALU (the Arab Lawyers Union) where she had proved her worth. During that same period she took part in a "United Nations Conference on Aging" on behalf of the ALU. She had also become chair of the CONGO, the umbrella organization of the NGOs. Lax thought it would be useful to have her on board. She invited Mahfouz, who was prepared to participate. Mahfouz on the committee seemed useful in many respects. For one thing, she was familiar with United Nations procedures. Lax was well connected in the psychoanalytic circles of New York and was on friendly terms with Otto Kernberg, whom she had helped in his election campaign for the presidency of the IPA. Afaf Mahfouz was a clever politician, and within no time she was co-chair with Ruth Lax. After a difficult year of shared leadership, Mahfouz in fact chaired the committee.

To Ruth Lax's distress and indignation, Otto Kernberg as president of the IPA made this official and decided on a reorganization of duties with vice-chairs from Eastern Europe and South America under the sole leadership of Afaf Mahfouz. As a result there was no longer a place for Ruth Lax as co-chair; this was a heavy blow for her. She felt that she had carried the committee, and Kernberg was a friend who now let her down. Marion Oliner, a friend of Lax, also resigned, but that was not only because of solidarity with her friend. In a letter dated November 16, 2001 to the president of the IPA, Daniel Widlöcher, Oliner looks back and states that Mahfouz was very assertive in her leadership that was politically biased:

> When I tried to reach the organizers of the Durban conference, early on, I was totally unsuccessful and Afaf Mahfouz told me that nothing was as yet organized. When I gave as one of my reasons for resigning my frustration in being able to make contact with the organizers, I was told by Afaf Mahfouz: don't worry, it has all been arranged. The message was clear; I was not to have any input.

Afaf Mahfouz was energetic in her leadership—and not without results. Within a year there was a psychoanalytic NGO, and this was considered very fast. The minutes of February 15, 2001 of the CUN showed little enthusiasm when a proposal by Paul Hoeffels

(UN Department of Public Information) was discussed. Hoeffels wanted to develop a service that would offer psychological assistance to UN employees working in conflict areas. In fulfilling this assignment the IPA saw an opportunity to make psychoanalysis visible in the discussion and thought that it could do even more: "To consider, advise and promote contributions that the profession of psychoanalysis might make in such areas of international concern".[2]

Daniel Widlöcher, who had become president of the IPA, knew that it would be difficult to have the committee accepted by the members and to obtain their approval to represent the psychoanalysts at Durban. Especially the Jewish analysts from New York were afraid that the committee would land in the political line of fire of the Arab-Israeli conflict and then explicitly or implicitly condemn the Israelis. Widlöcher showed himself to be quite diplomatic when he wrote to a worried Oliner before the conference. Oliner had asked him what the IPA would do if a "Zionism is Racism" resolution were to be presented, for it was clear to anyone who paid attention that preparations for such a resolution were visible. Widlöcher's answer of August 24, 2001 was formal and did not go into substantive objections:

> The specific resolution you mention is not to be on the agenda, according to a statement by government officials in South Africa. The IPA has no direct role. [...] The IPA's role is to make psychoanalysis visible in the debate, to interpret what is happening, to facilitate discussion [...] CONGO does not take position on substance. Currently the World Jewish Congress is Treasurer of the Association.

These are very political answers which were also used by the chair of CUN when it was under fire because of participation in the conference. The reasoning was practically the same, including the reference to the Jews, this time as participants in previous CONGO activities.[3] During preparations for the IPA participation in the Durban conference, the chair of the CUN emphasized:

> The issue of equating Zionism with Racism is one of many controversial issues, raised by some governments during the long process of preparation. The government of South Africa

announced last week that this issue will not be part of the agenda but as we know, things can change. As far as IPA is concerned, we do not represent any government, and therefore voting is not one of our rights there. As with many other NGOs we want to make a difference and our presence is important. Our absence would have no effect (APsaA OPEN LINE, August 21, 2001).

All this seems very nice and objective, but there is no such thing as not taking a position. No position is also a position. Taking part is also a standpoint. The government of the United States, through the Secretary of Defense Colin Powell, had already announced that it would not be present. For anyone who had eyes and ears it was quite clear how the conference would go.

Inside the APsaA (American Psychoanalytic Association) there was unrest about the IPA participation in the conference. This was expressed in an internet chat room, the APsaA OPEN LINE. A prescient comment about the appearance of objectivity was expressed by Irwin Savodnik in an e-mail to Zwi Lothane:

> What I would like to know is what specifically the IPA has to offer this group? Is there some theory of group process that will be applied? Perhaps such notions as displacement, reaction, formation or protection? This effort strikes me as ludicrous.
> Anyone who thinks that psychoanalytic reflections at a geopolitical conference such as this one will have the slightest benefit is seriously mistaken. And for a group that espouses "the Jewish Science" to a group, many of whose members are political anti-Semites, runs the risk of making things worse, being misquoted, and co-opted into their program (APsaA OPEN LINE, August 22, 2001).

The question is whether it was wise on the part of the psychoanalytic association to mingle with this company, or whether it was an overestimation of the capabilities of psychoanalysts who think that they understand politics because they sometimes have a good idea of what moves people in the treatment situation. I quote Savodnik once again: "Foreign affairs is not reducible to psychology. Debating platforms are not couches, and political ideology is not free association" (e-mail to APsaA OPEN LINE, August 27, 2001). I would like to add that it is like learning to swim in Niagara Falls.

The question whether the IPA could participate or act as a facilitator became the main issue in a lively debate that developed in the APsaA OPEN LINE. Observer, says one party. Participant in the process, say those who criticize participating but not acting it is an intense form of acting. Every time that someone—in the heated e-mail discussion that the American analysts have about this question—says that the IPA is a facilitator or acts in another official capacity, the general director of the IPA, Piers Pendred, writes "not true" in the margin, underlining his colourful handwriting. But the CUN was determined to participate. The e-mail discussion served at most to form opinions. The decisions about participation had already been made at the board level. The CUN makes sure that it is supported at the highest levels. That is not difficult because the IPA likes to show itself where decisions are being made.

The debate was already intense while the conference had not even started. Officially no one knew which direction the conference would go. The discussion in the IPA had not caught up with the facts. It was about participation or not, but that was decided long before. There were things about this conference that could be dangerous because they spelled trouble. A number of IPA members, especially American Jews, understood that there was a smear campaign brewing against Jews and Israel, and they wondered whether the IPA should be mixed up in that. Board members of the CUN preferred to read official documents and focus on them. The question was whether they shared the fear of the ordinary members. Opponents felt that the APsaA should pronounce a kind of veto against participation. At any rate they did not want to leave the decision to the IPA establishment but instead submit it to the organizations that together form the IPA.

Participation must be secured, and the members must not rally against it. Chair Mahfouz led the discussion inside the CUN. She explained what was going on according to her, and according to the report she did so in descriptive terms:

> Afaf informed on controversial issues re this conference. Some governments are upset about the decision to condemn Zionism as racist; others do not want to include the problem

of compensations for African-Americans or Palestinians. [...] It is crucial for a member of our committee to attend and help devize strategies that will make it easier for the governments to accept inclusion of this problem on the agenda. Afaf suggested linking it with assistance for children and/or women. The overall goal is for the parties involved in the discussion to unite (minutes of the CUN, April 18, 2001).

What is striking is that even at the first meeting the subject of the conference and the direction that it would unavoidably take were not considered problematic by the committee and that the obvious intention was to realize this objective.

In the e-mail discussion carried out on APsaA OPEN LINE that is intended as a permanent discussion forum, very penetrating arguments were exchanged. Robert (Bob) Tyson wondered if it wouldn't be more advisable to send the president of the IPA, Widlöcher, to Durban or else the chair of the committee that was supposed to recognize new groups in the IPA. Shouldn't APsaA as the largest contributor to the IPA be consulted before the IPA participates in such a dangerous conference? What should be done if a resolution meaning "Zionism is Racism" is accepted? Stay there and express disapproval? Stephan F. Bauer summarizes in an email:

> History is replete with innocent bystanders who claim to have done no harm ... and yet we all know what terrible harm has been done in the name of innocence or *Realpolitik* (APsaA OPEN LINE, August 22, 2001).

Two people will go to the Durban conference: CUN chair Afaf Mahfouz and secretary Isaac Tylim. Mahfouz is an Egyptian woman who has lived in the United States since 1985 and is an American citizen. Tylim is a Jewish American of Argentine origin who lives in New York. It is an illusion that the CUN could exert any influence among the 4,000 people who represent 12,000 NGOs in Durban. What counts is that the CUN goes, on behalf of the psychoanalytic community.

When the conference started, it was obvious that it was developing into what had been feared: one of the anti-Semitic high points of post-war history. A pogrom in which Israel and the Jews are pushed under the same blanket of insults and doublespeak. The scholarly part of my conscience tells me that I should carefully separate anti-Israeli, anti-Semitic, and anti-Zionist rhetoric and not confuse them. I would like to, but in this case it is impossible. Jewish speakers were shouted off the podium. The meeting of the Jewish caucus was made impossible. Jewish participants had to walk between rows of screaming and cursing participants in order to go to their meeting. The meeting could not be held because the room was stormed. The Jewish press conference was not allowed to be held. Jews had to take off their yarmulke if they wore one, and even those who walked around bareheaded were removed from any caucus that was not Jewish. There was an attempt to speak of "holocausts/Holocaust" in the final declaration of the conference. This was an attempt to make the Shoah as a unique event, unique in its size and in its aim to make a whole people disappear from the earth, into "a detail of history" (to quote the French racist Le Pen). The Canadian lawyer David Matas (2001) writes:

> One of the disturbing and frightening facets of Durban is that the main threat to human rights did not come from governments but from NGOs whose primary agenda was anti-Semitism and anti-Zionism. Bolshevik like, they manipulated and overtook a frail disorganized structure in the nongovernmental Forum, imposing their agenda of incitement to hatred on a forum structure that required good will and cooperation in order to function.

The *Protocols of the Elders of Zion*[4] was sold in booths at the conference. At registration a booklet with anti-Semitic *Stürmer* caricatures was passed out. This booklet had been produced by the ALU, the organization that at the time was led by Afaf Mahfouz. Posters with "Hitler should have finished the job" hung on walls. In the streets people shouted "Kill the Jews".

In the forum, the place where the CUN had secured its place, Jews, Israelis, and Zionists were equated with one another and were held responsible for just about all the problems of the world. In the closing statement of the conference Israel was portrayed as an apartheid state. Until the closing statement, Israel was accused from the floor of ethnic cleansing, war crimes, genocide, and racism. The whole thing became so upsetting that the chair of the conference,

Mary Robinson, was reduced to a powerless gesture during an official dinner. Pressing the booklet with anti-Semitic caricatures to her chest, she exclaimed: "I am a Jew". The booklet was not pretty. Jews have claws instead of hands and the usual hooknoses are omnipresent. In their claws they hold blood-soaked money. Things must have got out of hand for Mary Robinson, an experienced diplomat, United Nations high commissioner for human rights, a former president of Ireland, to be beside herself with anger. The triumph of Israel-haters had become the shame of the world.

Elie Wiesel (2001) says it more succinctly:

> The conference in Durban will be remembered as a forum that was governed not by anti-Israelis but by anti-Semites. [...] What is painful is not that the Palestinians and the Arabs voiced their hatred, but the fact that so few delegates had the courage to combat them. It is as if in a strange and frightening moment of collective catharsis, everyone removed their masks and revealed their true faces.

Mary Robinson managed to limit the damage, at least as concerned the official conference. She refused to accept the draft closing statement of the NGOs as an official UN document. In this way she avoided a repetition of the 1975–1991 trauma. During that time the official doctrine was the "Zionism is Racism" resolution. This resolution threw a shadow over all the other UN work.

Where were the analytic spokesmen during this conference? In their self-appointed role of facilitators they never let their voices be heard. They did not withdraw from the conference because it did not treat the subject for which it had convened. They did not step outside their neutral role as observers as—I hope—they would do if in their office they were witnesses to violence. They remained, did not stir, went home, and wrote a report. That report was one-sided but designed as if it were neutral. It caused a lot of excitement.

All the mistrust and anger that Ruth Lax felt towards her successor is evident in her questions about the booklet with the caricatures that was passed out at the conference. She had carefully kept the question of the authorship of that booklet and Afaf Mahfouz's involvement hidden and was ready with questions for the chair of the IPA. In her last public act within the IPA, a letter dated September 21, 2001 to Professor Daniel Widlöcher, Lax wants to know: "Did she

[Afaf Mahfouz] in any way object either verbally or in writing to their [Arab Lawyers Union's] activities? Did she resign in protest to their slanderous attacks on Israel?" For anyone who is in doubt, she adds a document that was signed by Afaf Mahfouz on behalf of the ALU. Her question is bothersome because it comes from the person who brought Mahfouz into the hierarchy of the IPA. Lax shows that she has no faith in the official impartiality of the CUN chair. Inside the IPA it is as if Ruth Lax has said nothing. The establishment ignored her, and the affair was disposed of as the nagging of a frustrated member. Even more importantly: the complaints of an individual member must not harm the higher interests of the IPA.

Ms Mahfouz answers later, following considerable criticism about her report on the conference. Part of her reaction was as follows:

> My membership in the Arab Lawyers Union (ALU) has been used by some[5] as a reason to discredit me and my representation of the IPA. The ALU is the largest association serving the Arab legal profession. Like most bar associations, human rights are among its many areas of focus, and when I joined in the 1970s, I helped establish its committee on women's rights, notwithstanding strong resistance and prejudice within the organization. [...] I had nothing to do with them in Durban and in fact never attended a meeting of any Arab-related organization while there.[6]

But I am ahead of myself. First there has to be a report on the conference. First it has to be presented to the board of the IPA and then it has to be disseminated among the members. It is peculiar that the report of the committee is sometimes written in the "I" form and in other places as "we". The "I" or "we" in question is Mahfouz. However, where it suits the purpose, secretary Tylim is claimed as witness. Her main point is:

> We were in no way involved in the contentious decisions that garnered international attention. We were there so that we could make our expertise available to people who want to understand racism and who want to discuss issues of its prevention and management. [...] We felt that our presence at this Conference

THE BATTLE OF DURBAN   175

would enhance our professional profile as potential experts and consultants with the United Nations in this field.[7]

She continues about the organization of the conference:

> The local committee was formed by the South African National NGO Coalition (SANGOGO), a coalition which reflected the long struggle by the South African National Congress against apartheid and the State of Israel (during apartheid, Israel had extensive connections with South Africa and therefore is widely perceived as having supported apartheid).

The words "widely perceived" are treacherous. To me they seem like two words that could be highlighted by experts to ask what this perception is based on instead of just copying them. As is known, much of the world, including neighbouring countries of South Africa, cooperated extensively with South Africa during apartheid. It is stated that one of the organizers was SANGOGO. What is left out is that it is a vehemently anti-Israel organization. With an organizer like that, it is clear that the conference will become a hate fest, and you participate if you share that hate. Even the excuse of the mayor in wartime, "to prevent worse", does not hold up if you are in the homeopathic ratio of two to 4,000 representatives. Elie Wiesel understood that better. As a VIP, he had been consulted in the preparation of the conference by the secretary of the United Nations, Kofi Annan, and the chair of the conference, Mary Robinson. They tried to convince him to be present at the conference. However, he figured out quickly how things would go and did not undertake the journey.

In Afaf Mahfouz's report, we find out very little about the conference as such. We do find out that clergymen had been lodged in the red-light district of Durban. She also recounts that the stay was an expensive one. She does not forget to mention that the documents were not translated into French. Fidel Castro's concluding speech is mentioned, and she does not neglect to mention that it lasted two hours and 20 minutes. She speaks about politicization, but gives no details. She does say that two of the 40 caucuses were absent, one of which was Jewish. The reason for their absence is not explained and is a mystery for anyone who gets his information about this conference from this document.

She then continues about the political tensions in the Middle East and their influence on the conference: "Mutual accusations from members of SANGOGO and the International Steering Committee, particularly around the Declaration and Plan of Action, were a continuing distraction". As analyst you wonder what these tensions consisted of, who kept them going, and why. But only a factual statement is given, with the implication that it takes two to tango. The cause was not difficult to find. SANGOGO wanted a declaration in the closing document stating that Israel is a racist, apartheid state: colonialist, guilty of war crimes, of genocide, of ethnic cleansing, and of human rights violations. SANGOGO asked for the reinstatement of the "Zionism is Racism" resolution. The board did not want it. You would have expected some comments from "facilitators".

Mahfouz applies the same technique of pseudo-objectivity to voting down an amendment that labels anti-Zionism as anti-Semitism.[8] She leaves out the fact that the conference was constructed in such a way that "a voice would be given to the victims of racism". Every group that felt it was a victim of racism could itself write up the paragraph about it. The *Dalits* (the caste of untouchables in India) did this, as did the Palestinians and the victims of AIDS. Logically, Israel and the Jews would also have had the right to a paragraph formulated by them. Afaf Mahfouz gives only the content of what the Jews wanted to put in that text and lets us conclude that this was a very strongly worded and controversial view.

Furthermore, she explains that to lessen the tensions, a former chair of SANGOGO was appointed as chair of the closing meeting instead of a representative of the conference organizers. Reassuringly, she adds that this person is now a director of Civicus. That means nothing to people outside the world of NGOs, but it does mean something that the organization is now domiciled in Washington DC. She reports drily that by 38 to two Israel was described as an apartheid state, and for the reader who so desires there is the suggestion that it is true and has now been officially determined.

According to Mahfouz's report, the IPA was mainly there to listen:

and [we] were present to further contribute to the basis for long-term relationships with the United Nations. [...] I did not engage in any matters related to the Middle East, nor was I in a position to do so. Isaac Tylim made a powerful intervention at a forum organized by the All-India Women's Conference on the legacy of Gandhi.

What she leaves out is at least as important as what she reports, and amidst all these acronyms and omissions there is a mention that the reports that were produced were "praised for their objectivity". The Dutch minister of foreign affairs was less positive. In his report he speaks of a conference that was marred by "Israel-bashing".[9] But the IPA report is favourable. Afaf Mahfouz's conclusion is:

Even though during these two weeks I often felt sad, angry and sometimes depressed, I considered that I was fortunate, privileged and enriched to be able to witness, to listen and participate. It was a unique experience.

The concluding sentence, like the whole report, led to unfavourable comment. Worried questions and remarks were sent to the IPA, and the president answered a very short email note from the well-known New York analyst Arnold Richards, dated September 19, 2001, as follows: "I hope that the IPA will be able to provide information about the participation in Durban to the members of the American",[10] and "I understand and share your concern about the Durban meetings. I have asked the Chair of our United Nations Committee to send me a detailed report on what happened in the NGO organisation" (e-mail dated September 21, 2001, from Susan Bouchet, Daniel Widlöcher's assistant). In an official declaration Widlöcher once more underlines the objective of the IPA ("to make psychoanalysis visible and heard in the United Nations system") and goes along with an illusion by saying that "our Committee was not engaged in political issues" (letter dated September 25, 2001, to all members of the IPA). The theoretical artifice that no position is taken by doing nothing (and that the report was neutral) is untenable. Mahfouz's sadness and depression may be genuine, but by being silent and glossing over she has become an accessory.

Subsequently, moving forward in the line of being officially in the right, there appeared an official four-point explanation from the president of the IPA.[11] The first two points state that the IPA is absolutely against all forms of religious and social discrimination and against all forms of racism, but is for democracy. The last two points state:

3. The chaotic and poorly organized conditions at the NGO Forum parallel to the UN World Conference in Durban allowed for the expression of unacceptable declarations of hate and prejudice as well as for some political manoeuvring which was totally contrary to the values and aims of the IPA.
4. The IPA, while represented at the Forum and the Conference was in no way involved with any political activities and completely dissociated itself from such political activities at the NGO Forum.

The last point contradicts the tone and content of the report that most certainly was biased, but the president does not give his opinion about that. There is also a reaction from Washington, this time from Warren Poland who voices his opinion loud and clear.[12] He wonders whether the sentence "Israel is widely perceived as having supported apartheid" belongs in a psychoanalytic report. Poland also wonders "whether personal biases entered unduly into the functioning of our committee in a battle that matters greatly and that is not psychoanalytic". Pendred writes "paranoia" in the margin. Poland then gets to his most important point: "We analysts [...] know that we communicate by our silence as well as by what we say". He wishes to thank the CUN for its valuable work and hopes that the committee's old members will be replaced by new ones.

Tylim, the secretary of the CUN, is fed up with being accused of "misrepresenting the IPA" by opponents of the CUN. He states:

> I am saddened by their naïveté and mean spirit. Dr. Mahfouz is a pioneer within the IPA. Her efforts on behalf of psychoanalysis in this troubled world are bound to leave a marker in the history of our discipline.

On October 26, 2001, Poland writes a letter to Daniel Widlöcher in which he calls the explanation of the IPA "too little and too late":

> While you propose a statement repudiating racism both at Durban and in general, you continue to accept the report of the IPA committee to Durban, a report that stunningly glosses over what happened in Durban, that glosses over their role in Durban. [...] Having the feeling that supporting the IPA at this time would feel like a betrayal of the values that I have always cherished as a psychoanalyst and as an individual, I resign my membership in the IPA.

He remarked in passing that the CUN report was still on the IPA website.[13]

In expressive language Michel Feldman touches the point where Arab and Christian hate meet the Jew. He writes to the president of the IPA as follows:

> May I tell you that what happened in Durban to my mind was a disaster, akin to what I as a Jewish boy that grew in Catholic Brazil witnessed: Every Easter the Catholic boys would build a dummy made out of old cloths and papers, they would dress it in old clothes, and in the Hallelujah Saturday (following Easter's Sunday) they would bring it to the streets and would invite all the neighbouring boys and girls to come and join "The Lynch Of Judas"—of course, Judas Iscariot, the Jew that sold Jesus for 30 coins. This Lynch certainly was made by beating the dummy relentlessly until it was half destroyed, and then it was hung up and burned. [...] Well, to my mind. Durban was a repetition of the Lynching of Judas. And the IPA was there, and said nothing. And Dr. Mahfouz was there and said nothing. [...] She apparently was not able to address there or in her report the real issue—namely, that again racism was being concretely performed live and fresh (October 30, 2001).

This letter coincides in time with an open letter from about 50 members who could not stand the whitewashing and the praising of the conference by the report. They write that "Durban practiced both organized racism and double standards in the name of opposing them". Then they continue:

> ... when Jews were dehumanized, booed, and physically threatened, our IPA committee, according to its own report, did not leave, did not effectively protest, did not ineffectively protest, did not try to protest, did not even send out a critical press release.

The members who feel that the CUN has not done its work well see a clear line "between the depths of Durban and the heights of what was once the World Trade Center". According to them it was not a simple fabrication:

> It [hatred] begins with projection. It is given voice as inflammatory speech. It is repeated to children, seeks out public approbation. It is encouraged by the silence of those who might oppose it, and, thus encouraged, lobbies for international sanction, which appears to give it external justification, and supports the transformation of feelings and of speech; the final response to this distortion does not constitute containment, but collusion.[14]

The letter concludes as follows: "We ask you to reconstitute this committee so that it may do good; or, if you refuse, to begin the process of disbanding it lest it do more harm and divide our organization further".

Afaf Mahfouz writes to Widlöcher that she has seen many expressions of support for her report (in the IPA papers that were sent to me, there were four or five out of about 90 that I saw about the affair). But Mahfouz also mentions some divergent opinions and writes: "I apologize if my parenthetically explaining the historical relationship that existed between Israel and South Africa in the past was seen as targeting Israel as responsible". She apologizes for saying it. However, she does not say that what she mentioned was not true, at least not exclusively. Then she gets to her most important defence: "Before I left for Durban, Professor Widlöcher, you instructed me not to take any public position on behalf of the IPA; to do so would require approval of the Executive Committee, which I did not have". That, in addition to her personal prestige as a professor and experienced lobbyist, gives her the courage to write, in a letter dated October 30, 2001 to Daniel Widlöcher:

> To give up the relationship with the UN may provide satisfaction to some, but the profession would be the loser, setting back the IPA pioneering effort to bring the process and power of psychoanalysis to bear in an appropriately balanced manner upon the international arena.

The affair had its consequences. Afaf Mahfouz was allowed to stay as chair of the CUN, and this could be seen as a victory for her. It was because of her argument that the board had instructed her not to take any position. This was accepted by the board of the IPA. A memorandum from the president, dated November 9, 2001, declared:

> The Committee in no way endorsed or supported the quite unacceptable activities at the NGO Forum in Durban, and the NGO Declaration, elements of which include inflammatory and profoundly offensive and discriminatory language related to Israel, which have infected the document and brought all of it into question.

The board accepted the blame for the CUN not leaving the conference. In a letter to Mary Robinson and Kofi Annan it dissociates itself completely from the final report of the NGOs. There is appreciation for what Mahfouz and her colleagues were able to accomplish for the IPA through their various activities for the United Nations.

Justice was done quietly to the furious opposition inside the IPA. Although the leadership of the committee remained in the hands of Afaf Mahfouz, temporary members were added for every future activity for the United Nations. In fact this meant that the governing board of the CUN was placed under strict restraint. For this purpose, senior consultants were appointed inside the committee. These were psychoanalytic and organizational heavyweights, among them two former IPA presidents, Otto Kernberg and Robert Wallerstein, a prominent theoretician, André Green from Paris, and Avigail Golomb from Israel.

A Contemporary Anti-Semitism Working Group was also created with Janine Chasseguet-Smirgel as chair. It was a committee that would get bogged down in a task that was too extensive. Its creation was clearly the result if the Durban conference. Its goal was to collect material about the outbreak of anti-Semitic incidents in the entire community of nations inside the representative structures of the United Nations and the governmental bodies connected to it. Understanding for the project would be needed, and suggestions for how to approach it had to be made.

The result was disappointing. Documents were produced, sometimes of excellent quality, but there was no final report. This was due not only to the monumental size of the task but also to a lack of common perspective inside the committee and the illness of the chair who no longer had the energy to compile it. Theoretical documents alternate with what is taking place in the authors' respective countries.[15] I am very tempted to quote from the theoretical discussions of several contributing authors because I am increasingly puzzled about the origin of the ever-present stigma of anti-Semitism, and some writers have a good understanding of it.[16]

With goals that were too extensive, between an analysis of the question and its attempt to solve the problem, the committee was unable to come up with a sensible report. Underneath it was the very knotty and very real IPA problem: the still unresolved relationship between the psychoanalytic and the Jewish heritage. More is needed for that than just a committee.

Notes

1. The author interviewed Ruth Lax, Marion Oliner, Warren Poland, and Arnold Richards.
2. From a concluding description of the activities of the CUN by IPA president Daniel Widlöcher.
3. Memorandum of Afaf Mahfouz, PhD, chair, Committee on the United Nations, dated September 14, 2001, to the IPA Executive Committee.
4. The myth fabricated under the Czarist regime in which Jews supposedly say that they want to rule the world.
5. Really? Only by the former chair of CUN! To me this seems a hidden but still clear hint at a Jewish conspiracy.

6. A letter dated November 1, 2001 to Professor Daniel Widlöcher, intended for the IPA message board and APsaA OPEN LINE.
7. In the following paragraphs I quote from:

> Afaf Mahfouz, PhD, chair, Committee on the United Nations. United Nations World Conference Against Racism. Memorandum to: IPA Executive Committee. Subject: Report on the Durban Conference—The World Conference Against Racism, Racial Discrimination, Xenophobia and Related Intolerance (WCAR). Date: September 14, 2001.

This is part of a series of official documents about the conference. The others are:

- Introductory memorandum from Daniel Widlöcher, IPA president.
- Statement from the president, September 25, 2001.
- Statement from the president, October 25, 2001.
- Statement from the president, November 9, 2001.
- Letter to the UN High Commissioner for Human Rights, November 9, 2001.
- Response from the UN High Commissioner for Human Rights, November 27, 2001.

8. "We are concerned with the prevalence of anti-Zionism and attempts to delegitimize the State of Israel through wildly inaccurate charges of genocide, war crimes, crimes against humanity, ethnic cleansing and apartheid, as a virulent contemporary form of anti-Semitism leading to fire-bombing of synagogues, armed assaults against Jews, incitement to killing, and murder of innocent Jews, for their support for the existence of the State of Israel, the assertion of the right of self-determination of the Jewish people and the attempts, through the State of Israel, to preserve their cultural and religious identity" (memorandum of Afaf Mahfouz to the IPA Executive Committee, September 14, p. 4).
9. Letter dated February 5, 2002, from the minister of foreign affairs to the presiding officer of the Second Chamber of the States General of the Netherlands.
10. Short for APsaA.
11. Circulated in various places, among other places on the website. The first time it appears in these documents is to the members of the CUN and is dated October 17, 2001.

12. Letter to Daniel Widlöcher and M. Gibeault, distributed on the APsaA OPEN LINE on October 19, 2001.
13. It was still on the website in 2007.
14. Open letter dated October 26, 2001, of almost 50 analysts to IPA president Daniel Widlöcher.
15. Germany, France, Greece, Austria, Sweden, and Finland.
16. An outstanding article is an old contribution (1990) by the chair, Janine Chasseguet-Smirgel. She reminds us of Freud's statement that his purpose was not so much to cure the sick but to "understand the mysteries of the world". Also worth reading are two contributions by the French political scientist Daniel Dayan after the meeting of October 6, 2002: (*Quelques Pistes, notamment méthodologiques à explorer en termes d"analyse et d"action; 13 remarques sur la judéophobie contemporaine, en France.*) There is much worthy of quoting here. The sentence that struck me most was that Jewish writers like Bernard-Henri Lévy, Finkielkraut, and Glucksmann participate in the public debate "dishonored by a yellow star". The German political scientist Gunnar Heimsohn delivered a lecture about *Seven Varieties of Anti-Judaism* and a 20 page lecture about *Why the Jews?*—both worth reading. My knowledge about the activities of the committee also dates from a visit that I paid to Janine Chasseguet-Smirgel half a year before her death in 2005. She recounted them and made the written documents available to me.

CHAPTER NINE

Conclusion

As I have already indicated in the introduction, the subject has shifted during the writing of this book. Originally I had thought of a history of psychoanalysis as a Jewish occupation. I wanted to observe the consequences of this perception in the non-Jewish world. The reason for the original concept was the extreme reactions that it always generated. From its beginning psychoanalysis always had to deal with absurd rejection and equally absurd adoration, irrational contempt and equally irrational glorification. Jews have always run up against a similar jumble. It is simple to give examples of the adoration and glorification. Freud-bashing is a clear example of the vilification. The glorification with the ironic undertone of the surrealists and of some analysts shows the other side of the coin. I have already written about Freud-bashing in a discussion of Crews. And I still agree with what I wrote as an editorial in the *Tijdschrift voor Psychoanalyse* (Journal for Psychoanalysis):

> The persecution of Freud as a person is becoming increasingly vicious and unrestrained. The same kind of stereotyping that is the fundamental structure of ordinary anti-Semitism is applied to him with all force. He seems to be not a man who has been

> wrong, but he is all wrong—his origins are no good, his work is a fraud, and he cannot stop lying. He is only interested in money, power, fame, and sex. Nothing he has done was right. The sympathy of later commentators with Emma Eckstein who was treated incorrectly by Fliess is the thin layer of ice on which floats the satisfaction about the mistakes that Freud made when he was consulted by Fliess. This old story is now told again as new for the tenth time.
>
> A new scandal has been found: at least for me. It is about a Mr Frank where it is not clear what Freud's role was in that unfortunate story, but the author knows his intent: *Freud's transparent aim was to get his own hands on some of the heiress Bijur's money* (Reijzer, 1996, p. 130).

I became more fascinated by the analysts' handling of the Jewish background of analysis, or more precisely by their handling of Jews and Jewish questions. I am shocked by Massud Khan's abusive treatment of his Jewish patients. I am concerned about Bollas's bias towards Israel as a Jewish state. Dutch analysts have come to my attention twice: the first time because of their treatment of Jewish analysts as refugees, and the second time as opponents of post-war compensation for material and emotional damage. At the highest IPA level the psychoanalytic community has shown itself to be a well-protected spectator of a large pogrom.

In reporting all these incidents, my thoughts went back to Freud's fit of rage (described by Wittels) against the Viennese-Jewish circle around him. Freud ended by exclaiming: "The Swiss will save us—will save me—and that will include you". That position turned out to be professionally correct, even though the Swiss, and certainly Jung, did not do much to save psychoanalysis. Yet, psychoanalysis is on the map, although its place on the map has always remained in dispute. And that is all the more so for the Jews in the profession who are the inhabitants of the marked landscape, even though they sometimes seem to control the terrain.

In the incidents and affairs described in this book there is, according to me, a thread that has to do with ordinary prejudices towards Jews and an attitude towards them that is meant to shape the distance between psychoanalysis and the anti-Semitic stereotypes that sometimes affect it. The Jewish analysts are involved in the situation

CONCLUSION 187

in such a way that they have to reconcile their Jewish identity with their analytical one, or distance themselves from it more or less pointedly if they want to feel at home in the analytic community.

Coincidence is not coincidental. Individuals and organizations show themselves in their doings, in what they reveal and in what they conceal. Utterances, events, large and small incidents have a meaning as expressions by individuals and have added meaning when you realize fully that they reflect a social reality. What I have described in the preceding chapters is about movements in the Freud, psychoanalysis, and Jewish legacy triangle. In that light I attach meaning to a CUN or a Freud Museum that each in their own way work on improving the world and incidentally want to elevate the status of analysis and to do this choose to undermine Israel's moral right of existence. I pay attention to people who slip up in unexpected contempt and hate, in which I do not primarily see the pathology of the anti-Semite but instead a clever positioning inside the psychoanalytic world and inside the greater world of which they are part.

Towards Jews I see an assumed right to feel superior, to make room for self-interest and for this to remove obstacles, with violence if necessary. It gives me a shock when a friendship of Pfister with Freud is not as intimate as it seems, but is strained by a misplaced feeling of superiority on the part of the minister. If the latter had not been friendly with Freud, no one would ever have heard of him. Yet he thinks he is better: steeped in love for and by Jesus. If I bundle the narrative lines into one outline, it is too rough to see an image of nothing but anti-Semitic aversion in it. I do not believe that, just as I do not believe the total lack of it after 2,000 years of preached anti-Semitism. In our secularized world I do see that there must be *Children of a Lesser God*: that is most likely an ordinary social phenomenon. But it is too bad that Jews get to fill that role so often and so insistently.

What the incidents have in common is that psychoanalysts, in order to make headway, have had to distance themselves as pointedly as possible from the appearance of being Jewish. Starting with Freud, Jews can be members of the psychoanalytic movement, but when they act as psychoanalysts they have to forget that they are Jewish and their Judaism is reduced to a religion. In principle psychoanalysts are not Jewish at all. There is nothing Jewish about psychoanalysis, because Judaism is not free, not enlightened, and not modern; besides, psychoanalysts *examine* religion, they have freed themselves from its practice.

What has struck me in studying the material is that biting anti-Semitism is carried out not only by a number of non-Jewish analysts but also by Jews. For non-Jewish analysts I think that it could be anti-Semitism, conscious or not; after all, why should that not occur among them? For Jews it is more complicated. I find the term "Jewish self-hate" insufficient for this form of damage to the self; it makes a social phenomenon too personal. If there is a question of a personal reaction, then "identification with the aggressor" seems more appropriate. But I think that the explanation is simpler. Inside the psychoanalytic world it is often a question of taking the appropriate steps to obtain entrance to the holy of holies: the status of approved psychoanalyst. Too great an identification with something else is not convenient for this. Moreover, Judaism is extra inconvenient because of its social connotations—disidentification is therefore required. Apparently that is not the case in New York. There, a number of analysts—primarily Jews—acted forcefully when they decided that their organization had made a mistake in the Israeli-Palestinian question. In Amsterdam there fortunately was the dissenting voice of "the five" who felt that "strong anti-Semitic outbursts" should not go unnoticed.

For psychoanalysis to become adult, it is necessary for it to distance itself from Freud. Freud also had to free himself from the circle around him and from his own ancestors. Hostility is part of that. I am not referring to ordinary Oedipal anger, but about a lashing out that is necessary to create space around oneself in order to be able to enter the larger world. It is also not the hostility that is part of freeing oneself in order to become oneself. Shaking off Jewishness is more violent. It can only be understood when the reputation of Jewishness, as contaminated by the undesirable, is kept in mind. Above all, it is not Sigmund Freud freeing himself from his father Jakob. That is too personal an explanation of an important social phenomenon.

Strong images are attached to the concept of Jewishness. There is, for example, Shylock's *three thousand ducats,* the caricature of the Jew that Shakespeare carved forever into the European mind. In *Operation Shylock,* Philip Roth (1994) shows how the Jews have lived under the curse of these three words for 400 years. According to the same source, in London in the second half of the 20th century *The Merchant of Venice* was the most frequently performed Shakespeare play after *Hamlet*. This and other images such as the evangelical "His blood be on us and on our children" have to a great extent determined the history of the Jews.

The Jews lived very visibly but isolated, with their own laws and customs. The image that they have of themselves is influenced by the other, the non-Jew. Being Jewish has for centuries been defined negatively, as being different: not Christian. That view, even when it was hostile, has become an integral part of the Jews' own experience. Freeing oneself from Jewishness is necessary in order to become part of what is modern, normal, and good. The fact that this is considered difficult lies in a hidden meaning of Judaism as a religion: old and worthy of respect is said admiringly, but also obsolete and vengeful. It is easy to add: not yet touched by the love that is part of the New Testament.

In chapter five I described how difficult it was to organize a congress in Jerusalem, and with how much fuss and fanfare and truly-felt relief the presence of the psychoanalysts in Jerusalem was celebrated in 1977. It was a homecoming in a house that had previously been declared uninhabitable. As a consequence of Jerusalem, the congress could go to Hamburg eight years later. A symbolic equality, as if the Second World War had been a struggle between two parties that could now be accepted once again on their mother's psychoanalytic lap. Germany has subsequently become so normal that Berlin could welcome the next congress in 2007. The Netherlands hosted the IPA congress four times, three of which were after the Second World War. For Israel it has remained a one-off. That is not a coincidence. It is a way of keeping as great a distance as possible from Jewishness, which is so dangerous and also dangerously close for psychoanalysis.

What had to be avoided at all costs and what Freud fought against has happened nonetheless: transference has descended on psychoanalysis as it did on Jews (Blumenberg, 1996). Blumenberg, whom I have quoted earlier, distinguishes two levels: first the analyst is seen as belonging to the group of persecuted and murdered Jews, and secondly it is assumed that the analytic theory is a "Jewish theory". One of the ways he demonstrates this is with a cover of the German weekly *Der Spiegel* of July 25, 1994, that figures a *Stürmer*-like portrait of Freud with the caption "Fraud or Healer?".

Again I refer to Philip Roth to describe what this can mean. In an extensive monologue in which Marx, Einstein, Saul Bellow, and Arthur Miller among others are tossed away like garbage, he let an anti-Semite say:

> Because there were no gas chambers, as we now found out. From chemistry. Which is hard science. Freud. That was soft science. Masson over at Berkeley has now proved that Freud's basic research was false because he did not believe these women when they talked about how they were abused. Sexually abused. Because he said society wouldn't accept it. So he changed it to child sexuality. That Siggy (1994, pp. 253–254).

The images that exist about Jewishness colour the images of the psychoanalytic, as I have stated in an extensive quote from Loewenstein and Frosh in my introduction.

The importance of this unconsciously known transference is at the root of a countertransference from the psychoanalytic organizations and their members. Within the profession people act as if they tacitly think: Freud may have been Jewish; it may be that the circle around him was Jewish; it may be that a number of psychoanalysts are Jewish; but psychoanalysis is a normal profession, and there should be nothing Jewish about it, and when nonetheless there seems to be, something needs to be done about it. I consider this mentality to be one of the motivating forces behind all the incidents that I have described.

When Wille (2005) constructs a psychoanalytic identity, he tolerates very little room next to it. Analogous developments can be found in organizations. They, too, have a history and pass through an evolution of what they are, what they want, and what they can do. They, too, have to take up a place in the world. And this has to be fought for inside the organization and against the other. By this I mean that the supposed Jewishness and the actual Jewish character of psychoanalysis have considerably hampered its development. It always had to watch out not to be too Jewish.

Gilman (1994) uses analysis—and Freud—as a key to understanding German and European anti-Semitism. In the second half of the 19th century, the concept of "race" was central in the social sciences. It was also assumed that Jews were a race, a lesser race to be exact. Race in that sense is a combination of physical characteristics and social circumstances and above all of ascribed characteristics. Illnesses that in a biological sense cannot be attributed to a race get, in a social sense, a meaning that does bind them. A number of physical diseases are genetically connected to Jews. Tay-Sachs disease and the Bloom syndrome are the best known. In the 19th century, hysteria was added as a race characteristic. If this is a disease that occurs primarily among Jews, then it is at least important to pay attention to the social position of that group. Gilman says that "[T]he most important question is how the category *Jewish diseases* was used to create the image of the Jew as contaminated and therefore likely a contagious member of the people among whom he lives". For this he uses a poem of Heinrich Heine, a pre-eminent expert on Jewishness. I quote Gilman's translation of the first three stanzas:

The Jewish hospital in Hamburg

A hospital for poor, sick Jews,
for people afflicted with threefold misery,
with three evil maladies
poverty, physical pain, and Jewishness.

The last-named is the worst of all the three:
that thousand-year-old family complaint,
the plague they dragged with them from the Nile valley,
the unhealthy faith from ancient Egypt.

Incurable, profound suffering. No help can be looked for
from steam-baths, shower-baths, or all the
implements of surgery, or all the medicines
which this house offers it sick inmates.

Gilman's point is that "[I]t was inconceivable that a practitioner of the social sciences would be able to free himself from the concept of race that was so central in the 19th century". The Jewish scientists, who were considered to be different, had to accept that this was true. As professionals they had to acknowledge that they were less by birth, or at least prove that this was not the case for them. They did this reluctantly because with their status as scientist they rose above that of Jew. Gilman lets science declare the following about the Jew of that time: "What I say is true because it is impartial, and what I say is that you are sick. And my impartiality gives me a special—and powerful—position in the new world that is defined by science".

For any practitioner of a profession this is an unpleasant and paralyzing position. It is particularly true for the physician because Hippocrates, in his description of *The Physician*, starts as follows: "The dignity of a physician requires that he should look healthy, and as plump as nature intended him to be; for the common crowd consider those who are not of excellent bodily condition to be unable to take care of others". To escape this, it is continually necessary to distance oneself from Jewishness, as we saw in chapter 1 in the incident described by Wittels and Sadger. Jews have to cleanse themselves by baptism or otherwise adapt to the non-Jewish reality so that they are invisible. No matter what, they have to know their place.

Gilman quotes from *The Essence of Judaism* by the psychoanalyst Otto Rank who wrote that the Jews had a "parasitic existence among the people with whom they were living" (op. cit., p. 25). In this quote the word "they" is a bit complicated. Rank acts as if he is studying a strange kind of insect and is revealing some of its characteristics to the reader. But Rank, one of the founders of the psychoanalytic movement and for many years secretary of the Wednesday evening group that gathered around Freud, was born a Jew in 1884. Rosenfeld was his last name, and he changed it to Rank. When he was 19, he changed his religion from *Jewish* to *none* on the civil registry form of the city of Vienna. This did not prevent Jones from calling him a "swindling Jew". Jones has always denied that he said that, but he could not deny that he had written that Rank's "general way of conducting business was distinctly Oriental". When this remark to A. A. Brill came to Freud's attention, he had already become a "swindling Jew" among the gossips. Jones called this remark highly exaggerated (Grosskurth McGrath, 1993).

Within the psychoanalytic world this distancing behaviour with respect to Jews is determined in multiple ways. Professionally there are all sorts of reasons not to get too close. Within the profession this distance is taken up socially as I have described in several instances. In the analytic processes the optimal "closeness while retaining distance" (Rümke) is an axiom. The patient is lying down; the analyst is sitting. The analyst must hold a blank mirror up to the patient—at least that was the starting point in Freud's time. You wonder what kind of dirt it might have had on it. By not calling each other by their first names, analyst and patient keep each other at a distance. There is an atmosphere of non-negotiability in psychoanalysis. Patients have to adjust their schedule to the hours that the analyst has available. As a rule, appointments cannot be cancelled or moved. For me it is beyond dispute that such an analytic contract is useful for treatment. But in the subject matter of this book I see above all a medicalization of the personal that is promised and eliminated. Psychoanalysis may treat unclean subjects, but the treatment is clean and is carried out with surgical precision by clean people with sterilized hands.

I see the wish to be autonomous, to have an independent sphere of activity and thinking, detached from the origin of its founders, as a significant motive in psychoanalysis to react against the element that is seen as Jewish: a very normal wish that has a special slant because of the Jewish connection. The acquisition of autonomy is the process by which the individual binds himself to his history by breaking away from it. In the present there are also tasks that have to be carried out to survive, to love, and to work. Later the individual gets something that can be called an identity. Father, mother, and the whole history of the family are of vital importance for what you will become and have become. Identity presupposes a knowledge of limits, knowing what you want and what you can do and knowing who you are, a continuity in the person. Within it are long lines of history that are realized in the present and stick out above it.

De Swaan (2005) describes very expressively how Israel's behaviour arouses "anti-Israel enthusiasm". Perceived misbehaviour by Israel causes a sigh of relief: now at least it is possible to lash out at that country, its inhabitants, and its government. Similar behaviour towards Jews can also be seen in the psychoanalytic world. There the opinion is expressed, hesitantly, that Jewish moaning should now stop. Who do they think they are with their traumas? At most, our patients. Chapter Six of this book and the interview with Meltzer demonstrate this in no uncertain terms. In short, Jews are accepted in the professional world, but they have to know their place and above all they should not drag psychoanalysis down with their own dubious reputation.

There is still another aspect of the distanced attention that psychoanalysis uses to look at its Jewish origin: with shame, whether or not vicarious. Psychoanalysts, no matter what their origin, do not want to be shamed by the Jewish stain as such. In the world around them, opponents of psychoanalysis—with hints that are not always comprehensible but certainly useful—use the association with Jewishness to distance themselves from psychoanalysis. The "Oberhuber" quote shows that Freud felt that if psychoanalysis had not been considered Jewish, its reception would have been better.

In the Netherlands the psychoanalyst Louis Tas has become a preeminent authority on shame. In discussing his diary from Bergen-Belsen, he tells the story about his Uncle Hans:

> As an adolescent, you hear adults say things that stay with you all your life. My father was a psychiatrist and had, as I mentioned before, an older brother, Uncle Hans, who was in business. Hans was a playboy type. He made no secret of the fact that he would have preferred not to be Jewish, but anyway ... Hans was interested in charity but not in social problems. Several months after *Reichskristallnacht* in 1938, some Jewish refugees who had just been released from concentration camps came to the Netherlands. Their heads had been shaved and they kept silent about their experiences. My father, Uncle Hans, and I (17) wondered why. It wasn't my father the psychiatrist but the more worldly Uncle Hans who figured out the explanation. In a tone that was unusual for him, Uncle Hans said: *They are ashamed because they were treated so badly*. The realization of belonging to a group that could be humiliated and mistreated with impunity caused feelings of shame (Vogel, 2000).[1]

An individual or a group does not want to feel ashamed or blush—and certainly not the psychoanalytic group that is the keeper of what is ordinary, normal, and healthy: the arbitrator who is healthy himself and who has at least worked through his unhealthiness. Shame appears when you are powerless when facing others and are no longer capable of giving form to your life. Psychoanalysis as treatment has as a goal to be freer from oppressive forces. That is why the psychoanalyst has undergone a training analysis, to be able to handle his unconscious more freely. Laplanche and Pontalis, the authors of the *Psychoanalytic Dictionary* (1973), quote Ferenczi as follows about training analysis, which "also serves to know and control hidden weaknesses of one's own personality, which is impossible without a fully completed analysis" (p. 283). In France psychoanalytic training is topped by a *Passe*: "a procedure introduced by Lacan, as the moment when the effects of a psychoanalytic treatment are verified by subjects who want to go from the position of analysand to analyst" (K. Libbrecht in Stroeken, 2000, p. 156). There should be no spots on so much perfection.

Finally a story that contains shame, perhaps also rebellion against parents, perhaps hate, but also political calculation. It is about the life of the psychoanalyst Heinz Kohut, whose biography should be read by those who want to know more about him (Strozier, 2001). There is a very strange aspect to the life of this Jew from Vienna. He emigrated to the United States in 1938, right after finishing his medical studies. He settled in Chicago where he became a psychiatrist and psychoanalyst. He was quite prominent in developing concepts and also in politics inside the psychoanalytic world.[2]

For this book the interesting thing is not that he was baptized, but that he showed a lack of knowledge about Judaism that was highly unusual even among non-Jews in Amsterdam, a large city where Jews have lived for centuries. The latter would most likely not order a ham and cheese sandwich with a glass of milk in a kosher deli and then make a scene when that request was not honoured. Kohut did this in the company of his friends, Paul and Anna Ornstein. When he ordered, the server said that the request could not be honoured because it was a kosher restaurant. Kohut then answered in a loud voice that this was a public place where whatever the client ordered should be served. When Strozier asked Kohut's son Thomas whether this story was correct, the latter could not remember the incident but did not doubt it: "Father did this sort of thing so often that he couldn't remember this specific time". The unusual thing about this anecdote is not that Kohut was Jewish but that he was reared in a traditional Jewish way, even though his mother went along with the custom in assimilated Viennese-Jewish circles to decorate their homes with a Christmas tree in December.

It also seems strange that the analysands did not know that Kohut was Jewish. Strozier tells about a man (Barglow), who was Jewish, from Europe, married to a non-Jewish woman, and was in training analysis with Kohut. From his relationship with Kohut he did not know that Kohut had started out as a Jew and that he, too, was a European immigrant. This could be psychoanalytical discretion. But Kohut also kept his Jewish background hidden as much as possible from the Ornsteins. Strozier describes this as follows:

> With Anna [who had survived Auschwitz], for the most part he seemed to try to bracket that part of her experience so it could be bypassed, ignored. He kept from her the full extent of his own Jewish past, but she knew that the Nazis had forced him to flee Austria. His failure to talk about the Jewish part of himself, to put it forward in some meaningful sense, left Anna feeling "betrayed by him".

To Paul Ornstein, who visited him monthly for supervision until Kohut's death and who became the editor of his *Collected Papers*, Kohut said: "Paul, you must often have wondered about my Jewishness. [...] I settled this issue for myself a long time ago. My father was Jewish. I am not. I made that choice a long time ago" (Strozier, 2001, pp. 187–188). That was simply not true. His mother was a member of the Jewish Lample family, even though she was mysterious about it. For him the analytic identity had to supersede his origins.

Psychoanalysis is not a Jewish science, of course not.

Notes

1. The fact that Loden Vogel is the pseudonym of Louis Tas is no secret. It was revealed in the introduction by A. van Dantzig and by the author himself. The book contains the candid report of the stay in Bergen-Belsen of Louis Tas and his father and mother. Eventually he writes a *Brief an eine Deutsche*, which contains this quote.
2. He developed a conceptual network that can be summarized under the heading of *Self Psychology*, was president of the most important American psychoanalytic organization, APsaA, and had a very good chance of becoming the president of the IPA, where he was already vice-president, until he encountered unexpected opposition.

REFERENCES

Abram, I. (2002). "Alle tranen zijn zout". Over multicultureel leren in opvoeding en onderwijs ("All tears are salty". About multicultural teaching in education and learning). In: J. C. C. Rupp & Veudelers, W. (Eds.), *Moreel-politieke heroriëntatie in het onderwijs*. Antwerpen-Apeldoorn: Garant, pp. 220–226.

Alexander, E., Popov, N. & Lange, M. (2003). Edward Said's parting shots. Grad Washington. Edu. May 20.

Antonovsky, A. M. (1988). Aryan analysts in Nazi Germany: questions of adaptation, desymbolization, and betrayal. *Psychoanalysis and Contemporary Thought, II*: 213–232.

Arendt, H. (1951). *The Origins of Totalitarianism*. New York: Harcourt Brace, 1973.

Arendt, H. (1961). *Eichmann in Jerusalem: a report on the banality of evil*. Introduction by Elon, A. New York: Penguin, 2006.

Ascher, J. & Wilgowicz, P. (2002). Judaïsme et psychanalyse (Judaism and psychoanalysis). In: *Dictionnaire International de Psychanalyse*. Paris: Calman Levy.

Auden, W. H. (1940). *Another Time*. New York: Random House.

Bakan, D. (1958). *Sigmund Freud and the Jewish Mystical Tradition*. Boston: Beacon Press.

Beland, H. (1988). How they know themselves: confronting the past—a contribution to the history of the German Psychoanalytic Association. *Psychoanalysis and Contemporary Thought*, *II*: 267–284.

Benjamin, J., Bowie, M., Bollas, C., Forrester, J., Green, A., Kristeva, J., Lear, J., Mitchell, J., Phillips, A., Pontalis, J.-B., Rose, J. & Safouan, M. (2001). Freud Memorial Lecture. *London Review of Books*, 23(6).

Berman, E. (2002). Beyond analytic anonymity: on the political involvement of psychoanalysts and psychotherapists in Israel. In: Bunzl, J. & Beit-Hallahmi, B. (Eds.), *Psychoanalysis, Identity and Ideology: Critical Essays on the Israel/Palestine Case*. Boston: Kluwer, pp. 141–177.

Bernstein, F. (1926). *Der Antisemitismus als Gruppenerscheinung: Versuch einer Soziologie des Judenhasses* (Anti-Semitism as a group phenomenon: towards a sociology of anti-Semitism). Berlin: Jüdischer Verlag.

Bernstein, P. F. (2009). *The Social Roots of Discrimination: the Case of the Jews*. With a new introduction by Bernard, M. S. van Praag. Piscataway, NJ: Transaction Publishers.

Bettelheim, B. (1979). *Surviving and Other Essays*. New York: Alfred A. Knopf.

Blumenberg, Y. (1995). IV Rezensionen (Four Reviews), Dührssen, A. (1994). Ein Jahrhundert psychoanalytische Bewegung in Deutschland: die Psychotherapie unter dem Einfluß Freuds (A century of the psychoanalytic movement in Germany: psychotherapy under the influence of Freud). Göttingen: Vandenhoeck und Ruprecht. *Luzifer-Amor: Zeitschrift zur Geschichte der Psychoanalyse*, 8(15): 153–175.

Blumenberg, Y. (1996). Psychoanalyse—eine jüdische Wissenschaft? (Psychoanalysis—A Jewish science?). *Forum der Psychoanalyse*, 12: 156–179.

Blumenberg, Y. (1997). Freud—ein "gottloser Jude"? Zur Frage der jüdischen Wurzeln der Psychoanalyse (Freud—a "Godless Jew"? The question of the Jewish roots of psychoanalysis). *Luzifer-Amor: Zeitschrift zur Geschichte der Psychoanalyse*, 10(19): 33–80.

Blumenberg, Y. (2006). "Der Jude ist selbst zur Frage geworden" (E. Jabès) oder: "Die Annahme des Vaters" (S. Freud) ("The Jew has become the question himself" (E. Jabès) or: "the father's acceptance" (S. Freud)). In: Hergener, W. (Ed.). *Das unmögliche Erbe. Antisemitismus Judentum Psychoanalyse*. Giessen: Psychosozial-Verlag.

Blumenthal, R. (2006). Hotel log hints at desire that Freud didn't repress. *International Herald Tribune*, December 24.

Bollas, C. (1992). *Being a Character: Psychoanalysis and Self Experience*. London: Routledge.

Bollas, C. (2003). Introducing Jacqueline Rose. In: Said, E. W. *Freud and the Non-European*. London: Verso, published in association with the Freud Museum.

REFERENCES 199

Brabant, E. (Ed.) (1993). *The correspondence of Sigmund Freud and Sándor Ferenczi. Volume I, 1908–1914*. Hoffer, P. T. (Trans.). London: Belknap.

Bräutigam, W. (1984). Rückblick auf das Jahr 1942: Betrachtungen eines psychoanalytischen Ausbildungskandidaten des Berliner Instituts des Kriegsjahre (Review of the year 1942: Reflections of a candidate for psychoanalytical training at the Berlin Institute during the war). *Psyche, 38*: 905–915.

Brecht, K. (1988). Adaptation and resistance: reparation and the return of the repressed. *Psychoanalysis and Contemporary Thought, II*: 233–248.

Brecht, K. (1995). In the aftermath of Nazi-Germany: Alexander Mitscherlich and psychoanalysis—legend and legacy: the first postwar legend regarding psychoanalysis in Germany. *American Imago, 52*: 291–313.

Brecht, K., Friedrich, V., Hermanns, L. M., Kaminer, I. J. & Juelich, D. H. (Eds.) (1985). *Here Life Goes on in a Most Peculiar Way ... Psychoanalysis before and after 1933*. English edition: Ehlers, H. (Ed.), Trollope, C. (Trans.). Hamburg: Kellner, and London: Goethe Institut.

Breger, L. (2000). *Freud: Darkness in the Midst of Vision*. New York: Wiley.

Brenner, F. (2003a). *Diaspora: Homelands in Exile, Photographs*. Amsterdam: Mets & Schilt. Original publisher, New York: HarperCollins.

Brenner, F. (2003b). *Diaspora: Homelands in Exile, Voices*. Amsterdam: Mets & Schilt. Original publisher, New York: HarperCollins.

Brinkgreve, C. (1984). *Psychoanalyse in Nederland: Een vestigingsstrijd* (The struggle to establish psychoanalysis in the Netherlands). Amsterdam: Uitgeverij De Arbeiderspers.

Carotenuto, E. (1982). *A Secret Symmetry: Sabina Spielrein between Jung and Freud*. Pomerans, A., Shepley, J. & Winston, K. (Trans.). New York: Pantheon.

Chasseguet-Smirgel, J. (1987). "Time's White Hair We Ruffle". Reflections on the Hamburg Congress. *International Review of Psycho-Analysis, 14*: 433–445.

Chasseguet-Smirgel, J. (1988). Some thoughts on Freud's attitude during the Nazi period. *Psychoanalysis and Contemporary Thought, II*: 249–265.

Chemouni, J. (1987). Freud et les associations juives (Freud and the Jewish Associations). *Revue Française de Psychanalyse, 51*: 1207–1243.

Chemouni, J. (1988). *Freud et le sionisme: terre psychanalytique, terre promise* (Freud and Zionism: psychoanalytic land, promised land). Malakoff, France: Solin.

Citroen-Brat, T., Citroen, P., Gomperts, W., Widlund-Broer, C. & Zeehandelaar, R. (2000). Ingekomen (Letters). *Mededelingenblad Nederlandse Vereniging voor Psychoanalyse, 15*: 192.

Clark, R. W. (1982). *Freud: The Man and The Cause*. London: Paladin.
Cocks, G. (1985). *Psychotherapy in the Third Reich: The Goring Institute*. New York: Oxford University Press.
Cremerius, J. (1997). Karl Abraham, Freuds Sündenbock und "Führer zur Wahrheitsforschung" (Karl Abraham, Freud's scapegoat and "Guide in the search for truth"). *Luzifer-Amor: Zeitschrift zur Geschichte der Psychoanalyse*, 10: 64–81.
Crews, F. et al. (1995). *The memory wars: Freud's legacy in dispute*. New York: The New York Review of Books.
Dahmer, H. (1983). Kapitulation von der "Weltanschauung". Zu einem Beitrag von Carl Müller-Braunschweig aus dem Herbst 1933 (Surrender of the "Weltanschauung". About a contribution by Carl Müller-Braunschweig in the autumn of 1933). *Psyche*, 37: 1116–1135.
Dahmer, H. (1984). Psychoanalyse unter Hitler—Rückblick auf eine Kontroverse (Psychoanalysis under Hitler—review of a controversy). *Psyche*, 38: 927–942.
De Klerk, E. (2003). Het trauma van Freuds besnijdenis (The trauma of Freud's circumcision). *Tijdschrift voor Psychoanalyse*, 9: 136–153.
Dershowitz, A. M. (1991). *Chutzpah*. New York: Touchstone, Simon & Schuster.
Deutscher, I. (1968). *The Non-Jewish Jew and Other Essays*. London: Oxford University Press.
Dezoncle, F. (2006). L'illusion de l'avenir "Et Moïse créa les Juifs ..." le testament de Freud (The illusion of the future "And Moses created the Jews ..." Freud's testament). Rey-Flaud, H. *Quid pro quo*, I: 3–15.
Diller, J. (1992). *Freud's Jewish Identity: a Case Study in the Impact of Ethnicity*. London: Associated University Press.
Dispaux, M.-F. (2000). Some reflections on the process of psychoanalytical training in the context of the psychotherapy/psychoanalysis debate. *International Journal of Psychoanalysis*, 67: 3–6.
Drews, S. (1996). Ein einmaliger Vorgang? Zur Debatte um die Ausstellung "Sigmund Freud, Konflikt und Kultur" der Library of Congress in der Presse (A unique event? The debate in the press about the exhibition of "Sigmund Freud, Conflict and Culture" in the Library of Congress). *Zeitschrift für psychoanalytische Theorie und Praxis*, 105–112.
Dührssen, A. (1994). *Ein Jahrhundert Psychoanalytische Bewegung in Deutschland: die Psychotherapie unter dem Einfluß Freuds* (A century of the psychoanalytic movement in Germany: psychotherapy under Freud's influence). Göttingen: Vandenbroeck und Ruprecht.
Eickhoff, F.-W. (1985). The formation of the German Psychoanalytical Association (DPV): regaining the psychoanalytical orientation lost in the Third Reich. *International Journal of Psychoanalysis*, 76: 945–956.

Eickhoff, F.-W. (1986). Identification and its vicissitudes in the context of the Nazi phenomenon. *International Journal of Psychoanalysis*, 67: 33–45.

Eickhoff, F.-W. (1989). On the "Borrowed Unconscious Sense of Guilt" and the palimpsestic structure of a symptom—afterthoughts on the Hamburg Congress of the IPA. *International Review of Psycho-Analysis*, 16: 945–956.

Eissler, K. R. (1965). *Medical Orthodoxy and the Future of Psychoanalysis*. New York: International Universities Press.

Eissler, K. R. (1978). *Sigmund Freud und die Wiener Universität: über die Pseudo-Wissenschaftlichkeit der jüngsten Wiener Freud-Biographik* (Sigmund Freud and Vienna University: about the pseudo-scientific character of the most recent Viennese Freud biographies). Bern, Switzerland: Hans Huber.

Elias, N. (1978). *The Civilizing Process, Vol. I. The Development of Manners*, New York: Urizen Books.

Ellenberger, H. F. (1970). *The Discovery of the Unconscious: The History and Evolution of Dynamic Psychiatry*. New York: Basic Books.

Elon, A. (2002). *The Pity of It All: A Portrait of the German-Jewish Epoch, 1743–1933*. New York: Picador.

Erikson, E. H. (1956). The Problem of Ego Identity. *Journal of the American Psychoanalytic Association*, 4: 56–121.

Erlich, H. S. (2003). Der Mann Freud: contemporary perspective on his and our Jewish and psychoanalytic identity. [Lecture delivered in Vienna.]

Falk, A. (1978). Freud and Herzl. *Contemporary Analysis*, 14: 357–388.

Falzeder, E. (Ed.) (2002). *The Complete Correspondence of Sigmund Freud and Karl Abraham 1907–1925*. Schwaracher, C. (Trans.). London: Karnac.

Fenichel, O. (1946). Elements of a psychoanalytic theory of anti-Semitism. In: Simmel, E. (Ed.), *Anti-Semitism: A Social Disease*. Madison, CT: International Universities Press.

Fitzgerald, M. (1998). The birth of pain. *Medical Research Council News*, summer: 20–23.

Fonagy, P. & Target, M. (2000). Playing with reality: 3. The persistence of dual psychic reality in borderline patients. *International Journal of Psychoanalysis*, 81: 853–873.

Forrester, J. (1997). *Dispatches from the Freud Wars: Psychoanalysis and its Passions*. Cambridge, MA: Harvard University Press.

Frank, P. (1968). *Einstein, sa vie et son temps* (Einstein, his life and time). Paris: Flammarion.

Freedman, N. (1988). The setting and the issues. *Psychoanalysis and Contemporary Thought*, II: 197–213.

Freud, A. (1936). *The Ego and the Mechanisms of Defense*. Madison, CT: International Universities Press, 1966.

Freud, A. (1978). Inaugural lecture for the Sigmund Freud chair at the Hebrew University, Jerusalem. *International Journal of Psychoanalysis*, 59: 145–149.

Freud, E. L. (1961). *Letters of Sigmund Freud 1873–1939*. London: Hogarth.

Freud, E. L. (Ed.) (1970). *The Letters of Sigmund Freud & Arnold Zweig*. London: Hogarth 1970.

Freud, M. (1957). *Glory Reflected, Sigmund Freud—Man and Father by his Eldest Son*. London: Angus & Robertson.

Freud, S. (1900a). *Interpretation of Dreams*. S.E., 5. London: Hogarth.

Freud, S. (1901). The Psychopathology of everyday life. S.E., 6. London: Hogarth.

Freud, S. (1909d). Notes upon a case of obsessional neurosis. S.E., 10, pp. 155–319. London: Hogarth.

Freud, S. (1914a). Observations on transference-love. *(Further Recommendations on the Technique of Psycho-Analysis III.)* S.E., 12, pp. 157–172. London: Hogarth.

Freud, S. (1914b). The Moses of Michelangelo. S.E., 13, pp. 211–239. London: Hogarth.

Freud, S. (1914d). On the history of the psycho-analytic movement. S.E., 14, pp. 3–67. London: Hogarth.

Freud, S. (1915). Thoughts for the times on war and death. S.E., 14, pp. 275–301. London: Hogarth.

Freud, S. (1917). Introductory lectures on psycho-analysis. Parts I and II. S.E., 15 and 16. London: Hogarth.

Freud, S. (1923). Two encyclopaedia articles: (B) the Libido Theory. S.E., 18, pp. 255–263. London: Hogarth.

Freud, S. (1925a). An autobiographical study. S.E., 20, pp. 7–75. London: Hogarth.

Freud, S. (1925b). Letter to the editor of the Jewish Press Centre in Zürich. S.E., 19, p. 291. London: Hogarth.

Freud, S. (1926e).The question of lay analysis. Conversation with an impartial person. S.E., 20, pp. 177–259. London: Hogarth.

Freud, S. (1927). The future of an illusion. S.E., 21, pp. 3–57. London: Hogarth.

Freud, S. (1930). Preface to the Hebrew translation [of *Totem and Taboo* (1912)]. S.E., 13, p. xv. London: Hogarth.

Freud, S. (1933a). New introductory lectures on psycho-analysis (XXXIV, Explanations and Applications). S.E., 22, pp. 136–158. London: Hogarth.

Freud, S. (1939). Moses and monotheism: three essays. *S.E., 23*, pp. 7–138. London: Hogarth.
Freud, S. (1940a). *An Outline of Psycho-Analysis. S.E., 23*, pp. 144–208. London: Hogarth.
Freud, S. (1915) Death and us. In: Meghnagi, D. (Ed.), *Freud and Judaism*, II-40. London: Karnac, 1993.
Frisch, S. & Vermote, R. (2000). A la rencontre de Donald Meltzer (A meeting with Donald Meltzer). *Revue Belge de Psychanalyse, 5*(36): 105–117.
Frosh, S. (2003). Psychoanalysis, Nazism and "Jewish Science". *International Journal of Psychoanalysis, 84*: 1315–1332.
Frosh, S. (2005). *Hate and the "Jewish Science": Anti-Semitism, Nazism and Psychoanalysis.* New York: Palgrave Macmillan.
Gans, E. (1994). *Gojse nijd & joods narcisme* (Goyish malice and Jewish narcissism). Amsterdam: Arena.
Gay, P. (1978). *Freud, Jews, and other Germans: Master and Victims in Modernist Culture.* New York: Oxford University Press.
Gay, P. (1987). *A Godless Jew: Freud, Atheism, and the Making of Psychoanalysis.* New Haven, CT: Yale University Press; in association with Hebrew Union College Press, Cincinnati.
Gay, P. (1989). *Freud: A Life for Our Time.* New York: Anchor Books, Doubleday.
Gicklhorn, J. & Gicklhorn, R. (1960). *Sigmund Freuds akademische Laufbahn* (Freud's academic career). Wien: Urban und Schwarzenberg.
Gilman, S. L. (1991). *The Jew's Body.* London: Routledge.
Gilman, S. L. (1993). *Freud, Race, and Gender.* Princeton, NJ: Princeton University Press.
Gilman, S. L. (1994). *The Case of Sigmund Freud: Medicine and Identity at the Fin de Siècle.* Baltimore: Johns Hopkins University Press.
Glasser, M., King, P., Laufer, M. & Hayman, A. (1995). Obituaries: Adam Limentani 1913–1994. *International Journal of Psychoanalysis, 76*: 1031–1035.
Godley, W. (2001). Saving Masud Khan. *London Review of Books*, February 23: 3–7.
Goggin, J. E. & Brockman Goggin, E. (2001). *Death of a "Jewish Science": Psychoanalysis in the Third Reich.* West Lafayette, IN: Purdue University Press.
Goggin, J. E. & Brockman Goggin, E. (2001). Politics, ideology, and the psychoanalytic movements before, during, and after the Third Reich. *The Psychoanalytic Review, 88*: 155–194.
Gomperts, H. A. (2000). *Een kern van waarheid* (A grain of truth). Amsterdam: Uitgeverij, G. A. van Oorschot.

Grosskurth, P. (1993). Reply by McGrath, W. J. "greatly exaggerated"? *The New York Review of Books*, 40, August 12 [In response to "Lost illusions", April 22].

Grubich-Simitis, I. (1997). *Early Freud and Late Freud*. Slotkin, P. (Trans.). London: Routledge.

Grünberg, A. (2007). Over Joodse en andere paranoia: Frans Kellendonk lezing 2007 (About Jewish and other paranoia: Frans Kellendonk lecture 2007). *Vrij Nederland*, February 17.

Grunberger, B. (1964). The anti-Semite and the Oedipal conflict. *International Journal of Psychoanalysis*, 45: 380–385.

Grunberger, B. (1998). On narcissism, aggressivity and anti-Semitism. In: Grunberger, B., *New Essays on Narcissism*. London. Free Association.

Hahn, A. (2005). Donald Meltzer (1922–2004). *International Journal of Psychoanalysis*, 86: 175–178.

Heenen-Wolff, S. (1987). "*Wenn ich Oberhuber hieße ...*": *Die Freudsche Psychoanalyse zwischen Assimilation und Antisemitismus* ("If my name were Oberhuber ...": Freudian psychoanalysis between assimilation and anti-Semitism). Frankfurt: Nexus.

Herzberg, A. J. (1980). *De Man in de Spiegel: Opstellen, toespraken en kritieken 1940–1979* (The man in the mirror: essays, speeches and criticism 1940–1979). Amsterdam: Em Querido's Uitgeverij.

Hirschfeld, H. & van der Sluijs, A. (2005). *Antisemitische Incidenten in Nederland: Overzicht over het jaar 2004 en de periode 1 januari-5 mei 2005* (Anti-Semitic incidents in the Netherlands: review of the year 2004 and the period January 1-May 5, 2005). Den Haag: Centrum Informatie en Documentatie Israel.

Hopkins, L. (2006). *The False Self: The Life of Masud Khan*. New York: Other Press.

Isaacson, W. (2007). *Einstein: His Life and Universe*. New York: Simon & Schuster.

Izenberg, G. N. (2005). Secrets of the soul: a social and cultural history of psychoanalysis. By Eli Zaretsky. *International Journal of Psychoanalysis*, 86: 926–931.

Jones, E. (1972–1974). *Sigmund Freud: Life and Work* (3 volumes). London: Hogarth.

Jung, C. G. (1936). *Civilization in Transition*. Collective Works. Vol. 10. Hull, R. (Trans.). New York: Pantheon, 1964.

Kafka, J. S. (1988). On Re-establishing contact. *Psychoanalysis and Contemporary Thought*, II: 299–309.

Kernberg, O. F. (1965). Notes on countertransference. *Journal of the American Psychoanalytic Association*, 13: 38–56.

Kestenberg, J. S. (1982). Introduction to "Persecutor's Children". In: Bergmann, M. S. & Jucoby, M. A. (Eds.), *Generations of the Holocaust*. New York: Basic Books.

Khan, M. M. R. (1974). *The Privacy of the Self: Papers on Psychoanalytic Theory and Technique*. London: Hogarth.

Khan, M. M. R. (1980). *Alienation in Perversions*. London: Hogarth.

Khan, M. M. R. (1983). *Hidden Selves: Between Theory and Practice in Psychoanalysis*. London: Hogarth.

Khan, M. M. R. (1988). *When Spring Comes: Awakenings in Clinical Psychoanalysis*. London: Chatto & Windus. [Published in the United States as *The Long Wait*. New York: Summit, 1989.]

Kirsner, D. (2000). *Unfree Associations: Inside Psychoanalytic Institutes*. London: Process Press.

Klein, D. B. (1985). *Jewish Origins of the Psychoanalytic Movement*. Chicago: The University of Chicago Press.

Klein, H. & Kogan, I. (1986). Identification processes and denial in the shadow of Nazism. *International Journal of Psychoanalysis*, 67: 45–65.

Kurzweil, E. (1986). Die Freudianer treffen sich in Deutschland (Freudians meet in Germany). *Psyche Zeitschrift für Psychoanalyse und ihre Anwendungen*, 40: 909–922.

Langer, W. & Gifford, S. (1978). An American analyst in Vienna during the *Anschluss*: 1936–1938. *Journal of the History of the Behavioral Sciences*, 14: 37–54.

Laplanche, J. & Pontalis, J.-B. (1967). *Vocabulaire de la psychanalyse (The Language of Psychoanalysis)*. Paris: PUF.

Lear, J. (1995). The shrink is in. A counterblast in the war on Freud. *The New Republic*, 2: 18–25.

Lifton, R. J. (1986). *The Nazi Doctors*. New York: Basic Books.

Limentani, A. (1986). President's address: Adam Limentani, London. *International Journal of Psychoanalysis*, 67: 5–7.

Lipschits, I. (1997). *Tsedaka: een halve eeuw Joods Maatschappelijk Werk in Nederland* (Tzedakah: half a century of Jewish social work in the Netherlands). Zutphen, Netherlands: Walburg.

Lockot, R. (1985). *Erinnern und Durcharbeiten* (Remembering and working through). Frankfurt am Main: Fischer Taschenbuch.

Loewenstein, R. (1952). Anti-Semites in psychoanalysis. In: Bergmann, W. (Ed.), *Error Without Trial: Psychological Research on Anti-Semitism*. Berlin: Walter de Gruyter, 1988.

Lothane, Z. (2001). The deal with the Devil to "save" psychoanalysis in Germany. *Psychoanalytic Review*, 88: 95–225.

Lothane Z. (2003). Power politics and psychoanalysis—an introduction. *International Forum of Psychoanalysis*, 12: 85–98.

Lowenberg, P. (1971). "Sigmund Freud as a Jew": A study in ambivalence and courage. *Journal of the History of the Behavioral Sciences,* 7: 363–368.
Maciejewski, F. (2002). *Psychoanalytisches Archiv und jüdisches Gedächtnis. Freud, Beschneidung und Monotheismus.* Wien: Passagen.
Mak, G. (2000). *De eeuw van mijn vader* (My father's century). Amsterdam: Uitgeverij Atlas.
Malcolm, J. (1982). *Psychoanalysis: The Impossible Profession.* London: Pan Books.
Marcus, S. (1984). *Freud and the Culture of Psychoanalysis.* Boston: Allen & Unwin.
Marcuse, H. (1969). *Psychoanalyse en politiek: Vier essays* (Psychoanalysis and politics: four essays). Amsterdam: Kritiese Bibliotheek Van Gennep.
Marr, W. (1879a). *Der Sieg des Judentums über das Germanenthum vom nicht professionellem Standpunkt aus betrachtet* (The victory of Judaism over the Germanic considered from a non-professional standpoint). Bern.
Marr, W. (1879b). *Vom jüdischen Kriegsschauplatz: eine Streitschrift* (From the Jewish theatre of war: a polemic pamphlet). Bern.
Masson, J. M. (1984). *The Assault on Truth: Freud's Suppression of the Seduction Theory.* New York: Farrar, Straus and Giroux.
Masson, J. M. (1995). *The Complete Letters of Sigmund Freud to Wilhelm Fliess 1887–1904.* Cambridge. MA: Harvard University Press.
Matas, D. (2001). *Anti-Racism after Durban.* [Revised remarks prepared for delivery to the Law Society of Upper Canada Equity Seminar, Toronto, Ontario, December 10.]
McGuire, W. (Ed.) (1974). *The Freud/Jung Letters: the Correspondence between Sigmund Freud and Jung,* C. G. Manheim, R. & Hull, R. F. C. (Trans.). London: Hogarth and Routledge & Kegan Paul.
Meghnagi, D. (Ed.) (1993). *Freud and Judaism.* London: Karnac.
Meltzer, D. (1967). *The Psycho-analytical Process.* London: Heinemann.
Meltzer, D. (1982). *Explorations in Autism: a Psycho-analytical Study.* London: Karnac.
Meltzer, D. (1988). *The Apprehension of Beauty.* London: Karnac.
Meltzer, D. (1992). *The Claustrum.* London: Karnac.
Memmi, A. (1962). *Portrait d'un Juif* (Portrait of a Jew). Paris: Gallimard.
Mendelssohn, F. de (2006). *Die jüdische Tradition in Freuds Werk* [unpublished]. Göttingen: Vortrag am Goethe-Institut.
Meng, H. & Freud, E. L. (Eds.) (1963). *Psycho-Analysis and Faith: the Letters of Sigmund Freud and Oskar Pfister.* Mosbacher, E. (Trans.). London: Hogarth and the Institute of Psychoanalysis.

Mitscherlich, A. & M. (1990). *Die Unfähigkeit zu trauern* (The inability to mourn). Munich: Piper, 1967.
Moscovici, S. (1967). *La psychanalyse, son image et son public* (Psychoanalysis, its image and its public). Paris: Presses Universitaires de France.
Moses, R. & Hrushovski-Moses, R. (1968). A form of denial at the Hamburg congress. *International Review of Psycho-Analysis, 13*: 175–181.
Müller-Braunschweig, C. (1933). Psychoanalyse und Weltanschauung (Psychoanalysis and world view). *Psyche*, 1983, 37: 1136–1139. Reprinted: Lohmann, H.-M. (Ed.) (1984). Psychoanalyse und Nationalsozialismus. Beiträge zur Bearbeitung eines unbewältigten traumas (Psychoanalysis and National Socialism. Contributions to process an unresolved trauma). Frankfurt: Fischer.
Nitzschke, B. (2003). Psychoanalysis and National Socialism: banned or brought into conformity? Break or continuity? *International Forum of Psychoanalysis, 12*: 98–109.
Nuland, S. B. (2003). *The Doctors' Plague: Germs, Childbed Fever, and the Strange Story of Ignác Semmelweis*. New York: W. W. Norton.
Nunberg, H. & Federn, E. (1962). *Minutes of the Vienna Psychoanalytic Society*. Nunberg, M. (Trans.). New York: International Universities Press.
Ostow, M. (Ed.). (1982). *Judaism and Psychoanalysis*. London: Karnac, 1997.
Ostow, M. (1996). Myth and madness: a report of a psychoanalytic study of antisemitism. *International Journal of Psychoanalysis, 77*: 15–32.
Ostow, M. (1999). Sigmund Freud, the Quintessential Diaspora Jew. *Jewish Museum* [lecture].
Oxaal, I. (1988). The Jewish origins of psychoanalysis reconsidered. In: Timms, E. & Segal, N. (Eds.), *Freud in Exile: Psychoanalysis and its Vicissitudes*. New Haven, CT: Yale University Press: 37–54.
Oz, A. (2002). An end to Israeli occupation will mean a just war: a withdrawal from Palestinian territories is now essential if a moral victory is to be achieved. *The Observer*, April 7.
Pfister, O. (1928). Die Illusion einer Zukunft: Eine freundschaftliche Auseinandersetzung mit Prof. Dr. Sigm. Freud (The illusion of a future: a friendly debate with professor Sigmund Freud). *Imago. Zeitschrift für Anwendung der Psychoanalyse auf die Natur- und Geisterwissenschaften, xiv*. Band: Heft 2/3.
Pfister, O. (1934). Neutestamentliche Seelsorge und psychoanalytische Therapie (New Testament pastoral care and psychoanalytic therapy). *Imago. Zeitschrift für Anwendung der Psychoanalyse auf die Natur- und Geisterwissenschaften, xx*: 425–443.

Presser, J. (1956). Heinrich Heine: "*Ich weiss nicht was soll es bedeuten*"; *een bloemlezing uit zijn poësie* (Heinrich Heine: "Ich weiss nicht was soll es bedeuten"; an anthology of his poetry). Den Haag: Bert Bakker/ Daamen.

Rabinbach, A. (1995). Response to Karen Brecht, "In the Aftermath of Nazi-Germany: Alexander Mitscherlich and Psychoanalysis—Legend and Legacy". *American Imago*, 52: 313–329.

Reijzer, H. M. (1993). *Naar een nieuw beroep: Psychotherapeut in Nederland* (Towards a new profession: psychotherapist in the Netherlands). Houten/Zaventem: Bohn Stafleu Van Loghum.

Reijzer, H. M. (1996). Redactioneel (Editorial). *Tijdschrift voor Psychoanalyse*, 2: 130–133.

Reijzer, H. M. (2003). Reactie op: Eddy de Klerk, Het trauma van Freuds besnijdenis (Reaction to Eddy de Klerk, the trauma of Freud's circumcision). *Tijdschrift voor Psychoanalyse*, 9: 148–152.

Rice, E. (1990). *Freud and Moses: The long journey home*. New York: State University of New York Press.

Robert, M. (1974). *D'Oedipe à Moïse: Freud et la conscience juive* (From Oedipus to Moses: Freud and Jewish awareness). Paris: Calmann-Levy.

Rose, J. (2003). Response to Edward Said. In: Said, E. W., *Freud and the Non-European*. London: Verso, published in association with the Freud Museum.

Rosenfeld, D. (1986). Identification in relation to the Nazi phenomenon. *International Journal of Psychoanalysis*, 67: 53–65.

Roth, P. (1994). *Operation Shylock: a Confession*. New York: Vintage.

Roudinesco, E. (1982). *La Bataille de cent ans: Histoire de la psychanalyse en France* (The hundred year battle: history of psychoanalysis in France), Volume 1, 1885–1939. Paris: Editions Ramsay.

Roudinesco, E. (1986). *La Bataille de cent ans: Histoire de la psychanalyse en France* (The hundred year battle: history of psychoanalysis in France), Volume 2, 1925–1985. Paris: Editions du Seuil.

Sadger, I. (2006). *Sigmund Freud Persönliche Erinnerungen. Herausgegeben von Andrea Huppke und Michael Schröter* (Sigmund Freud personal memories. Edited by Andrea Huppke and Michael Schröter). Tübingen, Germany: edition diskord.

Said, E. W. (1979). *Orientalism*. New York: Vintage.

Said, E. W. (1979). *The Question of Palestine*. [Republished, with a new introduction and epilogue]. New York: Vintage, 1992.

Said, E. W. (1992). Palestine, then and now: an exile's journey through Israel and the Occupied Territories. *Harper's*, December, p. 47.

Said, E. W. (1994). *The Pen and the Sword, Conversations with David Barsamian*. Monroe, ME: Common Courage, p. 50.

Said, E. W. (1998). Between worlds: Edward Said makes sense of his life. *London Review of Books*, May 7, p. 3.

Said. E. W. (2003). *Freud and the Non-European*. London: Verso, in association with the Freud Museum.

Sanders, E. (2004a). Jodenster (Star of David). *NRC Handelsblad*, June 14.

Sanders, E. (2004b). Jodenkoffie (Coffee with sugar and cinnamon). *NRC Handelsblad*, June 21.

Sanders, E. (2004c). Negerzweet (Coffee [slang]). *NRC Handelsblad*, June 28.

Sandler, A.-M. (2004) Institutional responses to boundary violations: the case of Masud Khan. *International Journal of Psychoanalysis*, 85: 27–42.

Sartre, J.-P. (1954). *Réflexions sur la question juive* (Reflections on the Jewish question). Paris: Gallimard.

Schalkwijk, F. (2003). Redactioneel (Editorial). *Tijdschrift voor Psychoanalyse*, 9: 134–135.

Schmidt, W. (1935). *Rasse und Volk* (Race and people). Salzburg: Anton Puster.

Schnitzler, A. (2002). *Der Weg in Freie* (The road to the open). Frankfurt am Main: Fischer Taschenbuch.

Schorske, C. E. (1980). *Fin-de-Siècle Vienna: Politics and Culture*. New York: Alfred A. Knopf.

Schröter, M. (Ed.). (2004). *Sigmund Freud—Max Eitingon Briefwechsel 1906–1939, Zwei Bände* (Sigmund Freud—Max Eitingon correspondence 1906–1939, two vols). Tübingen, Germany: edition diskord.

Schultz-Hencke, H. (1927). *Einführung in die Psychoanalyse* (Introduction to psychoanalysis). Jena, Germany: Gustav Fischer.

Schwaber, P. (1978). Title of honor: The Psychoanalytic Congress in Jerusalem. *Midstream*, 24: 26–35.

Semmelweis, I. F. (1861). *Die Ätiologie, der Begriff und die Prophylaxis des Kindbettfiebers*. Pest, Hungary: Hartleben.

Simmel, E. (Ed.) (1946). *Antisemitismus* (Anti-Semitism). Frankfurt am Main: Fischer Taschenbuch, 2002.

Simon, B. (2004). *Identity in Modern Society*. Oxford: Blackwell.

Solms, M. (1993). Translator's Introduction. In: Meghnagi, D. (Ed.), *Freud and Judaism*. London: Karnac, pp. 3–10.

Sösemann, B. (No date). Emnity towards Jews and anti-Semitism in France and Germany at the end of the 19th Century: Theodor Wolf, a liberal critic of both societies. [Lecture given at the University of Sydney].

Spanjaard, J. (1970). De psychoanalyse in Nederland (Psychoanalysis in the Netherlands). *Inval*, 3: 239–244.

Spanjaard, J. (1997). Tussen de Wereldoorlogen (Between the world wars). In: Ströeken, H., *Freud in Nederland; Een eeuw psychoanalyse*. Amsterdam: Boom, pp. 34–44.

Speier, S. The psychoanalyst without a face: psychoanalysis without a history. In: Heimannsberg, B. & Schmidt, C. J. (Eds.), *The Collective Silence: German Identity and the Legacy of Sham*. Oudejans Harris, C. & Wheeler, G. (Trans.). San Francisco: Jossey-Bass, pp. 61–72.

Steiner, R. (1989). "It is a new kind of Diaspora ..." *International Review of Psychoanalysis*, 16: 35–78.

Stern, A. (2004). *Le Savoir-Déporté: Camps, Histoire, Psychanalyse*. Paris: Éditions du Seuil.

Stoller, R. J. (1977). Primary Feminity. In: Blum, H.P. (Ed.), *Female Psychology: Contemporary Psychoanalytic Views*. New York: International Universities Press, pp. 59–79.

Stroeken, H. (1991). Der Einfluß von Freuds Judentum auf sein Leben und die Psychoanalyse (The influence of Freud's Judaism on his life and on psychoanalysis). *Forum der Psychoanalyse*, 7: 323–335.

Stroeken, H. (1997). *Freud in Nederland; Een Eeuw Psychoanalyse* (Freud in the Netherlands; a century of psychoanalysis). Amsterdam: Boom.

Stroeken, H. (2000). *Nieuw psychoanalytisch Woordenboek: Begrippen Termen Personen* (New psychoanalytic dictionary: concepts, terms, people). Amsterdam: Boom.

Strozier, C. B. (2001). *Heinz Kohut: The Making of a Psychoanalyst*. New York: Farrar, Straus & Giroux.

Stufkens, A. (Ed.). (1997). *Andere Kamers in het Huis van Freud* (Other rooms in the house of Freud). Amsterdam: Boom.

Suied, A. (1985). *La Poésie et le Réel* (Poetry and reality). Paris: L'Encre des Nuits.

Sulloway, F. J. (1979). *Freud, Biologist of the Mind: Beyond the Psychoanalytic Legend*. New York: Basic Books.

Swaan, A. de (2005). Anti-Israëlische enthousiasmes en de tragedie van het blind proces (Anti-Israel enthusiasm and the tragedy of the blind process). *De Gids*, 168: 349–369.

Thomä, H. & Kächele, H. (1986). *Psychoanalytic Practice*. Berlin: Springer.

Thomä, H. & Kächele, H. (Ed.) (1994). *Psychoanalytic Practice*. New York: Jason Aronson.

Van Amerongen, M. (2000). Freuds vele Vijanden (Freud's many enemies). *De Groene Amsterdammer*, May 6, pp. 48–51.

Van der Horst, P. W. (2006). De mythe van het Joodse kannibalisme (The myth of Jewish cannibalism). [Speech given on the occasion of his retirement from the University of Utrecht (including the passages removed at the request of the university), June 16]

Van Heerden, J. (1982). *De zorgelijke Staat van het Onbewuste* (The distressing state of the subconscious). Amsterdam: Boom.

Van Heerden, J. (2000). The omstreden erfenis van Freud (The controversial legacy of Freud). *Mededelingenblad Nederlandse Vereniging voor Psychoanalyse*, 15: 144–149.

Verhaar, H. (1998). Hans Gomperts 1915–1998. [Speech read in the Amstelkerk on October 24.

Verhage, F. (2000). Brief aan Jaap van Heerden (Letter to Jaap van Heerden). *Mededelingenblad Nederlandse Vereniging voor Psychoanalyse*, 15: 149–153.

Vitz, P. C. (1988). *Sigmund Freud's Christian Unconscious*. Grand Rapids, MI: William B. Eerdmans.

Vogel, L. (1946) *Dagboek uit een Kamp* (Diary from a camp). Amsterdam: Prometheus, 2000.

Von Dohnanyi, K. (1986). Opening ceremony: 34th IPA Congress, Hamburg, on Sunday, July 28, 1985. *International Journal of Psychoanalysis*, 67: 3–6.

Wallerstein, R. S. (1988). Psychoanalysis in Nazi Germany: historical and psychoanalytic lessons. *Psychoanalysis and Contemporary Thought*, II: 351–357.

Wallerstein, R. S. (1998). *Lay Analysis: Life inside the Controversy*. Hillsdale, NJ: Analytic Press.

Wangh, M. (1964). National Socialism and the genocide of the Jews—a psychoanalytic study of a historical event. *International Journal of Psychoanalysis*, 45: 386–395.

Wangh, M. (1986). Offener Brief an Dieter Ohlmeier vom 20. Dezember 1985 (Open letter, dated 20 December 1985, to Dieter Ohlmeier). *Psyche: Zeitschrift für Psychoanalyse und ihre Anwendungen*, xi: 902–906.

Weber, M. (1965). *The Protestant Ethic and the Spirit of Capitalism*. London: Allen & Unwin.

Weiner, J. R. (1999). Who is Edward Said ... really? "My Beautiful Old House" and other fabrications by Edward Said. *Commentary Magazine*, 108: September 2.

Weininger, O. (1997). *Über die letzten Dinge—Wien 1904* (About the last things—Vienna 1904). Munich: Matthes & Sietz.

Weinshel, E. M. (Ed.) (1986). 150th Bulletin of the International Psychoanalytical Association: Report of the 34th International Psychoanalytical Congress. *International Journal of Psychoanalysis*, 67: 87–131.

Widlöcher, D. (2005). The President's Column. *International Psychoanalysis, News Magazine of the International Psychoanalytical Association*, 14: 7–9.

Wiesel, E. (2001). *A Circus of Calumny*. www.aish.com

Wieseltier, L. (1998). *Kaddish*. New York: Alfred A. Knopf.
Wieseltier, L. (2003). Israel, Palestine, and the return of the bi-national fantasy: What is not to be done. *The New Republic*. October 27.
Wilgowics, P. (1999). Listening psychoanalytically to the Shoah half a century on. *International Journal of Psychoanalysis, 80*: 429–439.
Wille, R. (2005). De psychoanalytische identiteit: Psychoanalyse als intern object (The psychoanalytic identity: psychoanalysis as internal object). *Tijdschrift voor Psychoanalyse, II*: 233–248.
Williams, P. (1999). Internet discussion review of "Listening psychoanalytically to the Shoah half a century on" by Pérel Wilgowics. *International Journal of Psychoanalysis, 80*: 1063–1071.
Willoughby, R. (2005). *Masud Khan: The Myth and the Reality*. London: Free Association Books.
Wittels, F. (1924). *Sigmund Freud: His Personality, His Teaching, and His School*. New York: Dodd, Mead.
Yerushalmi, Y. (1989). Freud on the "historical novel": From the manuscript draft (1934) of *Moses and Monotheism*. *International Journal of Psychoanalysis, 70*: 375–395.
Yerushalmi, Y. (1991). *Freud's Moses: Judaism Terminable and Interminable*. New Haven, CT: Yale University Press.
Young-Bruehl, E. (1988). *Anna Freud: a Biography*. New York: Summit.
Young-Bruehl, E. (1996). *The Anatomy of Prejudices*. Cambridge, MA: Harvard University Press.
Zaretsky, E. (2004). *Secrets of the Soul: A Social and Cultural History of Psychoanalysis*. New York: Alfred A. Knopf.

INDEX

Abraham, Karl 32–33, 38, 42–47, 49
  as plagiarism 45
  salutation 47
Abram, Ido 20
Adlerians 86
All-India Women's Conferenc 177
ALU (the Arab Lawyers Union) 167, 172, 174
American Jewish World Congress 119, 121
American Psychoanalytic Association (APsaA) 41, 169–170, 183, 196
  OPEN LINE 171, 184
An Outline of Psycho-Analysis 67
Annan, Kofi 175, 181
anti-imperialism 143
anti-Israel
  enthusiasm 142, 193
  organization 175
anti-Semitic
  aggression 80
  arrows 67
  behaviour 121
  confrontations 130
  element 130
  enthusiasm 142
  feelings 110, 123–124
  patients 11
  prejudices 134, 143
  propaganda 145
  riot 53
  stereotypes 186
  watchdogs of the Netherlands 142
  writing 125
anti-Semitic outbursts 107, 114, 117–118, 121–122
  violent 119

anti-Semitic Vienna 12, 35, 48
  Jewish character of
    psychoanalysis in 48
anti-Semitism 11, 20–21, 27, 47, 68,
    73, 85, 103–104, 111, 114–116,
    118, 121–123, 125, 127, 130,
    134–136, 138–141, 143–144, 158,
    172, 176, 183, 185, 187–188
  attachment to 116
  Austrian 148
  authority on 24
  contemporary 182
  expectation of 41
  German and European 190
  Jung's 43
  manifestation of 21
  mindless 22, 121
  OPEN LINE 169
  vestiges of 24
anti-Zionism 172, 176, 183
APsaA *see* American
  Psychoanalytic Association
Arafat, Yasser 144, 147, 153
Arendt, Hannah 152
artificial reconciliation 92
Aryan declaration 109
Auden, W. H. 18

Barenboim, Daniel 147
Bauer, Stephan F. 171
Beethoven symphony 55
Belgian Association 141
Belgian psychoanalytic journal 136
Berlin Psychoanalytic Institute 52,
    68, 86, 98
Berlin psychoanalytic treatment 88
Bernays, Jacob 64
  dignity 65
Binswanger, Ludwig 46, 49
Blanton, Smiley 3
Bleuler, Eugen 44, 46

Blumenberg, Yigal 3, 12, 27, 98, 189
Bollas, Christopher 130, 134–135,
    145, 150–154, 186
Bolshevism 78
Bonaparte, Marie 78
Bouchet, Susan 177
Brenner, Frédéric 1–3, 6, 146
Brill, Abraham 32, 46, 49, 192
Brinkgreve, C. 14, 94, 110–111, 127
British Psychoanalytic Association
    110
British Psychoanalytical Society
    (BPAS) 41, 94–95, 131, 133–137

Carrefour Psychanalytique 136
Celan, Paul 102
Centre for Information and
    Documentation on Israel (CIDI)
    21, 143, 163
Chasseguet-Smirgel, Janine 17,
    85–86, 91–93, 102–104, 112, 182,
    184
Chayes, Michael 126
Chemouni, J. 12–13, 157
Chomsky, Noam 147
Chosen People 58, 73
Christianity 22, 39, 56, 62, 73–74,
    78, 156, 158
Christian-Jewish reconciliation 34
Chronology of the Verhage Question
    124
Citroen, Paul 117, 119
Citroen-Brat, Tilly 117, 119
Comparative Literature at
    Columbia University 145, 149
Contemporary Anti-Semitism
    Working Group 182
Cooper, Barrie 135
countertransference 11, 14–18, 28,
    69, 190
  definition 16

in *Observations on Transference Love* 16
Jewish element in 16
reaction 18

Dahl, Hartvig 6–7
Darwin, Charles 63
De Swaan, A. 142–143, 193
dedifferentiation of victims 92
Diaspora Jew 30
disidentification 24, 188
Dohnányi, Ernö 90
Dührssen, Annemarie 3, 98
Duijker, H. C. J. 112
Durban conference 166–168, 182–183
Dutch Association for Psychoanalysis (NVPA) 107–108, 111, 119, 125, 127, 129, 165
anti-Semitic incidents in 129
Dutch Association for Psychoanalytic Psychotherapy (NVPP) 112, 125
Dutch Organization for Psychoanalytic Psychotherapy 126
Dutch Psychoanalytic Group (NPAG) 107, 112, 126–127, 130
Dutch Psychoanalytic Institute (NPI) 111, 117
as training institute 117

East European Jews 7
Eckstein, Emma 186
Eickhoff, F.-W. 9–10, 91, 98–99
Eisenberg, Rabbi Chaim 37
Eissler, K. R. 40
Eitingon, Max 16, 46, 49, 65, 86
Encyclopaedia Britannica 75
Erikson, E. H. 26
European Christian civilization 59

Falk, Avner 35, 156
Fanon, Franz 155, 159
European colonialism 155
fascism 70, 78, 94, 138
Fascist State of Mind 151–153
Feldman, Michel 179
feminism 19
Fenichel, Otto
Psychoanalytic Theory of Neurosis 27
First Psychoanalytic Congress 32
Frank, Philippe 12, 57, 79, 186
Freud, Anna 2, 84–85, 89
Freud, Sigmund 2
anti-Semitism 158
authentic voice 80
Biblical Moses story 76
circumcision 37
correspondence with Abraham 33
death 33
dream 34
dream theory and symbol theory 113
exclamation 33
friendship with Pfister 51
Jew in Europe 29
Jewish atheist 85
Jewish organizations 12
Jewish religion and the Jewish people 70
Judaism of 27
letter to Arnold Zweig 75
letter to Pfister 54
letter to Ernest Jones 56
Memorial Lecture in Vienna 149
Moses and Monotheism 71, 154
Museum in London 130, 149, 154
non-European 154

obligations 39
Philippsohn family Bible 76
Prefatory Note 70
professional identity 9
psychoanalysis 2, 62
rationalism 53
relationship to Judaism 29
relationship to Pfister 56
salutation 46
spiritual heirs 5
Tenach (Bible) 58
The Moses of Michelangelo 77
theoretical game 156
Totem and Taboo 72, 78–79
traditional psychiatric line 47
transference 15
vengeance 38
Zionism 156
Freudians 2, 7, 18–19, 47
Freud-Jung-Abraham triangle 29
Friends of Psychoanalysis 32
Frisch, Serge 136
Frosh, S. 7, 11, 25, 42, 85–88, 98, 104, 190

Gans, Evelien 140
German Institute for Psychological Research and Psychotherapy 86–87
German Psychoanalytic Association (DPV) 88–89, 91, 96–98, 100
German Psychoanalytic Society (DPG) 86–87, 96–99, 103
Gicklhorn, J. & R. 39
Gilman, Sander 24, 76, 190–192
  recurring theme 24
Godley, Wayne 134, 162
Goggin, Brockman 85, 87–88, 99, 104
Gomperts, Wouter 115–117, 127
Göring, Hermann 87–88, 97

Greco-Roman and Hebrew antiquity 155
Green, Aaron 3, 6, 77, 181
Grossman, Marcel 13
Grubrich-Simitis, I. 68, 71, 75–77
  Moses and Monotheism 77

Hebrew University, in Jerusalem 5, 84
Heestermans, Hans 24
Heine, Heinrich 25, 42, 91, 161, 163, 191
Hellenism 21
Hindeloopen 120–121
History of Psychoanalysis in Germany 86, 95, 98
Holocaust 92, 102–103, 139, 144, 151, 159, 172
  education 20
Holstijn, A. J. Westerman 108–111
Hopkins, Linda 131–135, 162
Hopper, Earl 28
Hrushovski-Moses, Rena 101–102
Hupke, Andrea 33

Identification and its Vicissitudes 91, 101
Identification and the Nazi Phenomenon 101
institutionalization 32
International Journal of Psychoanalysis 41, 134, 162
International Psychoanalytical Association (IPA) 7, 32, 41, 53, 86–88, 94, 96–97, 100–101, 110, 126, 130, 165–166, 178
  Committee on the United Nations 165
  Congress 83
  Daniel Widlöcher, president of the IPA 167
  psychoanalytic community 186

INDEX 217

Israeli-Palestinian conflict 144, 146, 159
Italian Psychoanalytic Movement 78

Janet, Pierre 47
  allegations of pansexuality 48
Jerusalem congress
  Business Meeting of IPA 89
Jewish
  analytic entanglement 3
  characteristics 143
  circumcision 156
  dominance 149
  domination 143
  education 76–77
  family, Roman non-orthodox 94
  history 69, 81, 85, 144, 147
  isolation 55
  knowledge 12
  Lample family 196
  legacy 2, 86, 187
  man's identity 21
  narcissism 74, 140
  national affair 44, 49
  non-Jewish psychoanalytic mosaic 130
  organization 12, 29, 54
  physicians 39, 88
  press conference 172
  science 7, 11, 75, 84, 169, 196
  self-hate 23, 188
  social position 25
  society 21
  transference 12, 14
  victims 92
  wedding ceremony 36
Jewish identity 3, 10, 20, 26, 74, 79, 94, 156, 160, 187
  present-day 160
Jewishness 85, 94, 116, 161, 188–192, 194, 196

Jones, Ernest 30, 49, 56, 78, 96, 54, 56, 77–78, 80, 96–97, 110, 112, 192
Journal for Psychoanalysis 14, 112, 185
Judaism 3, 10, 19–21, 24–25, 27, 29, 36, 49, 56, 65, 67, 73, 75–76, 88, 159, 161, 184, 187–189, 192, 195
Judeo-Christian tradition 155
Jungians 86
Jung, C. G. 31–33, 38, 40–41, 43–49, 53–55, 62, 65, 67–68, 77, 80, 86, 97, 109, 132, 186
  active anti-Semitic National Socialism 132
  anti-Semitism 43, 47
  psychoanalysis 47
  salutation 46
  sensitivity 44
  spiritualistic tendencies 47

Kafka, John 92, 104
Kamm, Bernard 100–101
Kernberg, Otto 167, 181
Kestenberg, Judith 92, 104
Khan, Massud 130–131
  abusive 186
  anti-Semitic intervention 162
  anti-Semitism 135
  treatment 186
King Frederick II 55
Kirsner, D. 3–6, 123, 130
Klein, D. B. 10, 11, 40–41, 91, 105
Klein, Hillel 91
Klein, Melanie 117, 136
Koffler, Chaim 157
Kogan, Ilany 10, 91
Kohut, Heinz 195–196
Kranefeldt, Wolfgang 68
Kurzweil, Edith 93, 104

Lax, Ruth 166–167, 173–174, 182
Leibovici, Solange 74

INDEX

Lessing, Gotthold Ephraim 55
Lévy, Benny 2, 127, 184
Limentani, Adam 93–94, 100–101
London Review of Books 149
Lothane, Zwi 85, 98, 104, 169

Maeder, Alphonse 46, 49
Mahfouz, Afaf 166–167, 170–183
Malcolm, Janet 3, 6–7, 162
Malcove, Lillian 5
Marr, Wilhelm 22, 48
Matas, David 172
Matthias G. 87
Meltzer, Donald 130, 136, 138–142, 193
   psychoanalysis 141
Mendelssohn, Moses 55
Michael Balint Institute 96
Mitscherlich, A. and M. 92
Moses, Rafael 101
Moses and Monotheism 29, 35, 67–69, 71, 74–75, 77, 79, 154, 156–157, 159–161
   complication in 74
   Grubrich-Simitis view 75
Müller-Braunschweig, Carl 86, 96, 99

National Hebrew Library in Jerusalem 33
National Socialism 68, 78, 90, 98, 132
Nazi Germany 93, 109, 137, 141, 151
Nazism 10, 22, 68–69, 78, 91, 98, 102, 104
   glory 98
neurosis 12, 27, 36, 59, 72
New York Psychoanalytic Institute 3–4
   The Anointed 4
New York Psychoanalytic Society 2–3, 7

non-hierarchical psychoanalysis 138
non-Jewish emigration 160
non-Jewish Jews 161
non-Jewish patients 11
non-Jewish surroundings 36–37

Oedipal anger 188
Oliner, Marion 167–168, 182
On the History of the Psycho-Analytic Movement 47
Oosterhuis, Eugenie 124
Organization for Psychoanalytic Psychotherapy 126
Orientalism 145
Ornstein, Paul 195–196
Ostow, Mortimer 7, 25, 27, 30, 91, 93, 104
Oxford English Dictionary 23

Palestinian
   Arab 146
   exile 146
   Holocaust 144
   nation's war 144
   refugee 146
pansexuality 48
Pendred, Piers 170, 178
Pfister, O. 29, 51–57, 59–65, 187
   enthusiasm 54
   Freud, friendship 51
   Gay's characterization of 65
   theology 62
plagiarism 45
Poland, Warren 178–179, 182
political stigma (odium politicum) 30
Powell, Colin 169
Prince, Morton 32, 71, 131–132
professionalization 14, 32, 140
   process 140
pro-Jewishness 116

Protestantism 62
Protocols of the Elders of Zion 172
Prussian Academy of Science 55
psychic reality 15
psychoanalysis 2–3, 12, 27, 70
    anti-Semitic characterization of 7
    de-Nazification of 99
    history of 10, 86
    instruments of 15
    Israeli authority on 35
    Jewish character of 48, 190
    Jewish element in 41
    Jewish origin of 10–11
    Jewish transference on 12
    modern 9
    mythology of 25
    objectives of 25
    of psychoses and Primitivism 109
    opponents of 27
    practice of 14
    reception and the practice 11
    technical neutrality 16
    The New Yorker 3
    theory 18, 113
    Tijdschrift voor Psychoanalyse 112
    Totem and Taboo 76
Psycho-analysis in the Service of Education 53
psychoanalytic
    activity 26
    conference 10
    Dictionary 15, 195
    discipline 108
    identity 26–27, 190
    knowledge 46
    landscape changes 126
    movement 3, 11, 16, 26, 31–32, 47, 78, 85, 95, 110, 187, 192
    organizations 98, 117, 190
    publishing house 51
    theory, formation of 14
    thinking 14, 91
Psychoanalytic Association 97, 110, 113, 123, 127, 129, 169
    in the Netherlands 107
    members 110
Psychoanalytische Arbeitsgemeinschaft 96

Quadruple Alliance 42

Rat Man 32
Rayner, Eric 134
Reik, Theodor 71, 111
religious stigma (odium theologicum) 30
replacement theology 56
Rice, Emmanuel 34, 37, 77
Richards, Arnold 177, 182
Roazen, Paul 36, 110
Robinson, Mary 173, 175, 181
Rolland, Romain 61, 155
Rose, Jacqueline 150
    Freud and the Non-European 161
Roth, Philip 145–146, 190
    Operation Shylock 145, 188

Sadger, Isidor 33, 49, 192
Said, Edward 130, 142, 145, 147–163
    Agence France Presse 148
    Freud the Non-European 161
    Jewish circumcision 156
    Moses and Monotheism 156–157
    Nuremberg laws the Jews 159
    political pronouncements 146
    uncompromising attitude 147
Sandler, Anne-Marie 126, 134, 162
Savodnik, Irwin 169
Schmidt, Wilhelm 78
    Rasse und Volk 78
Schröter, Michael 33, 65

Schultz-Hencke, H. 97–99
    neo-analysis 99
Schwaber, Paul 83–84
Schweitzer, Albert 60
Second World War 10, 41, 70, 85,
    89, 95, 99, 101, 103, 107, 154,
    189
Segal, Hanna 99
self-evident superiority,
    demonstration of 121
Semmelweis, Ignace 13
sexual stigma (odium sexium) 30
sexuality 19, 44, 48, 53, 88, 190
Sharon murderer 142
Shoah 20, 85, 91–93, 101–102, 132,
    138–140, 143–144, 151, 159, 162,
    172
Shylock's *three thousand ducats* 102,
    188
social discourse 18, 140
Socratic training 138
Sösemann, Bernd 21
South African National Congress
    175
South African National NGO
    Coalition (SANGOGO) 175–176
Speier, Sammy 88–89
Spielrein, Sabina 49, 80, 132
Spock, Benjamin 19
Stein, Gertrude 2, 49
Stern, Anne-Lise 139
Stroeken's psychoanalytic
    dictionary 15
Suied, Alain 102
Swiss analytic association 110

Tay-Sachs disease 191
The Danger of the Jewish Legacy 86
The Future of an Illusion 29, 56–57,
    60, 62
The Interpretation of Dreams 30, 34, 38
The Man Freud 30

The Psychopathology of Everyday Life
    37
Totem and Taboo 58, 76, 78–79, 158
    theory 79
transference 2–3, 11–12, 14–19,
    27–28, 69, 88–89, 189–190
    Jewish in 11
transference-countertransference
    constellation 69
Treurniet, Nick
    reaction 118, 122, 124, 127
Tuynman, Jos 117, 125
Twelfth International Congress in
    Wiesbaden 90
Tylim, Isaac 166, 171, 174, 177–178

Ubbels, Jaap 122, 125
UN World Conference in Durban
    178
United Nations World Conference
    on Racism 130, 165

Van Amerongen 112–113
Van der Hoop, J. H. 108–110
Van der Horst, Pieter 21–22
Van der Sluijs, A. 142–144
Van Heerden, Jaap 113–114, 127
Verhage, Frans 113–114, 116–127, 133
    affair 108, 133, 141–142
    anti-Semitic character of 118
    anti-Semitic feelings 124
    letter of apology 122
    methodological polemic 114
    reaction of 119–120
    training authority 118
Verkuyl, Henk 24
Vermote, Rudi 136
Vienna Psychoanalytic Association
    32
Vienna Psychoanalytic Society 79
Viennese Freudian Association
    148–149

INDEX 221

Viennese Jewish circle 41, 186, 195
Von Dohnanyi, Klaus 90, 104

Wallerstein, Robert 39, 85–86, 92, 104, 130, 181
Wangh, Martin 93, 104
Weinshel, Edward 94–95
Western Jews 7
Widlöcher, Daniel 165, 167–168, 171, 173, 177, 179–184
Widlund-Broer, Christa 117
Wieseltier, Leon 139
Winnicott, Donald 133, 135
Wolff, Susan 102
World Trade Center 180

Yerushalmi, Y. 6, 34, 55, 64, 71, 73, 75, 77, 79–81, 157
Young-Bruehl, Elizabeth 89

Zaretsky, E. 18–19
Zeehandelaar, Ronet 117
Zeitschrift für psychoanalytische Pädagogik 96
zimmerrein 55, 65
Zionism 34, 132, 156–157, 168, 170–173, 176, 183
Zionist settlement in Palestine 159
Zweig, Arnold 52, 64, 75